LORD COCKBURN

A Bicentenary Commemoration

1779 – 1979

LORD COCKBURN

A Bicentenary Commemoration

1779 – 1979

Edited by

ALAN BELL

1979

SCOTTISH ACADEMIC PRESS
EDINBURGH

Published by
Scottish Academic Press Ltd
33 Montgomery Street, Edinburgh EH7 5JX

First published 1979
SBN 7073 0245 5

Printed in Great Britain by
R. & R. Clark Limited, Edinburgh

Contents

Preface

THESE ESSAYS are gathered together to celebrate the bicentenary of the birth of Henry Cockburn, Lord Cockburn, on 26 October 1979. Most of them make their first appearance here, but Sir James Fergusson's introductory essay was first published in *The Listener* of 24 February 1944; it is reproduced with the kind permission of Sir James's literary executor, Mr Adam Fergusson. An abbreviated version of my 'Cockburn in his Correspondence' was published in the 1979 volume of the *Scottish Literary Journal*, and a version of 'Cockburn's Account of the Friday Club', here re-edited from the original manuscript, was published in the *Book of the Old Edinburgh Club*, Vol. iii (1910). The reliance of this volume on the remarkable manuscript holdings of the National Library of Scotland will be readily apparent, and grateful acknowledgement is made to the Librarian and Board of Trustees for their permission to quote from the Cockburn letters and other documents in their keeping. Mrs Margaret S. Cockburn, owner of the family collection now on deposit in the National Library, is warmly thanked for her permission to quote from her letters and for her warm encouragement of this publication. Professor Miller's essay is partly based on Cockburn's poetical commonplace book now in the Osborn Collection, Yale University Library, where the assistance of Dr Stephen Parks and Mrs John C. Riely is gratefully acknowledged. The contributors are grateful to many other owners of manuscript material, including the Cockburn Association, the Faculty of Advocates, Mrs A. Frackleton, the Society of Writers to H.M. Signet and the Department of Manuscripts of the British Library, and wish to record their thanks for permission to make quotations.

I would like to thank Miss Christina Sharp and Mrs D. L. Mackay for their skilled and timely typing services, and my wife for much invaluable last-minute assistance.

ALAN BELL
Edinburgh,
December 1978

A great citizen of nineteenth-century Edinburgh

SIR JAMES FERGUSSON OF KILKERRAN, BT.

IN AN EDINBURGH drawing-room [of 1832], a group of people were eagerly discussing an historic piece of news: the election of the first Members of Parliament for the city of Edinburgh after the passing of the Reform Act. As they talked, a newcomer, a judge of the Court of Session, rushed into the room. He was seeking one of the ladies of the party, Mrs Fletcher, whose late husband had been an ardent reformer, to share with her the jubilation which they and their friends felt that day. 'Where's Mrs Fletcher?' he cried. 'She's the woman that I want!' He clasped her by the hand, and then, as her daughter afterwards recorded, 'they had a good greet together'.

The visitor was Henry Cockburn, and that anecdote is a perfect snapshot of him. It expresses three of his dominating characteristics: his zest, his strong Whig principles, and his delight in his friends. He had innumerable friends, for he was a lover of mankind and of human nature. He was also a successful lawyer, a keen politician, and a good literary critic: an outstanding figure in the Edinburgh of Sir Walter Scott's days and later. But that's not why we remember him. What wins Lord Cockburn a place in any gallery of famous Scotsmen is the books of reminiscences published after his death from the papers he left: the *Memorials of His Time*, the *Journal*, and the *Circuit Journeys*. He had himself published a biography of his friend Lord Jeffrey, and various pamphlets. But it is on his memoirs, including some final gleanings published [in 1932], that his fame rests, and particularly on the *Memorials of His Time*, one of the half-dozen best volumes of memoirs that ever came out of Scotland.

I shall not go into the details of Cockburn's life as advocate, judge, and reformer. All the same, he did have a rather distinguished legal career. He shone especially in criminal cases, and appeared in some celebrated ones, including the trial of Burke and Hare, the body-snatchers. He had an honourable record as a speaker and pamphleteer on Scottish parliamentary reform. He held firmly by his Whiggish principles, so firmly that his early career at the Scottish bar suffered during the period when only Tories could get advancement. His sympathies were wide, his humour unfailing, his tastes well cultivated. He wrote first-rate English and he spoke broad Scots, the decline of which among his contemporaries he called 'a national calamity'.

But apart from his own character, what draws the modern reader to Cockburn is his appreciation of the period through which he lived, and his brilliant descriptions of its scenes and characters. He chronicled a passing age, watched it die with sympathy but few regrets, and turned with courage and hope to the new one he saw opening. He combined a delight in the racy, picturesque eighteenth-century figures among whom he had grown up, and a passionate pride in the old Scotland and its traditions, with a forward-looking mind. Throughout his mature life, he showed a burning championship of the oppressed, whether they were starving Glasgow weavers, evicted Hebridean crofters, or political reformers whom a frightened government harried with ruthless prosecutions. He did not join in the Disruption, but he felt an intense respect for the hundreds of ministers and elders whom he saw walking down Hanover Street on that summer day of 1843, testifying, as Cockburn put it, that 'principle had really triumphed over interest'. He was, in a word, progressive. His mind embraced the past but moved with the present. He was modern. And to read some of his paragraphs today often makes it hard to realise that his lively, generous brain has been dust for [a century and a quarter.]

Speaking personally, Lord Cockburn is one of the writers for whom I always have a warm feeling of friendship. Some of my own forebears figure in his pages. I can even remember an old great-aunt who met him as a child, and who preserved to her dying day the feeling of outrage with which she read after Lord Cockburn's death his description of her father's house as 'a mere farm'. Most of all, I am grateful to him because he was the first writer who for me opened the door into the eighteenth century, and so brought home to me that neither it nor any other period in history is a glass case full of dried specimens, but a world of real people, moved by ideals, weaknesses and passions which were similar to our own and which often still influence us their descendants more deeply than we realise.

Cockburn himself was fully conscious of this continuity of history. He was proud of having witnessed the decline of the eighteenth century, and at the same time eager to watch and urge on the development of the nineteenth. So far was he from sentimental yearning over the past that he tended to overrate the present. The Edinburgh generation before his own had known David Hume, Adam Smith, William Robertson, James Boswell, and the two Allan Ramsays; had thrown up, almost without realising it, the genius of Robert Fergusson, and had hailed the genius of Robert Burns. Cockburn reckoned the four greatest Scotsmen of *his* time to be 'Dugald Stewart, Walter Scott, Thomas Chalmers and Francis Jeffrey': the order is his own. It was only a Silver Age in which he lived, but to him it was, at the least, silver-gilt.

But whatever his values, his appreciation was catholic. You can feel the same relish in his writing whether he is looking backwards or forwards. His pen-portraits of the old Scots judges are famous: Eskgrove, Hermand, Newton, Braxfield, Cullen and the rest. It is true that they are sometimes more artistic than strictly historical. Lord Braxfield was not quite so savage, nor Lord Hermand so eccentric, as they appear in Cockburn's pages; but they can never now be separated from the characters Cockburn's pen has given them—Braxfield will always be the prototype of Robert Louis Stevenson's Lord Hermiston, and Hermand will always be the judge who burst out to his brother judges, as they were deliberating over a case of manslaughter, 'Good God, my Lords! if he will do this when he's drunk, what will he not do when he's sober?' Cockburn's estimates of these veterans, as of many of his contemporaries, was coloured by his Whiggish views and by a sense of the proprieties which was distinctly Victorian. He had no tolerance for the hearty dining and drinking habits of Georgian days; and as for politics, it was as difficult for him to admit that a Tory could ever be able as that a Whig could ever be stupid. Yet in his descriptions of the Edinburgh of Henry Dundas, his humanity, his eye for the dramatic, and his sense of humour generally triumphed over his prejudices. Cockburn poured his greatest artistry as a writer into his sketches of the old Court of Session, or of the old Edinburgh ladies, of the City Guard, the water-carriers, the 'cadies'—all the principals and supers in the rich comedy of Edinburgh in the seventeen-nineties. And yet there is the same appreciation, the same gusto, in his account of the speed-up of

journalism just on the eve of the railway age. This is how he
describes the reporting of the speeches at an important dinner in
Edinburgh. 'The *Times* London newspaper', says Cockburn, 'sent
down reporters of their own. They left the room at twelve o'clock
at night on Monday, the 15th, and at one o'clock in the afternoon
of Friday the 19th that newspaper reached Edinburgh by the mail
with a full account of the proceedings. Post-horses, Macadam
roads, shorthand, and steam-printing never did more.'

Or again, this passage from his *Journal* in 1845 illustrates even
better the modernity of Cockburn's mind:

> Britain is at present an island of lunatics, all railway
> mad. . . . The ultimate miracles of railways are obvious.
> We are not now thinking of such places as London and
> Edinburgh, or even of Europe. Imagination speculates on
> America, Asia, and even Africa. It hears the bell of a
> station at Pekin or Timbuctoo, and sees the smoke of the
> engine trailing along the valleys of the Rocky Mountains.
> Distance is diminished twenty-fold. The world is not half
> the size it was a few years ago. The globe is in the course
> of being inhabited as one city or shire, everything known
> to and everything touching everybody. The consequences
> of the whole human family thus 'feeling in each thread
> and living along the line' cannot yet be foreseen fully,
> but there is no reason to doubt that on the whole the
> result must be good.

Would Lord Cockburn revise that optimistic opinion if he were
living today [1944] and could see the result of the shrinking of the
world? I don't think so. . . . The period covered by his life, from
1779 to 1854, was in fact remarkably similar to that now being
experienced by anyone born in the early nineteen-hundreds. His
period, like ours, was dominated by two great and interlinked
events: a world war and a political revolution in Europe. Again,
Cockburn's age was subject, like ours, to the far-reaching social
and economic changes produced by sudden enormous advances
in science and industry. What electricity and the internal com-
bustion engine have done to our age, steam did to Cockburn's.
His lifetime, like ours, witnessed the struggle of human society to
adapt itself to these changes.

Cockburn was very much a Scotsman, and patriotic without
being parochial. I have already mentioned his regret at the decline of the Scots tongue. He castigated attempts from London

to override the law of Scotland. He wrote in 1853, 'A direct attempt is making to assimilate the laws of our two countries by abolishing ours. If they were to adopt *our* law, the assimilation would certainly be for their advantage!' He cared most deeply for the national traditions of the Scottish people, and heartily despised what he called 'the insignificance of modern refinement' and the fashion which, he said, 'has cast all habit and character in one mould, of which London is the model'. That shows how free he was from provincialism, with all his love for Edinburgh, which in his time could still justify the proud title of the Modern Athens. His championship of a balanced policy of development of the city and preservation of the best of its old buildings saved much of its character for a later age to destroy. What he would say if he could see what our generation has done to Princes Street and George Street, and is now doing to St. Andrew Square, we can partly guess from his corrosive remarks on some of the early railway speculators [made in 1846]. 'Their principle is', he wrote, 'that nothing must obstruct their dividends, which is expressed technically by saying that "the public must be accommodated".'

Yes, we could do with some Henry Cockburns today: men with brains to match their hearts, and taste and tolerance to balance their zeal; men who respect the past but look to the future, without becoming obsessed with either.

Cockburn in his correspondence

ALAN BELL

KARL MILLER'S *Cockburn's Millennium* (1975) drew attention
to the large collection of manuscript letters by Lord
Cockburn which is held by the National Library of Scotland,
commenting that 'I don't think that it is the partiality of a biographer which makes me feel that they are among the best letters
of their kind that I have read'. This testimonial was to material
that was previously almost unknown. Cockburn's grandson Harry
A. Cockburn had published a few extracts from the family
correspondence in *Some Letters of Lord Cockburn* (1932), and there
was also available for specialists Cockburn's letters to Kennedy of
Dunure, published by the recipient in 1874 (against the wishes of
the Cockburn family) as *Letters on the Affairs of Scotland*: these latter
deal with political events in the Reform Bill period and are not
representative of the wider range and appeal of Cockburn's
general correspondence. His letters survive in considerable
quantities. Professor Miller's remarks were based on a collection
in the National Library which was augmented by a substantial
deposit from the Cockburn family just in time for the new documents to be incorporated in his study: there are now over six
hundred letters to various correspondents in the Library's
holdings. Professor Miller went so far as to recommend in print
that I should prepare an edition of them. I may one day do so, but
there is much further seeking-out and collecting of texts to be done,
much editorial routine to be performed, before such a possibility
may properly be considered. In the meantime, this essay attempts
to show something of the special qualities with which Cockburn
infused his extensive and highly individual correspondence, and
also to show the importance he himself attached to the letters of
his friends.

Unfortunately, the last point is best demonstrated by his
narrative of the destruction of the greater part of a lifetime's

accumulation of incoming correspondence. 'I have all my life had a bad habit of preserving letters, and of keeping them all arranged and docqueted,' he wrote in his *Journal* on 3 February 1845. These thousands of testimonials to friendship, he felt, imposed on him the duty of discretion, which could only be fulfilled in one way: 'seeing the future use that is often made of papers, especially by *friendly* biographers, who rarely hesitate to sacrifice confidence and delicacy to the promotion of sale or excitement, I have long resolved to send them all up the chimney in the form of smoke; and yesterday the sentence was executed.' With three exceptions, it was a thorough job, and the destroyed documents could now, 'thank God, enable no venality to publish sacred secrets, or to stain fair reputations, by plausible mistakes'. He had his regrets, as 'old friends cannot be parted with without a pang. The sight of even the outsides of letters of fifty years recalls a part of the interest with which each was received in its day. And their annihilation makes one start, as if one had suddenly reached the age of final oblivion. Nevertheless, as packet after packet smothered the fire with its ashes, and gradually disappeared in dim vapour, I reflected that my correspondents were safe, and I was pleased.'

Regrettably overprotective though this may seem to a later century's scholarship which realizes how his incoming letters would have enriched our understanding of Cockburn and his period, the bonfire is characteristic of the man. The three exceptions he made were the letters from John Richardson, Andrew Rutherfurd, and Francis Jeffrey. The letters from Richardson, going back to their salad days, and including some early poetical manuscripts, were retained and after Cockburn's death given by his executors to the surviving correspondent. Rutherfurd's letters, similarly returned, contain much on Scottish legal and political business at the time when Rutherfurd was Lord Advocate. Both groups have found their way to the National Library with their respective counterpart correspondences.

Cockburn had cherished the letters from Jeffrey long before they were to be essential to him as a biographer. Not many of them now survive in manuscript: only a selection of original Jeffrey letters escaped a later destruction, when the family papers were being weeded by Cockburn's son (without the paternal regrets) in the 1880s. These—with an extensive transcription in four large volumes—were presented to the Advocates' Library. The transcript had been made by Cockburn and his daughter Jane in 1835, and even at that early stage its value as historical evidence of the stirring times of the Reform negotiations was apparent to Cockburn. 'His letters are so excellent, and so illegible, that I have resolved to select and copy them,' he wrote. 'They are admirable as mere pieces of epistolary composition. Their matter however is more valuable than even their manner. They detail the progress of some of the greatest measures that ever engaged the reason or the passions of parliament or of the public.' As might be expected, Cockburn was lavish in his praise of Jeffrey's mind and style, as revealed by the copied letters: the reverential attitude was already established which was at the end of Cockburn's life to produce a biography which Karl Miller has likened to one Jonathan might have written of David.

They *are* good letters, which still await proper study by a political historian, and the transcript is of added interest for Cockburn's characteristic annotations which match the *Memorials* and *Journal* in their focus. Scott's friend William Clerk was 'rich and penurious—to a proverb. He made a fortune in twenty years out of £800 annually.' (Clerk's meanness is a standing joke throughout Cockburn's correspondence.) A report by Jeffrey of some awkward committee work in 1833 provoked Cockburn's reflection that 'Every hour of my official life has satisfied me—as it does every one—of this universal and mortifying truth. Enemies are easily managed, but wrong headed friends are the very devil.' Of Jeffrey himself we learn that 'No cat ever loathed the water so much as he does. His horror of sailing is dreadful. It was Love's greatest triumph to make Jeffrey cross the Atlantic for a wife.' And a long medical report from Jeffrey in 1841 produced the robust comment from his friend: 'No sensible man was perhaps ever so much in the habit of speculating on his own inside as Jeffrey. With more physiological knowledge than most men not medically educated, a restless fancy, and a nervous constitution, his imagination and descriptions of his health, sensations, and bodily system were so constant, and ingenious, and eloquent, that it is the best possible proof of his cheerfulness and strength of mind that he never fell under the tendency of all this to produce low spirits.'

There are sour little comments (Kinloch, the Dundee radical's, dying was 'the only useful thing he ever did') and longer appreciative passages (including one on William Adam of Blair Adam) which show Cockburn using this transcription of the Jeffrey correspondence in much the same way as he treated his *Memorials* and *Journal*. At first, however, the copying was a gesture of affection rather than a conscious instrument of remembrance. 'So the letters are done!' he had written to his daughter Jane when her work was finished: 'You have seen the best correspondence in the recent world; either as to heart, head, taste, or writing. But it can never see the light. To disclose these secrets would be perfidy. But it was a duty to transcribe, collect, and explain it.' Not that confidentiality and affection had prevented some mild joking about publication. In 1833, when Jeffrey was on the point of returning to Edinburgh, Cockburn had written to him that 'I must confess that I see our correspondence close with a pang. It has been to me a very great source of instruction and of gratification. When you are dead, or even turned out, I am thinking of turning a penny by publishing your letters. What shall the title be — "Pièces justificatifs, pour servir à l'histoire de la reformation parliamentaire en Ecosse", or "London Gossip—as detected by a stranger", or "Views of Scotch Lord Advocates—by one of themselves"? The only injustice some people think I have done you consists in the cautious parsimony with which I have kept you to myself. Not that the Faithful have not been duly benefited; but I always see that every thing transpires, especially if it be given as, or plainly be, confidential. It is a great deal to have had four letters a week from a man for three years, and yet to have brought him into no scrape.'

Cockburn's emphasis on safeness or confidentiality is as typical as his affectionate banter. Nearly indiscreet though his (post-humous) publications appear, he knew exactly how close he could sail to the wind, and he took a robust but well-judged view of 'safety'. As it turned out, when he came to use the letters for the second volume of the biography, he was disappointed by the result. He wrote to Mrs Andrew Rutherfurd, who had promised to look out further texts, that 'I have arranged a selection of epistles; but not good—chiefly because from his enormous length, and evanescent gossip, scarcely one can be given entire. Of nearly 500 to myself, I have not been able to select 20—and these only parts.' Jeffrey's flirtatious letters to ladies young and old added up to very little; 'I hope that those you have got', he added to Mrs Ruther-furd, 'have some plain sense in them, and little about himself.' Limited though their use was as a literary extension of the memoir —for they certainly cannot be reckoned an epistolary masterpiece

B

—Jeffrey's letters to Cockburn do survive in transcription (and
to a lesser extent in their originals) to be a probably very service-
able historical source for a long and complicated period of
parliamentary negotiation. The form in which Cockburn prepared
them for posterity shows us something of his attitude to his incoming letters, as he used this correspondence and the unusual
editorial apparatus he attached to it as yet another aspect of the
compulsive memorializing in which the particular cast of his mind
was most fully revealed.

His own letters, naturally enough, display this autobiographical
tendency, especially in his later years. They cover a much longer
period of Cockburn's life than the selected Jeffrey letters. Indeed
the National Library's various Cockburn collections begin with a
group to his friend Charles Anderson, minister of Gask, written in
1803, when Cockburn was rising 24. The earliest in the series has
the length born of greater leisure and the rather studied effects
characteristic of the apprentice letter-writer who has not yet
determined his ideal length, pace or tone. A visit is proposed—'the
pure and pious parish of Gask is to be polluted by the presence of
two vile pettyfoggers, who after feeding as fully as they can (poorly
enough however—Lord knows) in town upon the follies and vices
of men, retire to the country to create game for their winter's
pursuit.' This is stylized; it has yet to become stylish, but there are
signs even in these earliest letters that the writer is approaching his
characteristic mode. 'There is nothing new here,' he reported to
Anderson from Edinburgh in October 1803, 'except by the bye
what Christison would call a "fac" in the literary world—Thos.
Campbell is married. "Tam the hermit sighed, till woman
smiled"...'

Cockburn proceeded to narrate 'another very curious Fac':

We have often disputed about Brougham's poetical taste.
Now I lately heard him seriously, coolly, candidly declare,
in company, that excepting in Comus and *perhaps* Allegro,
Milton was not more poetical, possessed of more genius,
than Pope!!! Declared himself—without any affectation—
insensible to the merits—supposed merits I mean—of
Paradise Lost. This being said in such a way as to convince
me that it was true, settles the point, and turns Brougham
out with those who Beattie declares for not liking music
ought to 'Sneak with the scoundrel *Fox*, and Grunt (which
Brougham is very apt to do) with glutton swine'. These are

all the philosophical facts in this part of the world that
are new; tell me how many you have discovered equally
important in Gask.

Short, sharp, gossippy sentences with humorous literary allusion
are already beginning to show, as are the more studied passages
elsewhere on landscape and scenery poignantly recollected, along
with the over-serious metaphysical speculations of young adult-
hood.

Perhaps the reluctantly high-spirited tone of the 1803 letters is
due to their being written to a clergyman. Three years later
Cockburn's intimate friend John Richardson went to London
as a solicitor, where he soon established a good practice as a parliamentary agent—and also a lively correspondence with Henry
Cockburn of which, unusually, parts of the other side have survived. Phrases like 'laved the visage and went to Cranny's',
'arrayed in gold and green, like a ripe laburnum' begin to enter
his letters, these two examples coming from a letter in which he
wrote of the melancholy induced by re-reading an old commonplace book. 'I began', he told Richardson prophetically, 'to
lament I had never kept a minute diary of all the memorabilia of
my days. Such a thing would, if right done, be very interesting as
well as amusing.' The lucubrations continue rather lengthily, but
they are increasingly enlivened by the banter of friendship as well
as its more ponderous declaration; and literary news leavens the
legal and social record. 'Scott's Battle of Flodden is to be out this
week', he wrote on 18 February 1808: 'Report talks loud—louder
than specimen I think. At least this last herald has not made a
very stunning impression upon my poetic ears.'

James Grahame, author of *The Sabbath* (1804), is another
correspondent of this period, a Writer to the Signet newly turned
Anglican curate, and in need of reassurance about his literary
work as well as news of his Edinburgh friends. Frank criticism was
given—necessarily so, for the author, who died in 1811, never
again equalled his achievement in *The Sabbath*. The succeed-
ing years were to see the start of Cockburn's correspondences
with friends such as Sir Thomas Dick Lauder, the advocate
Andrew Rutherfurd and his army officer brother James, and several
others; the few surviving original letters to Jeffrey belong, however,
mainly to a later period, when the political events of the early
thirties were at last to separate the two friends physically and to
replace constant conversation by semi-official correspondence.

Later still there commenced the family letters, particularly to his daughters, and the very sprightly letters of his later years to Mrs Leonard Horner, to Dick Lauder's daughter Cornelia, and to a number of other female correspondents who brought out the frisky side of his nature so well; there are, too, the smaller groups of more serious letters of his old age on the preservation of ancient buildings and the avoidance of civic degradation, matters for which Cockburn is now so well remembered, particularly in Edinburgh. The six hundred or more items in the National Library of Scotland are by no means the whole of Cockburn's surviving manuscript letters, but they are enough to be representative of his special qualities as a letter-writer, particularly from about 1820 when the pattern of his correspondence is well established. By then the eager responsiveness of the dedicated letter-writer is fully apparent, and the right sort of literary familiarity has been established with several regular correspondents to draw out the best of Cockburn's very considerable epistolary skills.

One looks in Cockburn's letters for the features that are most typical of his published writings—a pungent, almost staccato, humorous turn of phrase, a strong sense of period and of place, and above all a tone of genial but edged reminiscence, laced throughout with a special feeling for character. The letters are rarely disappointing in one or most of these characteristics. 'Old Reid, Thomas's father-in-law, died a few days ago', Rutherfurd was told in February 1847, '—aged near 90. About twelve hours before his death, he asked for a glass of wine, and on getting it, smacked his lips, and declared he had never tasted better sherry. Soon after he took the Sacrament. Then played a rubber at Cribbage. Then died. Worthy of Hermand.' The reader is taken straight back to George Fergusson, Lord Hermand, a principal character in the *Memorials*, but the mixed sympathy, humour and brevity of the letter enable it to stand alone. In addition to such echoes of more considered biographical passages, there are the pawky Edinburgh phrases of letters such as an invitation to a dinner of the Academical Club—'Pray come and taste an academic egg here on Monday night about 10. . . . No silk stockings admitted —no ladies. Dominies and Directors.'

Good phrases—'worthy of Cockburn', it might be said— abound. Sometimes they may seem a little overdone to a modern taste, but they recall very accurately a period when puns reigned supreme and conversational elaboration was greatly prized. In 1836 his building work at Bonaly left him 'cheered morning and evening by the ring of masons' chisels—those larks and night-ingales of architecture. Yet in the surgency of one's own walls there is great delight.' Lord Moncreiff, newly on the bench in 1840, was doing well, though worrying away at his colleagues and cases—'too much of a terrier. A judge should be like a wise mastiff.' And in a fruitful Spring seven years later, 'the planes are pushing out their fresh, fat, green leaves—as a noble aristocrat used to push out his brood of young Tories, in the days when sinecures were as thick as midges'. Less elaborated than these examples are more spontaneous comments which perhaps recall Cockburn's conver-sational style—Lord President Hope's entertainments at Granton not being of claret and silver, but 'Hermitage and tin', or a letter written from the bench at Inverness in 1852, beginning 'Ivory is now under the luxury of a competition of Celtic lies (called a trial), so I may as well tell you that we are all well'.

Cockburn's expansive geniality is shown at its best in his letters, as in his life, when he was organizing one of his celebrated picnics at Habbie's Howe (or what was then generally regarded as the authentic Ramsay site) in the Pentlands. One of these breakfasts, 'in the grandest style', was reported to his daughter Jane in the summer of 1833. No less than twenty-three family and friends assembled in a choice bower in his beloved hills:

> Then began the lighting the fire, the setting the table, the building seats, the unpacking the stores, the sighing for its being ready, the children climbing up and sliding down, etc.; till at last our hermit fare was ready; and then what clattering, what scrambling, what disappearing of elements, what helping, what roaring, what upsetting of seats, what spilling. Oh Jane, Jane—thankful was I then that you were 400 miles off. The vulgarity of their mirth was shocking. Such frivolity! Would you believe it? In that tranquil scene, they laughed! Where the Scottish Theocritus wrote, they absolutely punned! Nay, I detected flirtation!—though in a delicate way. For Graham and Charlotte Lauder secretly removed a small stone from Mr Smith's seat, and tumbled him back, when he sat down, nearly into the burn. And he a decent agricultural Indian aged not above 60. For my part, I sat, on a stone retired, and reasoned high of Patie and of Ramsay. My

soul was with the Gentle Shepherd. But I trust that I kept
my temper sufficiently not to let them see how I despised
their low tastes. Their food (Oh! to think of food in such a
place) consisted of rolls, butter, honey, marmalade, jelly,
eggs, cold veal pie, tongue (no want of that) broiled
salmon—*hot*—(oh! oh! hot salmon, under the ray of an
August morning sun, in a pastoral, classical valley!), tea,
coffee, chocolate—closed on the part of the male, and a
few of the female, brutes, by a dram—(Oh Jane, blush
with me)—an absolute dram, God bless me! of whiskey!!!
    Having escaped from this dreadful scene, we came
home . . . Then we fell to bowls, then to a riotous dinner,
then to bowls again, prolonging it even under candle light,
then at 11 did I at last get to peace and my own
meditations. Next (that is, this) morning Pillans, who had
stayed all night, was up and out at 5!!! Walking, like an
idiot, till 9. Then appeared an Englishman—a friend of
Romilly's—to breakfast, after which Pillans, the Englisher
and I went up to Capelaw, and saw a glorious scene. We
dined here, and after dinner we took the bottles up to
Pisgah—and what a sunset!

Sometimes Cockburn's natural ebullience can erupt into a
Georgian robustness which must have struck primmer Victorian
ears rather oddly. 'I have been under what old Miss Auchterlonie
always called Bumlago', he told Rutherfurd in 1854. Earlier, in
1831, the removal of a public privy while the Royal Institution
building was preparing led him to write that 'On the 1st of March
—being the day on which the motion for Reform was made in
Parliament, the bōg began to be moved at the Institution. In both
it is a clean sweep. But I must confess that walking out yesterday to
the Foul Brig I saw the sun glittering three times on a large,
distant, whitish object, which, being neared, turned out to be a
bum.' And it was to Mrs Rutherfurd, when writing about her
husband's professional advance, that he passed on Mrs Cockburn's
remark upon his own judicial promotion: 'Odd—Preserve me this!
I never slept wi' a Lord o' Session i' my life!' Such full-bodied
expressions perhaps indicate conversational conventions prolonged
beyond their time. They may be socially interesting, and they at
least alleviate those heavier passages of agrestic contentment
which creep naturally enough into letters written from Bonaly in
the summer. 'And the blackbirds and mavises!' he exclaimed to

Mrs Rutherfurd in May 1851: 'I flatter myself that they know me—for they never think either of flight or of silence, how near so ever I get to them. I know the very branches where, at evening, they are sure to be perched; and no doubt for every songster there is an incubating mate close at hand. These faithful feathery husbands always remind me of Rutherfurd and myself, who spend our time piping to a couple of yawmmersome wives. (Delicate ground, so I get off it.)'

Expansive passages of rural bliss are often relieved, as rather archly in this example, by the effective use of good Scots words and phrases. Cockburn was widely reported as having had a good command of the doric, and he was able to use his skill with literary effect. (That fine word 'hurlythrumbo', in the *Circuit Journeys*, apparently denoting a bronchial catarrh, provides the unique recorded usage for the *Scottish National Dictionary*.) 'Hech!' is the most frequent exclamation of these highly conversational letters, and his rural retreat is well supplied with 'grozzetts' and 'rizzards' as well as the mavises he so keenly welcomed each year. He also appreciated older specimens of the language. 'Talking of the word cozie', he wrote to Mrs Richardson in 1812 after mentioning Scott's not being 'cozie in his own nest', 'I don't know a better translation than Zachary Boyd's account of Joseph's garment

> Now Jacob gied his dautie Josie
> A Tartan coat to keep him cozie.

Nothing in English could express this.'

When writing of the disrepair of Elgin cathedral, he is not one to 'scald [his] mouth with other folks' kail'; the reading of Jeffrey's early verse manuscripts is 'kittle'; after a journey back to London, young John Richardson's 'gebbie would be very toom when he reached Hampstead'. Such phrases were used unselfconsciously, and sometimes more recondite information is elaborated. A reference in a letter to Rutherfurd to the cockchafer, 'put me in mind of a very well made Scotch phrase of old Roby Craig's, anent a female friend of that structure. He used to call them "Nip-Doddles". Thus "Do ye ken Jenny Morison?—Lord! she's a fine lass! The best nip-dodle in the hail parish." ' (His views on the shibboleth *Scotch* are well known, and he pled vigorously for *Scotchman*; but his own practice is irregular.) Forensic practice provided him with plenty of dialect stories. In March 1840 'a little, old, wrinkled, sharp, honest, Irish woman' appeared as

witness in a murder case. Two judges tried to help her follow
counsel's questioning, but they were rebuked with an 'I hav' not a
voice for ye all three. You'l speak to me one at once.' Meadowbank's plea for greater clearness in her testimony was met with an
'Aye, Me Lord, but I canna' make it ony clearer; for Me Lord,
I'm no schollard, but just an ould wife like yoursell'.

Naturally enough the framework of the entire correspondence
is a legal one, except for the few years when electoral reform
questions dominate (to the immediate reduction of general
interest). Literary matters intrude only incidentally, and then
usually with a legal or Scottish historical bias (Cockburn was an
active member of the Bannatyne Club and a close friend of
Thomas Thomson). History was approached from a characteristic
viewpoint, as he wrote to Mrs Rutherfurd in April 1837:

> I am deep in John Knox, and the reformation, and Queen
> Mary—the subject of Tytler's late volume. A book which I
> have always liked; because it is the only readable connected
> history of Scotland. But then, it has always been an opinion
> of mine, that there are very few points in our history in
> which truth—I mean exact truth—is a bit more valuable
> than plausible blunders. The intolerable dogs are the nice,
> accurate, searching, restless, wretches who won't let our
> old beliefs alone.

John Hill Burton's *Life of Hume* was also well received in 1846—
'the biographer's part of it, though dullish, is sensible, short,
candid, and temperate. All that worthy, but unpromising looking,
man does, raises him. I am told that even his Bankrupt Law is
excellent.' Thus Cockburn reported to Jeffrey, having congratu-
lated the author a few days earlier on walking 'over the burning
ploughshares which fanaticism or faction will for ever set in the
way of any biographer of Hume with great felicity'. Burton was
warned to beware of angry reviewers:

> And let them do their worst. The humane purity of
> David's life, and the almost divine tranquillity of his
> death, have done more in favour of true religion, than all
> his speculative doubts have ever done against it. The real
> question is whether, *religion and his speculations being
> properly understood*, these two be at all inconsistent.
> Though the heathen therefore will certainly rage, and
> the bigots imagine vain things, they can do no harm to the
> biographer, who has performed his part with a more

complete avoidance of offence than one would have thought possible.

Jeffrey produced various English literary lions from time to time, and there are all too few glimpses of them in the correspondence. Thus of Dickens on his celebrated visit to Scotland in 1841 the badly-turned-out Cockburn reported to Mrs Rutherfurd: 'He with too bushy a scalp, but a very gentle, amiable, sensible, man, with a soft bright eye, and clothes better than even mine'. Macaulay, who was linked in local politics as well as by literary friendships, was reported to Andrew Rutherfurd in 1839 after a dinner at Craigcrook as 'A vulgar looking fellow—and a cumbrous talker; but pleasant, and natural—for him. He's like a heavy strong Flanders draught horse, beside the light fiery Arabianism of Jeffrey.' And in 1844 Cockburn wrote to Macvey Napier that

I rejoice in the anticipation of another birth from the Macaulay Muse. But, tho' I incur your contempt by the sentiment, I think the brilliancy of his style, especially on historical subjects, the worst thing about him. Delighting, as I always do, in his thoughts, views, and knowledge, I feel too often compelled to curse, and roar at, his words, and the structure of his composition. As a corruptor of style, he is more dangerous to the young than Gibbon. His seductive powers greater, his defects worse. But still I rejoice in all his deliveries.

Cockburn's respect for Sir Walter Scott was reciprocated on a social, but of course not on a political, level. Regular encounters in the Parliament House there must have been, and dinners of the sort Scott commemorated in his *Journal* (9 December 1826) with a warm tribute to merry Whig hospitality. He is mentioned all too rarely in Cockburn's letters, partly because of regular casual intercourse in the Parliament House, partly because of the different circles he moved in, as recorded at the end of December 1812: 'Rokeby is to be born in a day or two. Report speaks well of it—but Watty, I think, is a good deal lower in this intellectual city than he was. He has withdrawn himself very much from his friends, and not to be cozie in his own nest—for that he is not—but to share it with players and printers and low Torries.' There was regret, resentment almost, amongst Cockburn's circle at Scott's involvement in *Beacon* politics, but they all shared in the general astonishment and sympathy at the local results of the financial crisis of 1826. The *Memorials* are the source for Scott's dignified

appearance in the Parliament House after the revelation that he
had been inclined to 'dabble in trade' but had failed, and for his
remark when friends offered him money to arrange with his
creditors: 'He paused for a moment; and then, recollecting his
powers, said proudly—"No! this right hand shall work it all off!".'
Cockburn also reported it to Anderson in a letter of 6 February
1826, which is at once more astringent and more sympathetic.

> We are sadly annoyed here by Constable's failure. It is a
> great blow to Scottish literature—for no man here will
> venture to call up such spirits as he has done from the
> depths of genius and poverty. Several literary people have
> suffered—but none so much as Scott, who from being
> thought a man coining gold has come down to about
> £20,000 *below* zero, after all he can pay is made allowance
> for. He has behaved nobly—being cheerful and firm—
> delighted with his friends, and strong in unexhausted
> genius. Some of his friends went to him and offered him
> any money he chose. After a pause, he said 'No! this right
> hand shall work it all off!' Few better things have been said—
> at least few better thought. How little men are known. How
> few people thought that a man of his strong sense should
> become a bill merchant and printer, when by an easy
> process he could give out brains, and draw in gold,
> without risk, at his pleasure.

Although there is a formal quality about the measured cadences of
the concluding sentences, such a balance of expression is not un-
common in Cockburn's letters, and indeed the passage concerned
has more spontaneity than its more familiar parallel in the
Memorials. As the published work is known to have been revised
both by Cockburn himself and then by his executors, the letter
perhaps recalls the now missing original draft of the *Memorials*.

As with Scott's 'right hand', there is naturally some overlap
between the letters and the journal-based texts. The incident of the
Aberdonian wig, recorded in the *Circuit Journeys* on 22 April 1839,
was also conveyed to Mrs Rutherfurd a week later with much
additional circumstantial detail:

> We had an evening party at the Provost of Aberdeen's; an
> excellent, queer, old house, down a close; quadrilles, and a
> solid, leg of mutton, supper; he an octogenarian, she an
> undisguised Aberdonian; nice, kind, natural, happy bodies.
> Her head was so enveloped in ribbons and carfufles, that

nothing under them was visible to the world. Fancying that
his Lordship's wig was awry, and anxious for the honor of
the house, she dared to put it right, by an actual
imposition of hands. On which says he, solemnly, 'Madam!
I'll thank you to let my wig alone. *I never meddle with
yours.*' I don't believe that his wig will be touched by her
again.

A third version was sent to Cornelia Dick Lauder on 3 May,
briefer and a little more formal, but adding a few extra details. The
first letter omits the officers of the 74th who had been inimitably
summoned by their hostess ('I just sent up the lass to the barracks
an' bade them a' come doon'), the colour of the ancient wig, and
other facts to be picked up in the *Journeys*. On the other hand its
easier tone ('ribbons and carfufles' for 'too glorious with ribbons
and muslin') balanced by the mock solemnity of 'actual imposition of hands' makes it arguably better than the finished version
as written in Cockburn's journal, and shows how the published
works can often be supplemented in detail by related unpublished
correspondence.

As we shall see in a later essay in this volume, a number of
Cockburn's letters, particularly those from his later years, can be
related to another of his published works, the *Letter to the Lord
Provost on the Best Ways of Spoiling the Beauty of Edinburgh* (1849).
There are obviously parallels in contents, but even more interesting is the more strident pamphleteering tone which his letters
take on when dealing with the increasingly cherished topic of
civic degeneration. A fairly early example is one of 1 July 1835
addressed to Sir Thomas Dick Lauder, in which he wrote that
'. . . my whole time, thoughts, and soul, are engrossed, amidst
astonishment, horror, rage, disgust and indignation at a resolution
of the Town Council to make the front of the Calton Jail the
hanging place!!!' This is typical of the range of execration which
from about 1844 onwards he was to lavish on the city fathers,
on the administration of 'the d——d railway', and on those who
wished to interfere with the Princes Street gardens. A useful
memory reminded him that some thirty-five years before 'the
Town Council actually approved of a row of public privies along
the northern slope of the Castle Hill, fronting Princes Street; from
which truly magisterial decision we were rescued solely by the
energy of Mary Lady Clerk'. The Lord Provost's principle ('a
dangerous one for a magistracy') in approving a market to the

south of the Scott Monument, was *utility*. To which Cockburn added the comment, 'As if anything were more useful than public taste—i.e. the absence of brutality'.

Such gallant and consistently maintained crusading language went as far as (and, by the discreet encouragement of agents, perhaps farther than) judicial dignity would allow the strident defence of municipal fitness to venture. It was passionately felt, but buoyed up by Cockburn's notorious high spirits, which could rejoice in 'a glorious . . . God-like bouze' at the opening of a show of Grecian Williams's paintings as much as in the necessary discomfiture of a town council. This was the spirit which had animated those celebrated picnics at Habbie's Howe and his regular Sunday parties at Bonaly, well provided (like one reported to Macvey Napier in 1836):

> With two bottles of celestial punch, one of excellent hock, two of India sherry, one of port, and three of claret; with a rich, juicy ham, a pigeon pie cold, roast beef, a creamy salmon—to say nothing of reeking hotch potch, and mountains of salad and all your farinaceous stomatics. I mention these things just to make your fallow teeth water, and to show the anchorite lives of the Scottish Jurists. . . . The day was glorious—and we sauntered in the twilight of a mild, milky evening, amid a glorious profusion of breathing roses of every description.

A snowbound townscape could be similarly enlivened by his pen. Edinburgh in February 1831 was reported to Dick Lauder:

> Deep and universal snow here; silent streets—save when the house top avalanche comes plump on some startled wight, waiting in delicate raiment till the bell be answered; sparrows sitting chittering round the cans, but ever and anon descending, like Torries on a sinecure, round a ball of well laid horse dung, reeking through the clear air; two fools from Piers Hill making people think that they have been in Russia, by driving about, each with one nankeen horse, on sledges; hackney coaches hauling their noiseless wheels, through accumulated masses, by means of four horses proud of their strange grandeur; occasional bickers—a stray ball nestling, till it melts, about the tangling geer of a lady's neck, or excessively discomposing the comfortable primness of a poor yellow Bengalee, mincing his timid steps, 'to stop too fearful and too faint to throw';

the long white of the pavement interspersed with streaks
of glorious black slides—along which, to the delight of the
boys and the scandal of the decorous, a Solicitor General
is seen running and skimming.

It seems scarcely necessary to note that the law officer whose
dignity was in question was Henry Cockburn himself. His letter
to Lauder went on to evoke the companionship as well as the
coldness of an Edinburgh winter, as after various escapades he
found his way up to Court, to see 'judge after judge shake off
"their pouthery snaw", but not one of them lost life—tenacious
dogs, not a vacancy after all!'

However, Saturday it is! 'The long night of revelry and
ease.' Jeffrey alas! is gone. But here we are round Murray's
cornerless table. There sits Thomson's antiquarian visage
—addicted to old wine, old dates, old friends, old
principles; there the judicious Keay; see the Pundit's
sharp, iced steel—yet softened by heat and liquor; behold
Goliah's huge form—he of Morocco; hear Duloch's heavy,
hearty laugh, as loud and honest as a watch dog's; observe
the roseate countenance of our host, jolly in victuals, and
jollier in worth; there Playfair, in miniature Ionic; here—
but it is endless. Rave, ye tempests—fall, thou snow—
blacken, thou surly, dark souled night! Is it not Saturday?
Have we not coals and claret, talk and time? What want
we but Lauder—a heavy want—to reach whom by the pen
is but a cold substitute for the present, living, laughing
man.

This long letter, beginning with its description of Charlotte Square
under deep snow and ending with the nicknames and domestic
affections of his intimate circle of cronies, confirms an impression
of Cockburn's unusual command both of narrative skills and well-
chosen detail, whether describing buildings or personalities. It is
similar to, but naturally even less formal than, the easy style of
the *Memorials* and *Journal*.

Matching examples can be found at several different periods of
his life. In November 1824 he wrote at length to John Richardson
in London about the fires in Parliament Close, bringing out the
splendour as well as the frightfulness of the conflagration. Hearing
that the Tron Kirk was alight

I rushed out with many others, wigged and unwigged, and
saw the whole spire shrivelled to dust in one hour. Never

was there, though it was in the forenoon, a more beautiful
sight. The upper part was all wood, iron, and lead, and
burned and melted like paper and wax. It was a Dutch
thing two centuries old, and of course was full of edgy
ornaments, all quite dry. The fire ran along them as if it
had been led by art. The covering, being thinner than the
beams, was eat away first, and the beams left standing,
crackling and red. It was like a piece of hellish phillagree.
The highest stage of it, with a radiant and long triumphant
cock on its summit, at last bent inwards and made a
glorious plunge into the flaming gulf below. The handle of
the clock was pointing at a quarter from twelve, and of
course stood horizontally. When the heat destroyed the
muscular power of its machinery, the handle fell, suddenly
and silently, down, so as to stand at half past eleven. There
was something awful in the cessation of its powers, and its
thus dropping dead. It seemed to say, It is finished.

   The second stage fell in a little after this. The cutting off
of each of these sections left the tower better off in point of
architecture than before. . . .

Other Edinburgh events, such as the collapse of the floor at the
sale of Lord Eldin's pictures in 1833, or the laying of the foundation stone of the Royal Scottish Academy building in 1850, were
described with equal vigour and humour. Prince Albert's per-
formance of the ceremony at the Mound at the end of August
1850 was the culmination of plans which Cockburn and others
had long been making for the formal recognition of the artistic
community in Scotland. Cockburn had long given informal legal
advice and moral support to the Academy, and was particularly
gratified by the recognition accorded to the architect, his friend
William Henry Playfair.

   Think of Pluffy's felicity yesterday! At one o'clock Albert
laid the foundation of his Galleries, and at four The Queen
went over [Donaldson's] Hospital, *speaking much to the
architect himself*, and admiring everything. It was his great
day. And delighted, modest, and amiable he was—in spite
of all the laughter, and bad jokes, and parodies, that I
could exhaust myself in pouring out on him. Her Majesty
was charmed by the *site* of the Hospital; but, poor royal
creature, she had never heard of the Pentland Hills!— on
which she gazed with especial admiration. Think of a

crowned head never having heard of the Pentland Hills!
But her admiration shows that the head was not unworthy
of a crown. . . .

The Founding was beautiful. The Orators were His
Reverence Principal Lee, who prayed a good prayer—only
the sun blinded him, and was not heard five yards off;
Davie Bole [Boyle, Lord Justice-General], the handsomest
and youngest man there; and Albert, whose address—
whosoever composed it—was excellent, and excellently
spoken. All we—I mean of the Board of Trustees, etc.,
were introduced to him in the Gallery of the Royal
Institution, through which he walked. He particularly
admired my shoes. Everybody was in some sort of uniform,
or decent private dress; except three noble Lords, who
chose their superiority, and their familiarity with royalty,
by appearing as scurvy as possible. . . .

The Foundation stone is the great event. It greatly adorns
Edinburgh—and saves it from a fatal danger, which
nothing except the ornamental appropriation of the ground
could have averted; it marks, and promotes, the progress
of Art; it gives the Artists a dignity, and a permanency, of
station, which nothing but a connection with Government
could have given; and it refines and elevates the local
taste, and the local objects. I hope the Artists will show, by
their works, that they deserve it. Paton, I hear, is pretty
far on with a beautiful conception.

Sir John Watson Gordon, their President, was the most
picturesque gentleman in the ceremony. A full suit of
black velvet, lace frills and ruffles, silver buckles, and a
very handsome gold medal hung from his neck. He was
exactly an English nobleman, 250 years ago, going forth to
get his head taken off. What can I say more?

Extensive quotation shows one his command both of humorous
narrative and of his underlying seriousness of purpose, for the
promotion of the fine arts in Scotland was one of the great
campaigns of his life. The vivaciousness which stirred him to
'glorious bouzes' and snook-cocking slides was matched by a depth
of feeling which showed in his friendships and especially his
bereavements: the deaths of Dick Lauder and of Jeffrey upset him
deeply. The sudden death of Thomas Chalmers in 1847 was
another blow, and Mrs Rutherfurd received the elegy which

preceded a long passage about Chalmers in the *Journal*. Cockburn
wrote to her of his private loss as well as of the public man:

> His name was a tower. His voice a thunderbolt. Many of
> his opponents will now rail, and many of his own party
> chatter, who were dumb before him. How thankful I am
> that I was often within the flames of his eloquent
> enthusiasm; and that I was familiar with the honest smile,
> and the quaint, picturesque, oddities, of this most loveable
> original. He seems to have passed away almost as gently as
> Dr Black, for death had not made him even fall down on
> his bed, or relaxed his clasped hands from the apparent
> attitude of prayer. It is pleasant to think of his
> peculiarities, and his worth. The homage that he himself
> would prefer is that—very largely given—that proceeds
> from the hovels and the vennels.
>
> Our ranks are thinning. I clouded myself today on my
> way out [to Bonaly], sitting behind that faithful [driver]
> Geordie, by considering how the loss of two or three more
> would wreck me; and recalling the days in which—all at
> the gaiety of the bar, and not one of us dreaming of office
> —we closed a gay and not inglorious week, amidst the
> bowls, the claret, the talk, the boyishness of Craigcrook.
> But these visions are all nonsense. They are not for
> practical man. The only wise conclusion is, let those who
> remain cling the closer.

Such buoying comforts had been called out eighteen years
previously, when it became known that his artist friend Grecian
Williams was dying. At that time Cockburn had written to Sir
Thomas Dick Lauder

> These are sad privations. I tremble when I count the havoc
> of the last dozen of years. But don't you forget the true
> lesson to be learned from them. Repining, depression,
> moping, and despair are all the abuse, and not to the
> use, of these events. The business of the survivors is to act
> and to enjoy to act, so as to diminish the misery of others;
> to enjoy, by cherishing the remembrance of their departed
> friends, and continuing keenly engaged in the virtuous
> associations in which they delighted. The performance of
> the necessary business of life; the encreased cultivation of
> surviving friendships; and the bringing on, after our own
> meridian has been reached, of younger men, who may, in

their turn, be our new supports and associates—these are the proper tests and fruits of a right sense of what is due to a lost friend. But, Sunday tho' it be, I don't see why I should preach to you.

Whether we find him in a sombre mood of stoic gregariousness, or, as more commonly, in the exuberance of organizing a rout— or routing a provost—Cockburn's letters invariably deepen our knowledge of his life and writings. They are however more than merely a historical and biographical source, and deserve to be considered in their own right as very interesting—and above all specially entertaining—contributions to the art of letter-writing.

A NOTE ON SOURCES

Many of Cockburn's letters in the National Library of Scotland are included in the main collections, which have been indexed in detail. The principal concentrations (those which have been used in this article are marked with an asterisk) are of letters to Charles Anderson in MS.3546*; James Ballantine, MS.1660; Adam Black, MS.3713; J. S. Blackie, MS.2622; John Hill Burton, 3005*, 9394-5; James Grahame, MS.3519; Mrs Leonard Horner, MSS.2213-5; John Lee, MSS.3438-49 *passim*; John A. Murray, Lord Murray, MS.97; to and from John Richardson, MSS.2257, 3989*, 3990; and to and from Andrew Rutherfurd, Lord Rutherfurd, and his wife and family, 9687-8*. (A few quotations have also been made from Cockburn's letters to Macvey Napier, in British Library Add. MSS.34613-29 *passim*; and a letter on Bonaly architecture, to Dick Lauder in 1836, is one of a small group in the Advocates' Library, Edinburgh: the Librarian's permission to quote it is gratefully acknowledged). The Cockburn family's recent deposit (N.L.S. MS. Dep.235*) includes letters to his wife and his daughters Elizabeth and Jane; letters to and from Francis Jeffrey, Lord Jeffrey; to Sir Thomas Dick Lauder, John Richardson and several others. Adv. MSS.9.1.8-12* contain the letters and characteristically annotated transcripts of letters from Jeffrey to Cockburn; various legal papers collected by Cockburn are to be found in Adv. MSS.9.1.1-7; and a group of family and business papers relating to Cockburn's executry forms MS. Acc.3521. Many other single letters and small groups are to be found in the National Library, which is still adding to its holdings from time to time.

Reason and Dreams: Cockburn's practical and nostalgic views of civic well-being

ALAN BELL

—As to me, my *reason* is with the modern world, my *dreams* with the old one.

Circuit Journeys, Ayr, 19 September 1844.

—A wise man would like to have seen the past age, but to live in this one.

Journal, Edinburgh, 27 October 1847.

I

LORD COCKBURN is best known for his views on civic well-being from his *A Letter to the Lord Provost on the Best Ways of Spoiling the Beauty of Edinburgh*, first published in 1849, reprinted most recently as an appendix to George Bruce's *Some Practical Good* (1975), a centenary history of the Cockburn Association (the Edinburgh Civic Trust) named after the campaigning author of this locally influential tract. The challenge he issued in 1849 was taken up—many years after his death, it must be admitted—and the Association now flourishes (with, it must also be admitted, some fallow periods in its history) as a strident and often effective defender of the cause of Edinburgh, to which Cockburn devoted so much thought and energy in the last years of his life. Its current activities have been so well attuned to modern trends in conservation, the preservation of ancient buildings, the improvement of the amenity of urban environment, that one is tempted to apply each term to Cockburn's own views: that would however be anachronistic, and (with other general terms such as 'common good' having special connotations in Scotland) a less specific phrase, of 'well-being', has been chosen for a consideration of some of Cockburn's opinions and the varied experience which lay behind them.

Cockburn had rather surprised himself by writing his *Letter to the Lord Provost*. A career in law and politics had left him wary of tract warfare of any kind, and his judicial position meant that he was unable to enter into public controversy as fully as he might have wished. The high dignity of his office did not however mean that he was in any way indifferent to alterations which threatened the beauty of a city in which he took a lyrical, but a practical, delight. In August 1849, the threats seem to have been unusually many. John Macfarlan, a druggist on the South Bridge, tried to enlist Cockburn's interest in the agitation to preserve the architectural screen in front of the Register House, then threatened by a road-widening scheme; the argument of utility which had been adduced in support of its removal was later to be attacked in Cockburn's *Letter*. Macfarlan received a reply which debated the screen business fairly and went on to give some general views:

> Amidst such Edinburgh barbarities, or rather brutalities, as the extinction of Trinity Church and of Knox's House, it is consolatory to find one man, who, whether he be right or not, at least *takes an interest* in the preservation of that beauty on which the reputation of Edinburgh chiefly depends. . . .
>
> But though I don't agree with you on this matter [of the screen], I do rejoice in every sympton that such a matter is cared about at all. The Calton Hill—or part of it—is at this moment getting itself converted into a *public washing green*!!!!! with iron poles, and ropes, and wells, and streaks of worn grass—i.e. mud—and yellow, ragged blankets, and tubs, and stones, and bitches. All this on the Calton Hill! And not from right, or old usage; but by a voluntary magisterial act, cursed by a few, but applauded by many!!!
>
> Do keep your eye on all such pieces of Hunnism. And do not imagine, because I differ from you about the [Wellington] Statue, or because I cannot now agitate, that I am regardless of them.

A few days later, Cockburn wrote again to Macfarlan to emphasize his concern, and to lament the apathy of their fellow-citizens:

> I repeat that my zeal for the preservation of Edinburgh is as intense as ever it was. But I cannot now agitate. If I could, the very causeway stones should rise up against

certain most accursed projects. But why are others, with whom agitation would not be improper, so silent? The last Edinburgh papers report the dirt that issued from the mouths of certain presumptuous idiots who lately held a meeting in favour of *destroying* the screen. *I see, and hear of, no counter meeting.* Not that the thing will depend on such opinions either way—any more than a surgical operation would, or should. It is an architectural question. But it is scarcely fair, or safe, to expose those who must decide to hear roaring only one way. They should know that the wrong minded by no means represent the whole community.

But it must be confessed that the general apathy of Edinburgh on such matters is most discouraging and humiliating. I know well, by experience, how difficult it is to get even half a dozen of people to take the slightest trouble for any, even the most important, object of decoration, or of preventing abomination. The prevailing feeling is Indifference, or rather a paltry preference for any piece of mean utility, when it comes into competition with the noblest public adornment. Everything dignified and beautiful must be sacrificed to the lowest bodily conveniences of what is called 'the working man'—as if Judges and Druggists did not work, and were not entitled to have their tastes too. These people would have thought the garden of Eden wasted if it had not a distillery upon it, if one had been wanted.

Such fighting talk, with words like 'abomination' and 'Hunnism' that were to occur with some repetitiousness in Cockburn's private letters on the subject, indicated that he may then have been at the point of going as far as a judge could reasonably go in attempting to stir up a public discussion. His alarm at civic indifference was such that he soon composed his *Letter* for publication, recording in his *Journal* in October that 'If, as seems probable, publishing a pamphlet be one of the signs of insanity, I am mad, because I published one about ten days ago. . . . If any man doubts our dangers, let him read that letter. It has at least excited attention, and may do some practical good.'

The *Letter* to Lord Provost Johnstone (which was, incidentally, answered in print by at least one clerical defender of the Edinburgh poor, to whose plight Cockburn was far from indifferent) is much less shrill in tone than its author's private correspondence. He wisely adopts the moderate debating position of the avoidance of degradation, rather than advancing too many strident positive suggestions; and indeed 'the best ways of spoiling the beauty' of the *Letter's* title begs just the right number of questions and enables him to proceed from a definition of the beauty rather than entering immediately into the imprecation, overstatement and tendentiousness which sometimes renders suspect the arguments of his letters and journal. Only occasionally, as in his description of recent changes at the Castle, with its 'factory-looking erection which deforms the most picturesque fortress in Her Majesty's British dominions' do phrases like 'the most audacious piece of abomination in Europe' intrude. The tone generally is judicial: 'I listen to the plea of convenience nearly as if it were urged in recommendation of a crime.'

It is clear throughout the *Letter* that its views are based on old and growing misgivings, and informed by a wider experience of civic life and architecture, and by a much wider sense of civic well-being than merely antiquarian preservation, than the immediate circumstances of its composition might suggest. This essay attempts to identify the origins of some of Cockburn's opinions, notably in his experience of continental travel in 1823 and in his *Circuit Journeys* throughout provincial Scotland, before returning to examine his other writings on the specific Edinburgh matters which he dealt with in his *Letter to the Lord Provost*.

II

It is one of Henry Cockburn's curious limitations—a vulgarly narrow view might be disposed to consider it his peculiar glory— that his experience was almost exclusively Scottish. His topographical range was very limited. The restriction of his legal, literary, social, and artistic field of vision, except for matters of common educated experience, to Scottish national traditions gives his writings a localized sharpness of focus which increases their impact for a Scottish readership (while not necessarily diminishing their potential general appeal). Only once in his life did this commentator on the urban scene venture abroad, but the memory of the journey which he undertook in 1823 with John Richardson, Francis Jeffrey and some of the Jeffrey family, was to be as carefully cherished as the trip had been eagerly anticipated. It also provides a rare point of comparison against which we can assess the notions of urban layout and civic antiquity that he was to elaborate later in his life.

The journey itself, one of the principal events of his life, is dealt with at appropriate length in Karl Miller's *Cockburn's Millennium*, where particular attention is paid to the account of Venice (with a complete transcription of the relevant portion), since the history and traditions of the city and its doges had a special significance for him. The journal as a whole, which survives in a copy made by Jeffrey's daughter Charlotte (N.L.S., MS. Acc.3445), is the record of a jolly old tour with his friends—Jeffrey's flirtatious propensities are never ignored, and there is much ribbing, as if on a Habbie's Howe picnic. Cockburn's response to Rhenish and Alpine scenery is, as one would expect, immediate and wholehearted, and based (as Karl Miller emphasizes) on the expected romantic attitudes of the day. The grandeurs of the Swiss mountainous landscape impressed him deeply, but his recorded reaction to them is ultimately rather commonplace. It is however given a special domestic piquancy by the local references which punctuate his text—the Rhine, of which he had no previous conception, is for example described as 'in size it is just the Tweed below Melrose, or the Tay below Perth'. Similarly the horror of a first encounter with Flemish Catholicism enhanced both his reaction to the first cathedrals he saw and the contrasts he found with St George's Church in Basle, where he noted with relief the 'air of rude, provincial, simplicity, and of reverential attachment to the good cause which makes this ancient edifice far more interesting than those noble Cathedrals which have to boast only of their wealth and their art'.

Cockburn's own almost reverential attachment to rude, provincial simplicity makes his responses to the towns he visited both charming in their nationalist naïvety and informative about the development of ideas which shaped his view of Edinburgh as an architecturally appropriate capital city. From Ostend to Milan there were qualities of picturesqueness, visual variety, recreational spaciousness and civic vitality which he recorded with special pleasure, and they undoubtedly affected his attitude to Edinburgh as formulated a quarter of a century later. Novelty may have given the towns a special appeal, but the impact of this single long journey remained throughout his life and provided him with one of his few points of architectural and environmental reference.

Novelty certainly made even Ostend appeal to him (John
Richardson more prosaically remarked that 'it would be a great
misery to stay here a day, it looks so low and uninviting'). Cockburn
considered that

> It is the perfect model of a picturesque town. It is small,
> reddish, very clean and absolutely bristling in every part
> with rough ornaments. As we passed through the principal
> square we could not help exclaiming. The chimneys, the
> carved doors, the brass handles, the spouts, the gables, the
> tall roofs, every thing is old and picturesque. There is no
> form or colour that they have not exhausted in strange
> decoration, and the people themselves who were out in
> their Sunday attire, seemed as ancient in their air and
> raiment as their buildings.

Appropriate reaction to the urban picturesque was at that
period, I suspect, a good deal less codified than that to landscape
and mountainous scenery. Antiquarian notions of curiosity may
have more to do with it than reverential feelings of awe.
Cockburn's reports of the towns therefore seem much fresher, and
when in Brussels (where he noted approvingly a mixture 'of gaiety
and of antiquity, of old Gothic and of modern Grecian') com-
parisons with Edinburgh lent further point to his observations.
'Every one of the old houses throughout the whole town is
picturesque', he noted:

> I can scarcely conceive anything more striking than the
> long lines of irregularly ridged roofs which everywhere
> break the top edges of the narrow streets. Would that the
> planner of the new town of Edinburgh had seen them!
> How they would have changed the characters of our heavy,
> dull, lengthy uniform fronts!

At Antwerp a few days later, the notion of the special appeal of
the group of urban buildings began to take shape by contrast,
perhaps for the first time:

> The difference between Antwerp and the other cities we
> had seen is, that in the latter each individual house was
> generally insignificant while their combination made a
> collection that was striking from its irregularity; whereas
> the chief excellence of the former arises from the
> respectability of the private dwellings, which consist of
> detached, white painted, large doored, and large
> windowed, comfortable houses. Bruges and Ghent were

like moss roses, Antwerp only like a full cabbage.

Rotterdam, lacking much public ornament in the way of statues and municipal monuments, was 'singular and beautiful' none the less, because of—or in spite of—a lack of the architectural regimentation that feuing restrictions and the Dean of Guild decreed at home:

> Where there is a *mere* street without a canal, every house
> builder or owner seems to do as he likes—and the
> universal fashion is to erect a tall house, made of small
> bricks of every shade of red from pale yellow to deep
> scarlet, the different colours being placed into forms
> according to the different parts of the edifice. There is a
> good deal of wood about them, commonly employed in
> fantastic ornament and painted of various hues. These
> houses are invariably full of projections and irregularities
> which made them very picturesque—in so much that
> they are not anxious even to make the front walls stand
> straight up. They have often and throughout whole streets
> a fearful projection forward so that the result is that the
> whole town is roughened into beauty by mere independent
> individual caprice.

Such irregularities, though gratifying to the eye, were often offset in Holland by one characteristic which Cockburn found distasteful. The Hague was reported as 'quiet, genteel, and clean—But with all this, it is blighted with the Dutch curse. It is full of canals and every canal is a dead, green, stinking pool'. Compensations were to be found elsewhere, however. Amsterdam, otherwise disappointing in comparison with other Dutch towns, surprised the travellers by the quantity of trees in its streets: 'We found rows of them growing in streets not twenty feet wide and yet we are told George Street is too narrow for them.'

Further on their way, Darmstadt provided some of the formality which was to be wished for as a contrast with Dutch picturesqueness. Cockburn found the new part of Darmstadt the handsomest town they had seen since Brussels. 'The houses are large, white, blue, or pink, detached and with great cornices, and they and the street altogether in a very lordly style.' 'It is the only place where we have found a flagged foot pavement', he added, for such incidentals were reckoned as noteworthy as the more prominent architectural features. The 'pleasing and abundant fountains' which he observed even in the poorest of Swiss villages led him to reflect at Amsteg: 'Such an accommodation is one of the many points in which we have as yet everything to learn. There is scarcely a town containing 1,000 people on the continent, in which more has not been done for the recreation of the inhabitants, than in the largest British cities.'

The surroundings of Lake Como, viewed after an exhausting journey ('agreeable as scenery may be, there is really no enjoying it when it is only seen in a state of profuse perspiration') led to some opinions on ill-considered building sprawl:

It is no doubt beautiful but I scarcely ever saw a place in which I should have less desire to abide. . . . The margin of the Lake is crowded with villages and country houses, the latter of which are invariably styled Palazzos. . . . every gentleman's house seems to be elbowed by a parcel of low neighbours. . . . They look, in short, just like houses put down in the middle of a wide copse without external accompaniments, or separate boundaries. All this gives them a remarkably dead air. . . . Though it seems disrespectful, it really is not, to describe the houses as resembling square tea boxes or rather oblong ones standing on their ends.

Such a thirst for the picturesque, which was soon to make his reaction to Verona and Vicenza so interesting, was expanded even after so short an acquaintance with Italy:

There is nothing rough or picturesque in them [the Lake Como palazzos], nothing whatever. There is more roughness in one Flemish house than in all the Italian ones we have seen—when they do ornament, it is by correct cornices, or friezes, or pediments or the like. The result of all this is, that their buildings are plain, angular and simple and have generally a very architectural air. There are two things to which much of this is owing. One is, that their roofs are almost always set at a very pleasing angle. They are not flat but they are not much raised. They are broad and low; in which I wish our Scotch raisers of precipices of slate would imitate them. The other is, their addiction to straight horizontal lines. Their windows, roofs, doors, and every eminent object about the buildings, carry the eye along throughout the whole range of the same house, and often of all the houses on the same level, without shifting. In so much so, that even when a

town stands on a steep so that the horizontal line cannot
be preserved entirely throughout, it is preserved as far as
possible in stages—All this gives their buildings a severe,
but correct, air. There is nothing picturesque, but there is
much that is pleasing. Every thing is in the style of calm
elegant regularity.

Verona provided some admirable buildings, and Cockburn's
only regret was that it was only possible to see a little of them:

The Palazzos look inwards to courts, and it seems to be
generally the outer front that was intended to look best,
and they do look well, by being imposing in their
elevation, and rich and correct in their ornaments. They
seem to be set up as models and as mines, from which one
may see and extract all the elements of Italian
architecture. Whether it be from example or not I cannot
say but the whole town is rich in architectural decoration.
Their doorways, windows, wells, clocks, balustrades,
fountains, porticoes etc., though often mean and fantastic,
generally show quite plainly that a learned and ambitious
architect had been at them. . . .

Their architecture is greatly injured from the buildings
where it is displayed being almost never fully exposed
to view. All that is seen is an end, obscured by mean
encroachments, or a facade so close beside a high narrow
street that one's neck must be broken if it be long looked at.

The Palladian buildings of Vicenza, next on their route, were
excellently adorned: 'beautiful fronts generally ornamented as at
Verona with statues, which when seen in the skyline always look
well. Oh! for half a dozen of these facades in Edinburgh where
there would be room to see them, whereas here that is often
impossible.'

The architectural impact of Venice is not so well recorded as
that of smaller towns. He gave (as readers of Professor Miller's
chapter on the tour will know) a prolonged account of the deeply
moving experience of fulfilling a pilgrimage to a city in whose
history and traditions he seems to have been remarkably well
read. More space is devoted to the aquatic economy than to the
constituent buildings, but he did find time to write of the Palazzos
in general—and of the meanness of the interstices of the grand
buildings, of the decay and dirtiness, and the lack of show which
he himself probably found disappointing:

. . . things which would shock the eye of a person who went there expecting to see bright marble and great combined plans. There is nothing like marble, or cleanness, or care, or anything showy about them. They are of a whitish colour, or rather of a decaying grey, not unlike Burlington House, or the gate of Northumberland House. . . . In short these Venetian noblemen's palaces are like beggarly gentlemen's houses—richly ornamented and finely imagined, at first, but mouldering now into ruin.

Still however enough remains to show distinctly the original conception, and all the details. Not one of them is roofless, or has any appearance of falling down, in any part. So that if a person will rid his mind of the idea of bright marble, and living domestic purity; and will think of the carving, and the columns, the pilastres and the balustrades, the statues and the urns, of some centuries ago, and recollect that he is taking his last gaze of a city in its death-bed—he will overlook all these mean obtrusions on the scene, and will *in effect* behold nothing but a noble range of superb edifices, over which time has breathed only to give the character of venerableness to their original splendour.

The Place of St Mark . . . is perfect. . . . When I sailed down there and stood in the middle of that singular quad-rangle, my longing for novelty and for old architecture was for once completely satiated.

Venice was the culmination of his journey, spiritually and architecturally. Poor health on the return trip abbreviated his diary, but there was time to record his reactions at Milan and Paris, among other stopping places. At Milan he wrote of the cathedral that 'it is no doubt a magnificent edifice, but upon the whole I was disappointed with it. It wants simplicity and calmness if it be to be considered as of a grave cast, and if it be to be viewed as of the florid order then its floridity is not good.' These limita-tions were elaborated, and the principal blame was attached to the building material, white marble being 'too sparkling and showy for a great building'. The wealth of external statuary was felt to be distracting—it was too like 'a splendid toy':

this building being the first of the kind I ever saw has convinced me of the truth of what I have often heard, that good freestone is better for architecture than white

marble—the latter of which does not acquire its best
appearance till time has made it something like the former.
Freestone is softer and richer and simpler.
The interior of the cathedral—'dark, dirty and mean'—did not
occupy him long, and he 'thought nothing of the modern per-
formances' at the Brera, where he recorded that 'the rooms are
extensive and handsome, and this is a most honorable establishment for such a place. The whole community was freely admitted
gratis.' The adjacent library proved to be much more interesting:

> The books seemed numerous and excepting that many of
> them were, or had been, wormed, they were in exquisite
> order, being handsomely bound and perfectly free from
> dust. The shelves had no glass, wire, or cloth—but were
> quite open. They were all of mahogany, or of wood
> stained like mahogany. And round each room there ran a
> gallery of the same wood, with a plain, massive balustrade
> the effect of which from its gravity, and solidity and
> unfading purity, was admirable, and made me blush for
> our thin gilded iron railing in the advocates' and writers'
> library. This and the one at Brussels are the best libraries
> as to books that we have seen. The one at Venice made
> them both sink to nothing in point of gorgeousness of
> room.

Continental observation helped to crystallize his reaction to the
impractical magnificence of the Advocates' (later Signet) Library
building then under construction in Edinburgh. A final Edinburgh
parallel was provided by Paris, which he visited while recovering
from the illness which had laid him low on the journey back
through Switzerland. He quite enjoyed his five or six days there,
noting however that:

> its attractions are certainly confined chiefly to the court
> quarter of the town. It is impossible to lament that
> Napoleon did not get time to finish his designs for
> improving it. I was much struck with the miserable
> poverty of river, and with the total absence of all that
> blackguardism of air and manner which the revolution has
> taught us to associate with the populace of Paris. Even in
> the remotest and most crowded streets there was an
> uniform appearance of quiet and decency. . . . Their
> Champs Elysees are contemptible; poor, regularly cut
> trees, no grass and little space. But for its sculpture

Bonaparte's bronze pillar in the Place Vendome is not
equal to ours, taken from the same model, in St Andrew
Square.

Cockburn returned to England soon afterwards, noting (not
perhaps without surprise) that 'the ordinary statement that there
is nothing worth seeing or worth enjoying out of Britain, is an
absurd British boast'. The Flemish and Dutch towns, Paris and
above all Venice had all made their special impact providing him
with a fund of memory against which the settled architectural
opinion of his later years could be improved by an experience
broader than that afforded by the Scottish examples to which his
later life was to be confined.

III

The record of his *Circuit Journeys* which Cockburn compiled as a
memorial of his judicial travels between 1837 and 1854 contains
many valuable indications of his attitudes to architecture—urban
and rural—and to change and improvement in the provincial
towns of Scotland, which antedate his recorded opinions of
Edinburgh. This is perhaps surprising in a book which largely
consists of skilled evocations of country journeyings laced with
comments on judicial practice, ancient and modern, and on the
provincial amusements which delighted him. The handsome
octogenarian Miss Macpherson of Forres, who was 'always in
excellent spirits, and has a delightful northern accent and dialect,
with a willing flow of strong sense and acute observation, generally
of a cheerful character', can be seen as peculiarly sympathetic to
the author himself, in a work which a recent critic has called 'one
of the least pretentious masterpieces of Victorian travel literature'.

Rural bliss, in the agrestic mode of his own Bonaly and the
Pentlands, might be thought the most natural concomitant of
such provincial characters. Visiting Lord Abercromby at Airthrie
(now seat of the University of Stirling) in April 1840, when the
place was 'in the perfection of young vernal beauty', he recorded
that 'the verdure of Abercromby's grass, the bright, fresh, tenderness of his foliage, the clearness of his lake, the mirth of his lambs
and water-fowl, and the softened richness of his rocks and hills
were all blended into a scene of singular loveliness'. The *Circuit
Journeys* contains some of his lordship's lushest prose, but the
travels also allowed him to broaden his experience of ancient

monuments, and to become better acquainted with some of the great mansion-houses of Scotland, and with the ancient burghs which so delighted him—but which were so threatened by the rapid changes of the time in commerce, architecture and travel. His reactions often prefigure those to the much greater problems of Edinburgh.

The landscape, and not just the villages and small towns, was itself changing. His preference in arboriculture was indicated in his notes on Deeside in September 1846:

> The profusion of birch is beautiful, and of good old birch,
> with thick, honest, rough stems, such as I thought were
> only to be seen along Loch Ness; and weeping, not like
> poor contemptible solitary creatures, cultivated just in
> order to weep in a garden, but pouring and waving miles
> of tears, as if they thought the Dee could not flow without
> them. And the Scotch fir! profuse, dark, large, with arms
> tossed about as if defying even the oak, and looking as
> eternal as the rocks they have taken possession of. It is a
> glorious firth of wood.

The preference for thickness, roughness and *honesty* had its parallel in Cockburn's views of architecture, but such bucolic virtues were under threat. In 1838 he wrote admiringly of the Carrbridge-Inverness road, with its wood of Scotch firs, 'the branches being more gnarled and tossed about like those of forest trees, than any fir branches I ever saw', but he had also to observe that 'some monsters are *improving* the country (as they no doubt call it) by planting out these magnificent prospects, by lining the road with abominable stripes of wretched larch trees'. 'Our only hope', he added characteristically, 'is in the boys and the cattle.'

He was not, of course, opposed to 'improvement' when its results were aesthetically satisfactory. At Snaigow in Perthshire, his recently-dead friend James Keay's domestications of his policies were praised on a Spring visit in 1839:

> The place is one of the best examples of the triumph of
> taste within a short period over poor natural features, long
> aggravated into worse badness by detestable management.
> Fifteen years ago, it seemed absolutely irreclaimable, and
> its ugliness was in the worst style of dull, nasty,
> meaningless inconvenience. It is now a comfortable,
> respectable, sensible place, with all the old abominations
> of stone fences, single rows of wind-bent trees, and wet

grass fields removed, and a beautiful house, surrounded by
well laid-out and well-kept ornamental ground, thriving
evergreens, good lawn, and the former wood broken into
natural and useful shapes and positions, substituted in
their stead. But in all this satisfactory creation, the mind of
James Keay predominated, one of the most sensible of men.
Old affections perhaps influenced his view of these changes on
a small estate. Elsewhere the management of larger properties
incurred his wrath, absentee proprietors sometimes being treated
to withering scorn. Aboyne, in 1846, still exhibited 'all the signs
of dilapidation and insolvency. But while his woods are falling,
and railways are waiting to sleep upon them, the contemptible
old monkey-faced wretch of a beau, who danced at Versailles with
Marie Antoinette about sixty years ago, is still grinning and
dancing somewhere abroad, at the expense of creditors who can't
afford to let him die.' Landowners like Lord Huntly were castigated for a variety of offences, mainly of omission, in estate
management. Cockburn also encountered the Clearances when
on criminal business in Inverness in 1849, trying four resisters of
an enforcement. 'The popular feeling', he remarked, 'is so strong
against these (as I think necessary, but) odious operations, that I
was afraid of an acquittal, which would have been unjust and
mischievous'. Legal necessities had to be balanced against the
judge's distaste, but he was able to conclude that in this case 'the
slightness of the punishment, four months' imprisonment, will
probably abate the public fury'.

Cockburn's rage at the proprietors was concentrated on owners
developing—and often destroying—for sporting reasons. He admitted that the innumerable English tenants had their uses—'they
are kind to the people, they increase rents, they spend money, and
they diffuse a knowledge of, and a taste for, this country'—but
shootings interfered with footpaths, and previously accessible
countryside became shut off. Galloway provided a prime
example in 1844, where Lord Selkirk (the name is omitted from
the 1888 edition, but can be supplied from the *Journeys* manuscript now in the Signet Library) sacrificed all to 'the creation
of game':

His estate is a great preserve, it is absolutely crawling with
rabbits. For them, and for hares and pheasants, everything
else is neglected. The worse state his woods get into, he
thinks it the better, so as they be only suffering from

growing into tangled masses of branches and of underwood. Tall jungles are his object. I could overlook the meanness of his taste, for it is his own loss; and I could almost endure the cruel war which he and his mounted patrols of gamekeepers carry on against the people, because he gets properly cursed for it; but it is impossible to forgive the selfishness which bequeaths the beautiful scenery which has the misfortune to call him master in a state of decay to the next generation. We passed to-day through miles of the finest sweet chestnuts—all under sacrifice, in order that, during his hour, he may boast of his battues.

Passages such as these, though not immediately relevant to the theme of urban well-being, are interesting, and not just for the comparative study of Cockburn's execratory technique. They also show that rural improvements, far removed from the near-suburbanities of Bonaly, could occupy his mind and pen; and in the Galloway example quoted, themes of picturesqueness and the satisfactions the public gained through accessibility, are just as apparent as in his writings on architecture and on urban life.

The great landed proprietors came in for further uninhibited criticism for their neglect or maltreatment of the ancient buildings in their ownership. Cockburn's *Journeys* sometimes read like the work of a one-man historical monuments commission, and his reports are rarely favourable. Cawdor Castle, 'though pretended to be still maintained as a place of residence, is all in the most humiliating condition of paltry disrepair', with mean and vulgar repair work which would have disgraced a 'Findhorn fishcurer or Nairn grocer'. The poor state of the great ruins of Kilchurn in 1843 could be blamed on the Marquess of Breadalbane:

... still enough of turret, and window, and ivy remaining to render it perhaps in as perfect a stage for preservation, as a ruin, as it ever has been or can be. But what murder it is undergoing! There is little neighbouring population, and therefore there is little of the usual Scotch sheer filth. But except this, there is every other atrocity. Not one sixpence of money or one moment of care has ever been bestowed on either of the two duties of protecting or of cleaning.

The cause of the noble owner's negligence was divined as not avarice, nor ... ignorance, at least not in his case. It proceeds from want of thought, which creates the habit of

D

being reconciled to what ought to be felt shameful; till at
last he who would give £500 for a hearthrug, or £5000
for a Gothic dairy, stares at the idea of expending a
shilling on arresting the decay of the only thing he may
happen to possess which painting or poetry think worthy
of their notice.

A couple of years later, he recommended in his journal (regretting
that no-one had recommended it to the owner) that Kilchurn
should be pinned and pointed, cleared and grassed: all could be
done for £500, he opined. 'But suppose it cost £5000. Would not
the Marquis spend twice this in defending one of his grouse knolls,
or even his marquisate?'

Religious buildings, with even more potential appeal as picturesque ruins than Kilchurn, were often in equally negligent lay
ownership. Beauly was sadly neglected: 'a spot more absolutely
abandoned to abomination never disgraced a community.
Rubbish, nettles, and that filth so dear to Sawney, have there
their triumph over decency.' Of Dunkeld, in 1844, he wrote that
'its keeping—absolutely within the ducal shrubbery—is most
disgraceful'; destructive reformation from popery was all very well,
'but what defence is it to dukes who can afford to give £5000 a
year of their estate to the deer?' The beautiful ruins of Pluscarden,
once threatened merely by an excess of ivy, had been reprieved
only by a nobleman's dire financial straits. 'What a mercy it is
that Lord Fife became bankrupt some years ago!' Cockburn wrote
in 1844: 'Long may he continue so! An old abbey still in adequate
preservation may, innocently, and even with good taste, be kept
up as a residence, if this be done properly. But this poor, insensible,
ignorant wretch was making Pluscarden into a *shooting-box*!' It
had been part slated and some register stoves installed when, as
Cockburn put it in a letter to Jeffrey, 'God justly smote him
bankrupt'.

Jedburgh, owned by the Lothian family, was contrasted un-
favourably with Dunblane, in public custody, which Cockburn
felt 'does the Woods and Forests great credit'. But Jedburgh was
'disgracefully, most disgracefully, abused'; the conversion of half
the building into a parish church, and the continuation of family
burials in unsuitable new tombs, were both regrettable, and the
grand old building was jostled by others. In 1845 Cockburn
described it as an 'abomination' and laid about him in the *Journeys*
with his usual vigour:

It cannot be described. And under the very lock and key
of the noble house of Lothian, to whom it belongs, and
who live within five miles of the smell of it! nay, over the
very dust and prostrate statues of their own ancestors!
They can dine off plate; and they can build Puseyite
chapels in Jedburgh; but they cannot lay out one shilling
in protecting a ruin, the ownership of which does them
more honour than their title does, from pollution at which
the snout of a famished hog would revolt . . . how they can
resist the mere romance of the matter I cannot understand.
This over-energetic rhetoric, perhaps recalling the verbal batter-
ing of a jury in his days as counsel, was characteristic; the editors of
the published *Journeys* were able to record a change of heart by
the owner, and Rowand Anderson's extensive restoration work
in the 1870s.

His view of Melrose brought in the question of the desirability
of public access. Structurally he found it clean and respectable,
and the old attendant who had shown it for forty years (despite a
'very whiskyfied visage', and amusingly pretentious diction) was
an adequate guide. 'Shall we never see these Scotch fragments
waited upon by attendants worthy of them?', Cockburn asked in
1841: 'By the respectful, well dressed, reverential old man, the
nice, tidy, decent, kindly woman, or the gentle and intelligent
girl?' Four years later he was distressed to see a party of respectable
farm-workers having to pay to visit Melrose Abbey: 'instead of
having the door thrown open, and being encouraged to humanise
their minds by the spectacle of such an edifice, they were sternly
barred out, and those only let in (which to their honour was the
whole of them) who would first pay a penny.' Once again, it was
the noble proprietor (in this case the Duke of Buccleuch) who
was excoriated.

Attitudes to the preservation of ecclesiastical antiquities were
changing even in Cockburn's own day. Dundrennan Abbey in
Kirkcudbrightshire (from which Cockburn's brother-in-law
Maitland took his judicial title) was in 1839 distressingly neglected.
Although the owner himself was 'a most liberal and right-minded
gentleman', Cockburn felt that 'the mischief proceeds from no
positively improper object, but from that absence of right feeling
which, on such subjects, seems to be nearly universal among
Scotch proprietors'. On returning to Dundrennan five years later,
Cockburn gave himself some credit for the improvements; in this

case family affinities had allowed him (which never happened
with the nobility) to 'freely administer verbally ... the objurgation'
written in 1839. The result was that

> the Commissioners of Woods and Forests have cleaned out
> the rubbish, and drained the ground, and made some
> judicious repairs, and cleared away the abominable offices
> of the manse, and enclosed the whole. It is still far from
> what a reverenced ruin ought to be, because its
> preservation requires much more pinning and cementing,
> and purity; but compared to what it once was, it is
> humanity to barbarism. It is another of several examples,
> that none of the hallowed architectural remains of
> Scotland, except those belonging to the Crown, will ever
> be kept in decent order. . . . It is plain that every private
> ruin is destined to disappear.

The country nobility and gentry could rarely be trusted to look
after their modern, let alone their ancient, habitations. Of ducal
mansions Inveraray merited only Cockburn's (very much over-
used) 'abominable' *tout court*; Blair had been shut off with pro-
hibitory notices; and Drumlanrig, in an aesthetically neglected
setting, was rumoured to be 'dangerously frail'. Perhaps the best
thing for the last would be 'to leave it as a ruin, [and] to get a
noble design for a new castle from Playfair', a typical urging of a
close friend whose merits were always to be contrasted with
Burn's repetitious and inappropriately-set work. Sir David Blair's
new house at Blairquhan was described as 'too ostentatious and
too large for the place, and architecturally ... nothing', and
Cockburn lamented other Burn houses at Faskally, Lude and
elsewhere, 'none of them in keeping with a rough climate and
situations of romantic wildness'. A brief mention of the old house
at Faskally, and a comment of 1853 on Balmoral, then rebuilding,
that it 'may be better than the old one for residence, but I don't
anticipate that it will equal the old one in picturesque beauty',
shows where Cockburn's preference lay. Taymouth was regretted
as an Inveraray derivative, when 'old Grandtully Castle still
stands, for hints, but a few miles off . . . a good old mass, main-
taining a feudal atmosphere around itself.' And his friend Sir
Harry Moncreiff's Tulliebole perhaps represented the ideal of
picturesqueness—

> an admirable small castle. A delightful castle inside and
> out. The date, 2d April 1608, and two scriptural texts

carved above the door, a tower, walls seven feet thick,
turrets, odd, small windows, queer irregular little up-and-
down bits of stairs, and a general air of quaint solidity and
primitive awkwardness, give it all the charm of ancient
habits, which, in this instance, is not disturbed by the
slightest attempt at modern innovation.

There is a good working description of the picturesque baronial
impracticalities which Cockburn and Playfair were to aim for at
Bonaly itself.

Regular judicial tours gave Cockburn plenty of opportunities
for exploring villages and towns, as well as for delighting in rugged
or well-improved Scottish rural scenery. Generally speaking, it
was the picturesqueness of the urban setting which was particularly admired—old squalor was to be pitied, ancient variety to be
praised. The urban world of the Scottish provinces as he had
known it was under threat; 'manufactures' were advancing, and
Galashiels, which Cockburn records in the *Memorials* as once
having been 'a rural hamlet' had become 'the Glasgow of Selkirk-
shire'. And in 1847 he grieved for the Ayrshire village of
Dalmellington:

It has the appearance and the reputation of being a
singularly virtuous and happy village; and I am told is
perhaps the last place in Ayrshire where, with a good deal
of old primitive manufacture, rural simplicity and
contentment still linger. But it is now to taste of
manufactures in an *improved* state. The devil has disclosed
his iron, and speculation has begun to work it. . . .

Larger towns, like Arbroath, were also threatened: in 1844 it was
'what they call rapidly advancing, that is, its steam-engine
chimney-stacks are multiplying. But its old character is dis-
appearing.' Railways were a particular danger, removing provincial peculiarities, making places *too* accessible: 'the country is
an asylum of railway lunatics' is a frequent complaint, and the
engineers and speculators were doing their worst.

Elgin represented in many ways Cockburn's ideal of a burgh.
There was a notably well-kept Cathedral—'certainly by far the
best kept old ruin, public or private, in Scotland'—which owed
its state much to the exertions of John Shanks, a local shoemaker
and devoted guide to the building, whom Cockburn himself saw
was adequately commemorated after his death. Of the town
itself, Cockburn wrote in 1839 that

I am not sure that, except Perth, there is a nicer
provincial town in Scotland. Placed in a delightful country,
with a climate not exceeded in mildness, and a soil not
equalled in dryness, by any that we have, it is dignified by
the survivance of many of the old ecclesiastical dwellings,
of which numerous obvious vestiges are to be seen in the
streets; and the affection of its successful sons is attested by
munificent bequests, which their beautiful public buildings
show that the existing inhabitants have intelligence to use
rightly, while over all there presides the spirit that yet
hovers over the ruins of their glorious Cathedral. Old
Henry Mackenzie, who married a Grant, and had much
intercourse with Morayshire, described Elgin in its old
state, before its modern improvements began, as 'a
melancholy and gentlemanlike place'. So it was, being
respectable, ancient, and silent. It has now far more new
life, graced by due antiquity. The scenery of Perth is
better, but it has weavers. Montrose, in its main street at
least, is grander, but it has ships. Stirling has every interest,
a history, picturesque streets, ruins, prospect and its
castle, but the town is squalid and cursed by charity.
Kelso, Melrose, and Jedburgh have each its river and its
ruin, but they are all paltry, sinking, insignificant places.
I cannot recollect such a union of ancient venerableness
with modern respectability, and provincial seclusion as in
Elgin.

Like Perth, mentioned here as almost Elgin's equal in his affections, its size and standing were deeply satisfying. 'It is comfortable to have a few Goshens', he once remarked of Perth, 'a
few spots where taste, and intellect, and peace can enjoy themselves in their old way, undisturbed by steam-engines, mobs and
upstart temporary wealth.' Yet vigilance was essential; he was
distressed to hear prominent Perth citizens envying Dundee its
trade: 'We must have manufacturing towns. But there is no
necessity for their being made out of the ruins of natural beauty,
or the retreats of academic learning.'

Aberdeen, with its limited commercial development and its
academic establishments, proved in many ways that the two did
not sit happily together:

The old town is striking and interesting, with its venerable
college, its detached position, its extensive links, and

glorious beach. But the new and larger city is cold, hard
and treeless. The grey granite does well for public works
where durability is obviously the principal object, but for
common dwelling-houses it is not, to my taste, nearly so
attractive as the purity of the white freestone, or the
richness of the cream-coloured.

The inappropriate textures of such hard building materials were
often adversely commented on, not least a granite statue of the
Duke of Gordon: 'the *freckled face*, if the granite be grey, or the
pimpled or *blotched* face, if it be red, are insuperable objections.
The duke's visage looks as if it had been rubbed over with oatmeal.'
Granite, however, might be thought to have special affinities as
an architectural medium used by civic authorities; and Cockburn
once remarked after remonstrating with the burgesses of Aberdeen
about the re-siting of their ancient cross that 'Town Councils and
taste rarely draw together'.

A similar example of his perpetual mistrust of municipal administration is provided in Cockburn's admonition to his friend
Kennedy, who as Commissioner of Woods and Forests had various
responsibilities for public buildings, in 1851: '*Never take your eye
off St Andrews*. There's a Provost there—a hater of old stones.' As
a place which had been 'Pompeiied, saved by circumstances from
being superseded, or dissipated, by modern change', it was very
satisfying, architecturally and academically—but also perhaps a
bit dull?

There are very few shops, and, thank God, no trade or
manufactures. I could not detect a single steam-engine, and
their navy consisted of three coal sloops which lay within
a small pier composed of large stones laid rudely, though
strongly, together upon a natural quay of rock. The gentry
of the place consists of professors, retired Indians, saving
lairds, old ladies and gentlemen with humble purses,
families resorting here for golf and education, or for
economy, or for sea-bathing. Nobody comes for what is
called business. Woe be on the ignorant wight who did!
He would die of lethargy in the first week.

An 'asylum of repose', little disturbed (then) by 'the repugnances
of later ages', enlivened by quiet sociabilities and (even then) by
a dominant staple of golfing: much to be desired, but equally
much to be watched. The old buildings of the United College had
been added to:

They have rashly laid out about £12,000, being all they
had, in a wretched new building, containing only four
class-rooms. If they ever get more, I anticipate a brief
survivance of the remaining old portions of the college.
They will all be torn down, not repaired, in order to make
way for some poor substitute by the Burn or the Reid of
the day—the two masons who have had most of the recent
spoiling of this venerable place. There are many things
well-deserving of preservation; but what can be expected
of poverty too great to keep even the monuments of
Bishop Geddes and of Archibishop Sharp in order?

Cockburn's concern for the future of St Andrews was a genuine
one, and (despite the bugaboo references to unfavourite architects)
not unmerited. He saw the place, if left unchanged, as providing
'a lettered retreat' to preserve, in spite of what others may have
considered an intellectual stagnation, 'the taste and the means of
learning' while others concentrated on the provision of professional education.

Endearing though he found such oases, it should not be thought
that he was opposed to urban improvement, provided it was well
managed. Small changes making a welcome but inexpensive
addition to municipal amenities were to be encouraged as well as
large architectural schemes. He once told the Provost of Stirling
that much local annoyance would be dispelled by having multiple
spouts on the public water-pumps, and in Dundee he was 'delighted to see some comfortable iron seats placed on different
parts of the green, near the infirmary, marked "for the sick poor".'
Such indications of municipal thoughtfulness were always welcomed, and larger endeavours were also praised, as in Dumfries,
where the newly-erected Crichton lunatic asylum met with his
approval in 1839 (although a passing urchin cast doubts on the
treatment by describing one of its functionaries as 'the *breaker* . . .
the man that *breaks* the daft folk'). Dumfries had also converted a
windmill into an observatory—'which means a windmill-looking
tower, with a bit of shrubbery round it, ginger-beer in the ground
floor, a good telescope in the second storey, and a camera obscura
in the third. So the astronomical dignity of the establishment is
not great, but still it is an agreeable and civilized institution.'
There could be many worse epithets than 'agreeable and civilized'
to characterize civic improvements.

The South Circuit took him frequently to Ayr, a town which

was full of memories for him; his later visits, recorded at a time when reminiscence was increasingly taking the place of topographical repetitions in the *Journeys*, are full of nostalgia. The old seasonal world of gentry jollifications had vanished, but the recollection was pleasant, impaired though it was by a visit to the lower quarters of the town ('they have a very Hibernian air'). It was gratifying to look back to the social life of his days as a junior at the bar:

> These were the days of no roads and of detached
> communities. All things are now melted into one sea, with
> a strong Corryvreckan in it sweeping everything towards
> the metropolis. And this has been the process in all
> provincial capitals. Improved harbours, railroad stations,
> better trade, and larger masses of migratory people have
> succeeded, and those who prefer this to the recollections
> of the olden time will be pleased. As to me, my *reason* is
> with the modern world, my *dreams* with the old one. And I
> feel that as to the ancient days there is much of their
> enchantment that arises from distance.

IV

It was of course on Edinburgh that Cockburn's views on urban layout and amenity were concentrated. Many of them derived from his limited but influential travels on the continent in 1823, and from his regular provincial journeys as a circuit judge: his preference for picturesque irregularity of what is nowadays called 'townscape', the historical authenticity and associations of ruins, varied and refreshing arboriculture, may with other opinions all be ascribed to such sources. The city of Edinburgh had been a major part of his experience for very much longer. The best-documented portion of his observation and agitation dates from the last decade of his life, but his interest in such matters was of much longer standing. At the Theatrical Fund Dinner of February 1827, famous for Lord Meadowbank's revelation of the identity of 'the author of *Waverley*', one of the lesser speakers produced laughter when he mentioned Cockburn's non-appearance at the banquet; his subject was Edinburgh Improvements and the possibility of siting a new theatre on the North Loch, to the south of Princes Street. Cockburn's sustained work on the *Memorials* not long after this cannot have failed to concentrate his views on civic change, as informed by nostalgic memory.

Just as his visits to Ayr had revealed a divergence between his reason and his dreams, so his memory's view of Edinburgh was modified by his recognition of current practicalities: 'a wise man', he wrote in his *Journal* on 27 October 1847, 'would have liked to have seen the past age, but to live in this one'. Lord Dunfermline, John Richardson and himself could then reminisce comfortably enough, though admitting the superiority of modern domestic life over the crowded arrangements of the Old Town. A single upper class—noble, landed and professional—living in close proximity, had its special social and cultural advantages, especially when 'the people had not arisen'. There was no Public in the Edinburgh of that 'final Scotch century' which Cockburn and his cronies had been just in time to witness. Yet they recognized the inevitability of change, and had enough confidence in their own position not to lament an inevitable intellectual decline during their lifetimes. The 'variety of eminence and agreeableness' had been increased, and the community, however much altered, had not been destroyed.

It had been the rise of the New Town, Cockburn admitted early in the *Memorials*, that had 'obliterated our old peculiarities with the greatest rapidity and effect. It not only changed our scenes and habits of life, but, by the mere inundation of modern population, broke up and, as was then thought, vulgarized our prescriptive gentilities.' The social impact he came to find less disagreeable than the architectural: the passages on the New Town in the *Memorials* show how his views had been moulded by his brief continental experience:

> In addition to the varied forms exhibited [in Scotland] by
> our forefathers, almost every city on the Continent supplied
> us with specimens of striking and cheap town architecture
> perfectly adapted to the purposes of ordinary life. Yet we
> went on as if these examples were ridiculous, and as if the
> common sense of building consisted solely in making it
> mean, and all mean in the same way. . . . We were led
> into the blunder of long straight lines of street, divided to
> an inch, and all to the same number of inches, by
> rectangular intersections, every house being an exact
> duplicate of its neighbour, with a dexterous avoidance, as
> if from horror, of every ornament or excrescence by which
> the slightest break might vary the surface. What a site did
> nature give us for our New Town! Yet what insignificance
> in its plan! what poverty in all its details!

Such opinions read rather oddly nowadays, when the New Town has been sanctified by contrasts with later work. It is, moreover, difficult to picture it in its original form of a straight, stark grid in which the gentle curve of Abercromby Place was viewed with wonderment as a departure from the rectangular pattern. 'It will take many years', Cockburn wrote in the *Memorials*, 'to lessen the baseness of the first ideas. We have now some pillars, balconies, porticos, and ornamental roughening; and money, travelling and discussion will get us on.' By 1823 the same *Memorials* could regret the development of housing on Lord Moray's pleasure grounds to the north of Charlotte Square, long a source of rural delight to Cockburn and his friends, who had been misled by the glory of the summer evening prospect from Queen Street into a fallacy:

> We had got into the habit of believing that the mere
> charm of the ground to us would keep it sacred, and were
> inclined to cling to our conviction even after we saw the
> foundations digging. . . . But it was unavoidable. We
> would never have got beyond the North Loch, if these
> feelings had been conclusive. . . . It would be some
> consolation if the buildings were worthy of the situation;
> but the northern houses are turned the wrong way, and
> everything is sacrificed to the multiplication of feuing feet.

Cockburn's distress at the advancement of Moray Place was aggravated by the removal of trees which, as was thought, it necessitated. 'One lamentable error we certainly have committed, are committing, and, so far as appears, will ever commit. We massacre every town tree that comes in a mason's way; never sacrificing mortar to foliage.' Memory was all that remained of the old aristocratic gardens of the Canongate, and he wrote of many other special trees or groups of foliage which had been destroyed in his lifetime. Later on, a little way from the city centre, further destruction while the Dean Cemetery was constructed in the grounds of the old Nisbet mansion-house caused him much distress. 'How the savages were smashing the wood to-day, as if for mere pleasure!', he wrote in his *Journal* in 1845. 'I thought that venerable trees and undying evergreens were exactly what a burial-ground would long for. But here they are in perfection; plenty hollies and yews, apparently a century old; and how did I see these treated? As a drove of hogs would treat a bed of hyacinths.' It is in this cemetery that Cockburn now lies, simply and worthily commemorated, but without the benefit of

the sympathetic evergreen boskiness which he so strongly commended.

The mansion-house of Bellevue (where Drummond Place now
stands) had its wooded policies removed in the same way; 'all that
art and nature had done to prepare the place for foliaged com-
partments of town architecture, if being built upon should prove
inevitable, was carefully obliterated'. As always with Cockburn,
whether with friends, buildings or scenery, the loss of particular
items made him cherish the more strongly those that remained.
One of the most lush passages of his *Journal* is the long account of
the mansion-houses adjoining Edinburgh: at the end of 1845 he
wrote lovingly of houses such as Merchiston, Bruntsfield, Grange,
Caroline Park, Lauriston and Craigcrook. In such buildings
the curiosity and historical suggestiveness of ancient structures
was combined with the spacious recreational amenity of well
planted and sometimes publicly accessible policies. The associations of such places were enhanced by friendship—for example, a
Charlotte Square neighbour, Thomas Allan, at Lauriston Castle,
where he was succeeded by Cockburn's intimate friend and
protégé Andrew Rutherfurd; and above all Jeffrey's Craigcrook,
'morally the Paradise of Edinburgh villas'. There was something
about such buildings which recalled the glories of houses such as
Niddrie, remembered in the early pages of the *Memorials* as one
of the delightful experiences of his youth. And woe betide any
attempt to interfere with their individual character, when a
proprietor was accessible enough to remonstrated with. In the
mid-1820s Thomas Allan at John Law's seat of Lauriston received
a strong protest, in which Cockburn announced his intention

> to invade you this summer, in order to evoke the ghost of
> old Mississippi to resist the horrible project of letting a
> modern mason demolish the scene of his early speculations.
> I require nothing to convince me that the plan is bad—
> and I am perfectly determined not to be convinced that it
> is good. I never yet have seen any one old monument
> destroyed, under any temptation, or in any circumstances,
> without being followed, when it was too late, by sorrow
> and reproach. The last you won't escape—God save you
> from the first. The worthy old tower! How often have I
> seen it nodding to old Sol, and old Sol to it, as the said Sol
> was sinking into his western repose. Depend upon it, the
> demolition is totally unnecessary, and even necessity, or

what is called so—that is, the temporary convenience of a
new domicil—is no justification. If you can clap two
centuries of time on top of a new house the day it is built,
it may not be profane to extinguish two centuries by
pounding an old one.

Cockburn's protest, fully informed both historically and senti-
mentally, with its early declaration of the inadmissibility of
arguments based on mere utility and its threat of ultimate
retribution, was couched in terms which are familiar from other
letters. It may well have been effective, for on 3 December 1827
Sir Walter Scott was able to record in his *Journal* a visit to
Lauriston, where Allan 'has displayed good taste—supporting
instead of tearing down the old chateau, which once belonged to
the famous Mississippi Law. The additions are in very good taste,
and will make a most comfortable house. Mr Burn, architect,
would fain have had the old house pulled down, which I wonder
at in him, though it would have been the practice of most of his
brethren.'

The accessibility of such retreats on the fringes of Edinburgh
was seen as a particular civic asset by one who took a pedestrian's
view of the city. When he was promoted from being an Outer
House judge to the Second Division of the Court in November
1843, Cockburn was inclined to groan at a minor promotion
which most of his brethren considered specially desirable. The
different timetable did not offer him the old compensation of
'independence and long walks'—

Adieu! Salisbury Craigs, and the top of Arthur Seat, and
Duddingston, and the point of Leith Pier, and Corstorphine
Hill, and Caroline Park, and the Grange, and Braid, and
a hundred other long frequented and hallowed resorts. I
shall visit you again, and often, but never as my daily
Elysiums after Court.

Such sentiments led him to take a special interest in the open
spaces surrounding Edinburgh. The Calton Hill was an obvious
site for monumental enhancement as well as for general recreation,
but its adornment had to be carefully scrutinized. The National
Monument, proposed in 1816 as a war memorial, remains a
splendid project, a monument probably more interesting in its
incomplete form than as a roofed Parthenon serving as a
Westminster Abbey for Scotland. It formed in any case a worthy
addition to so prominent a setting, which the new jail started

there in 1808 could never have been held to be, although its
placing did lead to the successful completion of the Waterloo
Bridge to improve the long prospect from Princes Street.

Cockburn was not one to hold that the Calton should have been
left entirely free of buildings, recognizing that the view that 'it
should have been left to what is called nature [would be] as a
piece of waste ground for blackguards and washerwomen'. The
site was too important for it to be debased. In 1834 he protested
successfully against an application to build a privately-operated
Camera Obscura there. And in 1835 there was another proposal,
an obvious accompaniment of the prison, that provoked his wrath
in a letter to Sir Thomas Dick Lauder:

> My whole time, thoughts, and soul, are engrossed, amidst
> astonishment, horror, rage, disgust and indignation at a
> resolution of the Town Council to make the front of the
> Calton Jail the hanging place!!! There's a scheme for you!
> The Parthenon of Edinburgh—the Westminster Abbey of
> Scotland—the National Acropolis—the scene hallowed by
> the ashes of Hume, Burns, Playfair, and Stewart—to be
> voluntarily brought into connection with Jack Ketch and
> his subjects. And for what? To remove an established
> nuisance from the Old Town, from which a majority of
> Councillors proceed, to the New Town! If the said New
> Town be not degraded below the lowest dirt in spirit,
> it will rise into rebellion. All which I tell you in time,
> to warn you against rashly committing yourself in this
> probably coming discussion. What beasts!!

Salisbury Crags was another open space to be watched, where
an end was put to irresponsible quarrying just before the skyline
was damaged beyond recall. In 1833 a protest was entered at the
project of the new road from Musselburgh through Duddingston,
'destroying the privacy of the walk and scene, cutting the loch off
from the hill, creating a nuisance of coal carts, etc.' Such a protest
against the threat to 'privacy' by no means implied a restriction
on public access, for Cockburn was well aware of the recreational
value of such open spaces for all classes. The celebration of Queen
Victoria's coronation in 1838 was marked by the opening of many
otherwise closed places to the populace at large, and the working
people of Edinburgh took their ease soberly and moderately,
confounding those who had foretold damage and abuse. As
Cockburn wrote in his *Journal*, 'If the people were trusted, and

felt that it was their own interest to protect the means of their enjoyment, publicity would be the true safety of objects of taste and recreation, *provided that mischief and disorder were always severely punished'*. Seven years later, another long passage in the *Journal* (6 April 1845) records the formation of a society to protect the traditional footpaths around Edinburgh from various encroachments. The society was commendable, but Cockburn reckoned that it had been formed half a century too late.

When I was a boy nearly the whole vicinity of Edinburgh was open. Beyond the Causeway it was always almost Highland. Corstorphine Hill, Braid Hill, Craiglockhart Hill, the Pentland Hills, the seaside from Leith to Queensferry, the river-side from Penicuik by Roslin and Hawthornden to Lasswade, the valley of Habbie's How, and innumerable other places now closed, and fast closing, were all free. Much of this was the indulgence of private owners certainly, but much more of it was because, by the long usage of an unenclosed and very ill-ploughed country, the people had acquired prescriptive rights. But when improvement began ways were taken in. . . . The public was gradually mantrapped off everything beyond the high road. . . .

The true thing to humanise the people, and *save property*, is to have a footpath through every field. The alleged mischievousness of the Scotch, *when they are trusted*, and have an interest in preserving what they are allowed to enjoy, all my experience induces me to deny. . . . Would that our dun sky could borrow some of the Italian blue; but much of the coarseness of our climate would be abated if we turned the good that is in it to better account.

As a proprietor himself of a small property in the area referred to, Cockburn was in a special position to observe the threats which an expanding Edinburgh posed to his Pentlands retreat. The requirements of the civic water supply would interfere with the beloved Linn which occupied so prominent a place in his agrestic life. He wrote to Mrs Leonard Horner in November 1846 about the proposed construction of a series of reservoirs, 'all that the people of Edinburgh may get their faces better washed'. A year later he referred the matter to a neighbouring proprietor, Sir William Liston-Foulis, who actually owned the Linn and a favourite elm nearby:

The Water Company have begun their operations close
beside [that elm,] and are soon to have a great number of
Paddies and other devils, who will be working there till
the end of the year. You are aware of an Irishman's love
of Shillelas. This love is so strong that nothing except
warning and threatening can save a leaf of that tree. I have
spoken to the foreman, who *professes* fairly enough. But as
he knows that the tree is not mine, of course he estimates
all my threats at very little.

Fully aware that liberties would be taken around the agreed limits
of construction work, Cockburn begged his neighbour to issue
very firm instructions to the Water Company.

It is interesting to see how Cockburn the supporter of public
access to the countryside reacted—humorously—when confronted
with an attack of the people. In 1847 his young friend, the glass
painter and dialect versifier James Ballantine, produced in his
The Gaberlunzie's Wallet verses praising Bonaly and the liberal
hospitality of its master. Cockburn replied to Ballantine:

If you happen to be acquainted with a Gaberlunzie who
goes about with a wallet full of scraps of meat and of
verse, I wish you would thank him, in my name, for some
very good, and very complimentary lines which he . . .
has lately published about this humble spot.

But I suspect that he feels I have been negligent of
him, and takes this method of punishing me. And an
effectual punishment it is. Because from the moment that
he announced that my yett [gate] was open to all, I have
been unable to call my own my own. . . . The wee raggit
laddies I dont object to—nor to anyone male or female,
who really enjoys the hills in decorum. But there is a
species of riotous, devil may care, half and half genteel
blackguards, that are very odious. Odious to others of their
fellow creatures, to mavises, to burns, to roses, to cows,
sunsets, lambs, and everything reasonable. Therefore I
mean to put up a placard saying 'No passage this way
without leave from the Gaberlunzie!!' And if the body can
turn a penny, or fill his bag with heuk banes, for selling
indulgences, like the Pope, I shall be very glad. Without
some such check, a popular yett is a very inconvenient
thing near a large town.

By the mid 1840s, when this letter was written, Cockburn's

views on urban, as well as suburban, subjects were becoming firmly settled. He had never been shy of expressing himself when he felt the well-being of the city was involved. Some subjects, such as the row of public privies proposed for the ridge of the Castle Hill, engaged his humour (it was the opposition of Lady Clerk that was effective in this case); others, such as new monuments or old buildings, engaged his expertise. The Scott Monument was a matter of special interest to him, not just as an erection (he wrote to Mrs Rutherfurd in 1840 that 'it will be a most picturesque and singular object, and will add greatly to the peculiarity of this surface-varied city'), but because of various consequential threats to the south side of Princes Street. In 1844, for example, the Council was denounced in a letter to Dick Lauder as encouraging an attempt to make the flat ground to the south of the Monument into a market. 'The Provost's principle', Cockburn commented, 'a dangerous one for a magistracy, is utility. As if anything was more useful than public taste—i.e. the absence of brutality.' Some of his characteristic notions, and phrases, had long been prepared.

The North Loch site (to the south, or unbuilt, side of Princes Street) was a cause for perpetual concern, and it was probably anxiety for its future before its inviolability was legally established, and for the various linkages between Old Town and New, which was to be the principal cause of the *Letter to the Lord Provost*. The Princes Street valley west of the Mound seemed the more attractive to one who recalled it ill-drained and foetid, a disgrace whose removal was duly praised. The Mound itself needed vigilance, with attempts at piecemeal building to be rejected, and bold and striking schemes like Trotter of Dreghorn's proposals to be commended in the *Memorials* (where he remarked on its being 'too magnificent for execution'). Further along, to the east, the North Bridge had to be watched, a proposal in the summer of 1845 for widening it and erecting shops being denounced in the *Journal* as 'a most abominable conception', and rousing Cockburn's civic ardour almost to the point of writing a pamphlet about it. George IV Bridge and the related Improvements put forward by the Commissioners had before that provided years of debate in which the Cockburn party's view had eventually prevailed, securing the openness of Princes Street and the Mound in return for the new southern access scheme. Looking back on the history of this project in the *Memorials*, he could point to 'jobbing, and mismanagement, and trick, and ill humour, and folly', but he also

E

remarked justifiably the general success of the scheme.

There had been objections to the opening-up of George IV Bridge from defenders of some older property which had to be destroyed. Cockburn was a trifle dismissive of them, but preserved a balanced attitude:

Some people let their picturesque taste get so sickly that they sigh over the destruction of every old nuisance or incumbrance. But they never try to live among these fragments, nor think of the human animals who burrow there. Everything that has an old history, or an old ornament, or an old peculiarity, if it *can* be preserved, ought to be preserved in spite of all living inconvenience. In these matters mere antiquity is better entitled to be respected than existing comfort. It is not once in a thousand times that the two are really incompatible. But it does not follow that present necessities and tastes are to be sacrificed for the preservation of every tottering gable that would look well in one of Weinrotter's etchings.

The *Memorials* (and to a lesser extent the *Journal*) contain many passages which weigh old and new against each other, reminiscing lavishly, but usually prepared to see the practical advantages of certain recent innovations. Of the old Parliament House, location of some of his warmest professional recollections, he remarked that 'no one who remembers the old exterior can see the new one without sorrow and indignation'. Anciently and interestingly ornamented, the old fronts had been removed 'in order to make way for the bright freestone and contemptible decorations that now disgrace us ... there was such an utter absence of public spirit in Edinburgh then, that the building might have been painted scarlet without anybody objecting'. Yet internally the new arrangements were spacious, unobstructed and artistic, more suited to the dignity of judicial business than the promiscuous tumult of the disorderly schoolroom that preceded it.

The location of the new jail on the Calton Hill, of which building started in 1808, was, as we have seen, regretted but viewed as a welcome opportunity for improving and completing the vista of Princes Street to the east. But the removal of the old 'Heart of Midlothian' in the High Street was considered with mixed feelings:

A most atrocious jail it was, the very breath of which almost struck down any stranger who entered its dismal door. . . . But yet I wish the building had been spared. It was of great age: it once held the parliament (though *how* it could, I can't conceive): it was incorporated with much curious history, and its outside was picturesque. Neither exposing St Giles, nor widening the street, nor any such object, ought to have been allowed to extinguish so interesting a relic.

Of all the ancient buildings of Edinburgh, that which Cockburn reckoned the most 'picturesque deposit' left by time was the old Trinity Hospital. The *Memorials* record at length a visit he made to that picturesque and curious almshouse in 1826, describing buildings and inmates with a Trollopian softness. But even so distinctive a structure was threatened, and a note had to be added to the final text of the *Memorials*:

> In a short time, [Edinburgh] shall know it no more! But the public will be gratified by a railway station. Trinity College Church, too—the last and finest Gothic fragment in Edinburgh—though implored for by about four centuries, will disappear for the accommodation of a railway! An outrage by sordid traders, virtually consented to by a tasteless city, and sanctioned by an insensible parliament. I scarcely know a more curious instance of ignorant insensibility than the apology that is made for this piece of desecration. It is said that the edifice is to be replaced *exactly as it is*, in some better situation. And it is really thought that the Pyramids would remain the Pyramids, or Jerusalem Jerusalem, provided only their materials were replaced in London. Oxford would be Oxford, though in Manchester, if its stones were preserved. These people would remove Pompeii for a railway, and tell us they had applied it to a better purpose in Dundee.

It was of course the rapidly spreading railways which provoked some of his most mordant comments, filled him with such apprehension for so many aspects of Scottish life and culture that he felt were under threat. Throughout the 1830s and 1840s his *Journal* and letters record his mounting distaste for this innovation. The threat was a general one, from the industrial revolution as a whole and not just the railway boom. In April 1835 he had noted with contempt in his *Journal* that the town council had approved a committee report suggesting 'projects for the introduction of *manufactures* into Edinburgh'. Perish the thought!

> ... all sane persons see that the idea of forcing such a
> thing is absurd, and that, if left to herself, Nature has too
> much sense to tolerate such an abomination in such a
> place. Weavers and calico-printers, power-looms and
> steam-engines, sugar-houses and foundries in Edinburgh!
> These nuisances might increase our population and our
> pauperism, our wealth and our bankruptcies; but they
> would leave it Edinburgh no more.

The city had declined in wealth, to be sure:

> But I rejoice that we cannot excite it by steam. We must
> try to survive on better grounds, on our advantages as the
> metropolis, our adaptation for education, our literary
> fame, and especially on the glories of our external position
> and features; improved by the bluish smoke of human
> habitation, and undimmed by the black dirty clouds from
> manufactures, the absence of which is one of the principal
> charms of our situation.

As the advance troops of this industrialisation, railways were
seen as an especially disruptive force. In May 1836 Cockburn
summed up his early feelings about them in a letter to Kennedy of
Dunure.

> Not being a merchant, and thinking that all letters, and
> all strangers, come a great deal too soon, I groan over
> these railways. They will destroy all privacy, all provincial
> nature. The whole island will be a workshop; and all the
> peaceable independence and picturesque peculiarities, and
> salutary self-importance of little places will be melted in
> the general fusion of society.

This was a theme on which he had written at greater length in his
Journal only a month previously, when the speculative fever of the
current railway mania recalled for him something of the financial
crisis of 1825.

The land-grabbing destructiveness of such developments was
soon apparent. Lady Glenorchy's Chapel, Trinity Hospital, the
old Botanic Garden and many other interesting buildings to the
east of Princes Street gardens were to be swallowed up; elsewhere,
as in the threat to the South Inch at Perth, the problems were the
same. Much could be put down by him to the apathy and
interestedness of civic administrations. Nowhere was the problem
seen as graver than in Princes Street Gardens, when in 1837 it was
first proposed to bring the Glasgow railway along the valley and

under the Mound: railway buildings would follow, the peculiar qualities of the east end of the space would be threatened, building on the south side of Princes Street might come to be seen as less abhorrent. 'Could a Judge agitate, I should raise the very stones against this project', Cockburn wrote in his *Journal*, reserving his condemnation for his private correspondence ('I would rather see the Reform Bill repealed' he told John Murray). As it turned out, the 1837 project failed, foundering on the heavy opposition of the Princes Street proprietors, who (as he remarked in the *Journal*) 'petitioned against the scheme on the ground of its hurting their *property*, but not a whisper of opposition was heard from the town generally on the immovable ground of its destructive consequences in reference to taste'.

The railways were to prove irresistible, especially when growing commercial success elsewhere and a renewed wave of investment and speculation in the early 1840s strengthened their position. On 10 April 1844 Cockburn wrote to Francis Jeffrey, imploring him to

> put in any well placed word you can, in salvation of Edinburgh from the d——d railway. Think—dream—curse—over the idea of a street being drawn . . . so that, in place of henceforth looking from the principal Mound to arches of the North Bridge, these arches are to be hid by a beastly Station House and a raised street, which are to hold up their ugly heads in defiance of both old town and new. Yet our poor, constituent-cowed members for Edinburgh, Leith and the Shire will all support this—as they would a distillery on the top of the Calton, if their masters bade them.

('Kemp the Architect of Sir Walter's monument was drowned', Cockburn added, 'drunk as usual, in the canal.')

It was natural that Cockburn should do his best to approach the town council, 'haters of old stones' though he might not unjustifiably have considered them as men to be mistrusted as an interested mercantile oligarchy indifferent to local grandeur. He had had many brushes with them in his time, notably in 1827 during the Improvements Bill negotiations. By January 1848 the implications of the Glasgow railway's extension, with its proposed 'new roads, tunnels, station houses, etc., on the eastern division of the North Loch', were clear enough for Cockburn to address himself to the Lord Provost, then the publisher Adam Black, in terms which anticipate his printed pamphlet issued some twenty months later. 'If these designs be carried,' he wrote to the chief magistrate, 'no further thought need be given, by the real friends of Edinburgh, about the preservation of that beauty which is its only wealth—

> There is no one on whom such of the people of this place as are not railway mad are so much entitled to look for protection as your Lordship. For it was chiefly your evidence that accomplished what I always predicted was the fatal step of letting these beasts set their hoof on that valley. You meant them to have a mere right of *transit*. But you see the ell that the inch ends in.
>
> The present scheme is *absolutely destructive*. . . . The only remedy is to resist ALL *further encroachment*. The instant that they are allowed, on any pretence, to come west of the little Mound, it is all over. So long as they have their Dalry Station they have, or may make, room enough for their goods. And if not—then this only shows the more what must be the result of letting them in upon the new ground east of the Mound. In a few years it must be all covered with buildings and roads.
>
> I do trust therefore that you will not lose this opportunity of raising yourself still higher with the rational portion of the public, by a vigorous resistance, and a marked separation of yourself from whatever portion of the Council, or of the Lunaticks, may be favourable to *any part* of the accursed scheme.
>
> So many people are interested in this railway, and so many more are crazy about furious communication, that I fear that any public meeting that could be called, would be favourable to any accommodation to any railway. But I cannot doubt that a strong remonstrance might be obtained from a great number of the disinterested and the sane. Do you only lead them.
>
> Excuse all this from one who is mad on the other side, and who—*deliberately*—would rather see all the railways in Scotland bankrupt, than that one fragment of this projected Hunnism should be perpetuated.

Such a letter, written from the confidence of local eminence, with dignity, information and humour, and a carefully gauged tone of diffidence, apology, flattery and calculated rant, is in Cockburn's best argumentative style. The pattern was laid for the pamphlet *Letter to the Lord Provost* as published in 1849.

The *Letter* should be read as a unit, and even lengthy quotation would reduce its impact as a campaigning piece. It is well-shaped and well-controlled, lacking the frequent imprecation which fills his *Journal* and correspondence on the subject. Occasionally he bursts out: the new buildings on the Castle Hill (admittedly a Government rather than a municipal enterprise) are denounced as 'the factory-looking erection which deforms the most picturesque fortress in her Majesty's British dominions, by the most audacious piece of abomination in Europe'. Elsewhere the tone is much less strident, more suited to an appeal to the town council as civic leaders to instruct the taste and direct the attention of the people to the unique natural advantages of their city. There is irony in Cockburn's pleading thus with a magistracy of whom he privately had so low an opinion, but any tactical subtlety would be lost on a body of men who had repeatedly shown themselves indifferent to their natural and their architectural heritages.

Much of his argument can be traced back through his other writings, although the praise of Edinburgh's natural setting, which has been implicit throughout the environmental commentary of the previously written (but only subsequently published) *Memorials* and *Journal*, is now crystallized in moving passages of topographical analysis. And from this exposition he can point to one of the most dangerous of fallacies—a sort of municipal quietism, it might be said—the attitude of 'Let them do what they like, they can never spoil Edinburgh'.

The examples he gives of 'some of the dangers from which we have, and some from which we have not escaped' are familiar enough to readers of his works. The attempt to erect the privies on the Castle Hill; the threat to the south side of Princes Street; the public gibbet proposed for the Calton Hill; the scheme for widening the North Bridge—all had been given full consideration in his correspondence and journalising. The whole problem of trees in the urban setting is discussed at some length; a more immediate matter, the adjustment of the screen fronting the Register House, is introduced both as an urgent current problem and as yet another demonstration of the fallacy of arguments based on mere utility. And it is Trinity Hospital and its Church which are adduced as examples of the regrettable destruction of historic buildings in public ownership (rather than in then uncontrollable private hands), where civic conscience should have dictated otherwise. Up-to-date in his reading, Cockburn used Ruskin's *Seven Lamps of Architecture* (1849) to reinforce his argument—and to hint at changes of attitude in the future: 'The glory of a building is not in its stones, nor in its gold. Its glory is in its age; and in that deep sense of voicefulness, of stern watching, or mysterious sympathy, even of approval or condemnation, which we feel in the walls that have been long washed by the passing waves of humanity.'

Yet for all his defence of ancient monuments, for all his spirited attempts against the intrusion of the railway into the very centre of the town, Cockburn remained enough of a realist—his reason with the modern world—not to fail to take account of some of the advantages which some new work offered to the local environment. It was the reasoner and not the dreamer who wrote that

> The better modern spirit is manifest and gratifying. Heavy
> uniform lines are rapidly breaking into variety; scarcely
> a street is contented without its ornamental edifice;
> respectable chartered companies, with a proper social
> pride, vie with each other in the splendour of their offices;
> sculpture aids architecture; and, besides handsome secon-
> dary buildings, there are several of a higher character, and
> of the greatest excellence.

A curiosity of informed antiquarian taste is transformed into a manifesto for a Victorian Society. Buildings were specified; designers such as Hamilton, Graham, Kemp and Rhind, applauded; particular praise was reserved for Playfair, his warmly attached friend. Great improvements had been effected on Arthur's Seat and Salisbury Crags, and on the Mound, where a great, and fitting, repository for the nation's art was soon to be sited. And the Dean Cemetery was forgiven the defoliations of its projectors; inhumations as well as aesthetics were the beneficiaries of a revival in taste: 'The improving spirit has evinced itself in nothing more agreeably than in the reformation of our last homes. The contrast between the old loathsome town churchyards, and the recent spacious, pure, and breezy cemeteries, is creditable both to the taste and to the feelings of the age.'

From banking-halls to burial grounds the environmental argument was advanced with skill, moderation—and probably very little effect, at the time. But the underlying concern for civic well-being was much more widely based. In spite of the architectural concerns of his Letter, it should not be thought that Cockburn's view of civic well-being was confined merely to building preservation, even in its widest sense. The gratifying 'better modern spirit' which he detected at work in architectural matters was to be found in equally commendable contributions to the public good. Some were individual, more were corporate. The advocate James Simpson was presented with a silver testimonial by the working men of Edinburgh, to whom he had given free lectures during many years of quiet but persistent activity as 'an apostle of the poor'. Simpson, who had long been 'rather an object of ridicule with the upper classes in this his native place', was in fact a widely-known and much-appreciated teacher in other walks of life; Cockburn found his moral example admirable. As a corporate effort, the institution in 1821 of the School of Arts for the instruction of mechanics, conceived and in its early years directed by Cockburn's close friend Leonard Horner, was similarly praised. Other 'useful associations' made their contribution; in the *Memorials* for 1812, Cockburn instances three which helped in 'marking the advance of the place, and indeed of the age'— Playfair's Astronomical Institution, the Society for the Suppression of Public Begging (an 'early step in the philosophy of pauperism'), and the establishment of the Lancastrian School in spite of clerical opposition to a useful scheme in popular education. The New Town Dispensary (1815), much opposed at first by existing medical interests, and the Horticultural Society a few years earlier, also had a beneficient influence in their very different ways. Cockburn looked to the latter as having its greatest success 'in the moderate place, the villa, and especially in the poor man's garden; in the prevalence of little flower societies; its interest as a subject of common conversation; and the cheap, but beautiful and learned practical works that are to be found in the houses of the humblest of the people'.

It was not just the technological and horticultural instruction of artisans which was to be encouraged. The Edinburgh Academy, of which Cockburn was a leading projector (along with Horner, Scott and others), was also seen as an instrument of civic renewal and adaptation. With his view of education irremediably coloured by his own experience of the High School, Cockburn cherished lofty aims for the Academy, explaining it in his *Life* of his fellow-director Jeffrey as 'a proprietary day school, instituted with the view of raising the quality and the tone of education, in its higher branches, for boys of all classes'. Cockburn took a sustained practical interest in the management of the school, assisting in the appointment of senior staff and taking an informed interest in its deliberately anglicized classical curriculum. He and Jeffrey were comfortably satisfied with its progress.

The other Academy in which he took a keen interest, seeing it likewise as a major contribution to civic, and national, life, was the Scottish (later Royal Scottish) Academy of Arts, which he helped with informal legal advice and skilled arbitration between the different factions of his many artist friends. The division between the Royal Institution and the Scottish Academy, and Cockburn's timely intervention and wise advice to David Octavius Hill, the Academy secretary, and others, have recently been discussed in Esmé Gordon's *The Royal Scottish Academy* (1976). His intervention in the petty disputes of these fractious artists was backed by a belief in the importance for Edinburgh of the development of the fine arts. In 1838 he had written in his *Journal* that 'I see no ground for doubting that Scotland may become as splendid in art as it has been in literature', and the struggle both to achieve the public recognition which a royal charter would assure the new foundation and to keep the warring factions from each others' throats, were felt worth while. Perhaps even more than the achievement of a legal settlement and a real status was the laying in 1850 of the foundation stone of Playfair's building, which symbolised for Cockburn the central place that the arts had come to occupy in the life of the city—and of the nation. A building for his artist friends by an architect who was one of his intimates was deeply satisfying. Moreover the building filled a disputed site to the best possible advantage and indicated a possible renewal of general interest in the architectural setting of the city which might be thought encouraging.

The challenge to the inertia of the citizenry which Cockburn's *Letter* presented had been taken up by at least one citizen, a Mr W. A. Parker, who wrote to him in October proposing the foundation of an 'architectural association' for Edinburgh. His suggestion met with the expected welcome, Cockburn remarking that 'the propriety of some sort of Association for the promotion of this object, has often occurred to me also. But it is a matter that would do more harm than good, if it were not organised, and conducted, very cautiously. And it is clear (to me at least) that any Judge taking a lead in it, would be objectionable.' Despite these personal reservations, Parker's attitude was one to be encouraged. 'I am glad that you take an interest in preserving, and extending, the beauty of Edinburgh,' Cockburn wrote: 'The friends of this cause need all the aid they can get.'

Cockburn and the Church

IAIN F. MACIVER

THROUGHOUT his long legal and political life Henry Cockburn's work as a public man was intertwined with the affairs of the Church of Scotland. Cockburn was not merely a passive observer of the actions of the Kirk through its General Assembly; as advocate, politician and judge he was often an actor in church cases, and in the bitter controversies that culminated in the major 'Disruption' of the Established Church in 1843 and the formation of the rival Free Church. To the modern general reader this involvement may seem to stretch out at tedious length, particularly in the pages of the *Journal*, whose volumes are full of detailed description and analysis of increasingly complex and tortuous ecclesiastical affairs. Cockburn himself would not have been the least apologetic about this. The *Journal* may lack some of the autobiographical power of the *Memorials* and the descriptive charm of *Circuit Journeys*, but it is the record of his own prime years of achievement in public affairs. It captures the excitement of the Scottish Whigs as they emerged from a quarter-century of political impotence, and the creation of what Cockburn saw as his and Francis Jeffrey's supreme monument, the Scottish Reform Act of 1832, which, though flawed in construction, did create a new political nation in Scotland.

Cockburn was also alive to parallel stirrings in the Church, which had been divided on party lines since the mid-18th century into Moderates and Evangelicals. The era of secular reform coincided with a change of control in the General Assembly of the Church out of the hands of the *ancien régime* Moderates to the Evangelicals, who were the party of movement and potential change.

In 1834 Cockburn resigned his office as Solicitor-General for Scotland, held since 1830, on his elevation to the Court of Session, but he was not raised out of the arena of church politics, for in the next decade the Court was to hear a succession of explosive cases

brought forward and sustained by supporters of the Moderate
party to challenge the civil validity of Church legislation inspired
by Evangelicals passed in the General Assembly of 1834. All were
based on specific local suits spread geographically through
Lowland Scotland from Ayrshire to Banffshire: the Auchterarder
case (1837–1838), Lethendy (1838–1839), Marnoch, or Strathbogie (1838–1841), Cusalmond (1841–1842), and Stewarton
(1843). But in essence they came to represent a final desperate
effort by the Moderates to reverse the loss in 1833–1834 of their
seventy-year hegemony in the General Assembly and in the
Church as a whole.

Both Church parties operated as political groups largely in the
General Assembly, though, as the conflict became sharper, the
district and provincial courts of the Kirk, the presbyteries and
synods, became more politicised. It was in the Assembly of May 1834
that the Evangelicals had exposed a vulnerable legal flank by
passing an act 'anent Calls', better known as the 'Veto Act', em-
powering presbyteries to reject the presentee of a lay patron to a
vacant parish if a majority of the communicant 'heads of families'
handed in 'reasons of dissent'. Equally important was the act
'anent Chapels of Ease', erecting the chapels (additional churches
built within existing civil parishes) into ecclesiastical parishes
quoad sacra, whose ministers and elders were given seats in the
church courts. The first measure could ensure the rejection of
'unpopular' candidates (often Moderates) and the second greatly
inflated Evangelical majorities in the Church courts with the votes
of the chapel men. Both measures, however, could be held to
encroach on civil property rights, and were open to challenge in
the civil courts.

John Hope, Dean of the Faculty of Advocates, a legal colleague
for whom Cockburn shows fairly consistent dislike, was none the
less an astute ecclesiastical politician, and the *éminence grise* of the
Moderate party. Hope appreciated quickly that the two Assembly
Acts of 1834 could result in the gradual extinction of the moderate
interest in the Church. He immediately entered his formal dissent
in 1834 to the 'Deliverance on Calls' which became the Veto Act,
and was adviser and counsel for the pursuers in the Auchterarder
case. He was equally alive to the implications of the Chapel Act,
whose effects were resented bitterly by the Moderate leadership.
One Moderate chief, Dr George Cook of St Andrews, articulated
the instinctive erastianism of many of his party in January 1839,

writing of patronage as being the only cement joining an essentially
republican Presbyterianism to the state, and without which, he
informed Robert Dundas, Lord Melville, 'a Presbyterian Establishment cannot harmonise well with a Monarchical Government'. Cook genuinely feared the implications of the Evangelicals'
resolve to challenge the right of the Court of Session to set aside
the Veto Act in their Auchterarder case decision of 1838, con-
demning his fellow-churchmen for 'creating agitation, and
something approaching even to insubordination and rebellion'.
He also found time to condemn the great current expansion of the
Kirk inspired by the Evangelical leader and orator, Thomas
Chalmers, and to link all this unseemly agitation with 'the number
of new ministers popularly elected, and who have got into the
Church Courts' who were 'the cause of the present ferment'.*

Cook's point of view was that of an 'Old Moderate', and more
strongly erastian than some of the other 'Residuaries' who chose
to remain in the Established Church in 1843. The Moderates did
not lack personal and pastoral virtues, but as an ecclesiastical
party they had come to represent a constitutional immobility,
dictated probably by their identity in ideology and self-interest
with conservative 'lairdocracy', and allied sections of the legal
profession and the old mercantile élites in the burghs. Cockburn
had little sympathy with Moderatism as an ideology, identifying
Moderates with unregenerate Toryism, not an inaccurate
attribution given his own definition of Scottish Toryism in the
Memorials as a creed which 'seldom implies anything with us
except a dislike of popular institutions'. He saw them as a party led
in the General Assembly by men of elegant speech and intellectual
ability, but subordinating their virtues to the pressures of political
expediency. They had abandoned the independence and wider view
of their great leader of the previous generation, William Robertson,
the Enlightenment historian, a process exemplified for Cockburn
by their treatment of Professor John Leslie in 1805, when the party
attempted to exclude the latter from a chair at Edinburgh
University on a continued charge of religious scepticism, in order
to install their own nominee. Cockburn was particularly repelled
by what he saw as the hypocrisy inherent in this action of a party,
as he said in *Memorials*, 'more indifferent about scepticism than
their opponents, yet liking power above all things'. He particularly

---

* For sources of material quoted in this account see 'Notes on Sources' at the
end of the text.

disliked the Moderate leader, Principal George Hill of St Andrews, recalling him waspishly many years later in *Circuit Journeys* as 'most graceful and externally elegant, but the meanest of political priests'. Dr John Inglis, the Edinburgh Moderate chief, was more respected by Cockburn—though he felt that the 'qualities which he has thrown away on the ignoble task of attempting to repress the popular spirit of our Church would have raised him high . . . in any department of public life'.

There is no doubt of Cockburn's doctrinal, though not personal, dislike of the Moderates as an ecclesiastical party. In his *Memorials* description of the state of the Kirk in 1807, written with the benefit of some hindsight in the 1820s, he condemned their entire management of the Kirk:

> Until Chalmers and his consequences arose, the theological philosophy and eloquence of the Church seemed to be worn out. And no wonder. Nothing can inspire religious duty or animation but religion. . . . But a stern system of patronage, rendered more illiberal by its union with Toryism, tended to exclude all clergymen who were known to cherish a taste for the people and their piety and to reserve pulpits for those whose ambition ended in pleasing their political masters. . . . A new Presbyterian revolution was approaching, which brought out new men, and new dangers, and new popularity, with a necessary elevation of those who shone in it. But about this time the old thing was dead.

Cockburn's view of the Moderates is clear enough: they were anachronistic, and being incorrigibly opposed to any popular reform of the Kirk they had forfeited their claim to govern the Church.

In 1835 Cockburn, announcing the demise of the party, summed up his views of it in a balanced and thoughtful *Journal* passage:

> The old Moderate party is extinguished . . . and I am sorry for it, for as a minority they might have been useful sedatives. The time may come, however, when the reader of Scotch history may ask what a *Moderate* was. My answer is that, speaking generally, he was a Tory in politics, and in religion not in the Scotch sense religious. But his Toryism had very little purely political in it. It began (speaking only of clergymen) by an early obsequiousness to an expectant patron, probably as a tutor in his family, or

in that of some of his friends. After obtaining his living, in which the people were seldom thought of, and never consulted, he naturally subsided into an admiration of the system to which he owed his bread, and into a general sympathy with the opinions and objects of the lairds. . . . Thus his Toryism was not that of direct political principle or party, but a mere passive devotion to the gentry. But he was not necessarily irreligious. On the contrary, he might be, and often was, a truly pious man; but . . . his clay was perfectly impervious to the deep and fervid spirit which is the soul of modern religion. He had no personal dislike to the people, who always found kindness at the manse; but he had no taste for the people as desirous of either political or religious advancement. It was this that destroyed them.

For Cockburn, Moderatism was an historically obsolete creed, and despite being 'socially speaking . . . better fellows' the Moderates' fate was sealed once 'the people would not continue submissive to their rulers and lukewarm in their religion'. Club-bability and easy social intercourse with the upper classes were no substitute for neglect of the popular imperatives of Presbyteri-anism, and so 'the structure . . . founded on no rock, has crumbled into dust'.

Regarding the rival Evangelicals, Cockburn's attitudes were based on a far more complex amalgam of his own religious views and prejudices, the influence of private friendships, his concepts of Scottish history and identity, and the interaction of his Whiggism with all these elements. Cockburn was both fascinated and re-pelled by Evangelicalism. As Karl Miller has said, in his introduc-tion to a recent (Chicago 1974) edition of *Memorials*, he was neither a Moderate nor an Evangelical, but many of his basic political and emotional instincts responded to Evangelical points of view, and it is this critical empathy that makes him such a penetrating com-mentator on the Church and its role, particularly in the 1830s and '40s when Evangelicalism dominated the ecclesiastical scene.

Many aspects of the 'Ten Years' Conflict' between the Evangeli-cal majority in the Church and the civil courts and government, leading to the Disruption, alienated intellectual Whigs. They scented demagoguery and theocracy in the impassioned utterances of many of the more enthusiastic devotees of 'Non-Intrusion' and 'Spiritual Independence', and the *Edinburgh Review* reflected this attitude by loftily ignoring the great events taking place on its doorstep. But Cockburn had no patience with this attitude, writing to Jeffrey on 10th May 1844 regarding the foundation of a rival periodical, the *North British Review*, by Whig Evangelicals now in the new Free Church (he repeated some of these remarks in the *Journal*):

The Pundit [Macvey Napier, editor of the *Edinburgh Review*] affects to despise his rival; but is really alarmed. ... I can't say that there is much *in the No.* to disturb him. But there is a great deal *in the circumstances* which have produced a new review. He has brought it partly on himself by the paltriness of never even alluding in the Edinburgh to the late great national struggle. His Review could not sympathise with the fanaticism of the Wild; but as little could it justify the extravagances of the courts and the suppression of the people; and a wise middle man was just what was wanted.

Cockburn's Scottish nationalism was as well developed culturally as it was suppressed politically by his Whig unionism. As a man well-read in Scottish Church history, the current 'great national struggle' was to become for him a legitimate expression of national protest against metropolitan interference. Reflecting in the *Journal* on the commemorations of the two-hundredth anniversary of the General Assembly of 1638 which abolished Episcopacy in the Kirk he wrote:

Our forefathers believed that presbyteries such as they set up, and particularly with an independent spiritual government in the Church, was the only ecclesiastical system warranted by Scripture. For holding this opinion they were long and sorely oppressed by Popery and Prelacy; and when, after a struggle that did them honour, they triumphed, the feelings and recollections of the flames they had passed through descended with their creed to their posterity. ... We owe much to the Covenanters ... because it so happened that they could not maintain their Presbyterian principles without advancing principles of civil liberty. ... If the Auchterarder case had occurred in 1638, or at any time for a century afterwards, the patron would have been set in a white sheet at the church door, the presentee deposed, and the Court of Session excommunicated. Some hold this to be a proof that wise men ought to discourage the vices of old Presbytery that

F

still prevail. So they ought. . . . But it does not follow from
this that whatever is offensive to the wise must be offensive
to the people, and still less that *Governments* are ever
entitled to trample on religious principles which the people
imitate their fathers in venerating. Every sect on this
principle might crush its rival by force. . . . The antiquity
of the Scotch creed, and even its picturesque peculiarities,
considering how intensely and how generally it is clung to,
are the very circumstances which make it oppression to
interfere with it, except by gradual change. Those who
fancy themselves philosophers may sneer at religious
enthusiasm, but while our present human nature endures,
it can never be discounted in the practical management of
human affairs.

Thus Cockburn was able to swallow his dislike of many features
of contemporary Evangelicalism in the belief that it encapsulated
the vital claim of historic Presbyterianism, particularly in its
recognition of the rights of the ordinary members of the Church.
This was the constitutional justification of the Established Kirk to
Cockburn, appealing both to his Whiggism and his sense of
national history and identity. To cut at these roots with the tools
of erastian legalism was a sacrilege akin to the philistine destruction of venerable trees and buildings, an attack on the national
past and an impoverishment of its future, and in this instance
Cockburn could give his romantic nationalism full scope, secure in
the knowledge that it was reconcilable with Whig ideas of political
liberty.

Cockburn also appreciated the need for 'religious enthusiasm',
or a widespread sense of personal religious commitment within a
Church, which he considered to be best provided by Evangelicalism. He appreciated Evangelical preaching when its fervour
was harnessed by oratorical skill and restrained by natural
discipline from slipping into forced emotionalism, as witness his
short but memorable *Memorials* picture of the aged and bowed
Evangelical leader Henry Erskine under whom the Cockburn
family 'sat' at Old Greyfriars Kirk in Edinburgh: 'he was so
earnest, though with none of the Presbyterian roar or violence,
that when his gown encumbered him, as it seemed often to do, he
let it drop off, and went on almost erect with animation.' But on
his own profession Cockburn found Sir Harry Moncreiff, laird of
Tulliebole, minister of St Cuthbert's, Edinburgh, and leader of the

Evangelicals in the Assembly until his death in 1827, to be 'the oracle of the whole Church in matters not factious, and the steady champion of the popular side. In comparison with him every other Churchman who has appeared since I knew the world must withdraw. Nothing that I could say would express one half of my affectionate and reverential admiration of this great man.'

Sir Harry's urbane brand of Evangelicalism dispensed at evening supper-parties described vividly in the *Memorials* obviously influenced Cockburn considerably, and this sympathy was increased by lifelong friendship with Sir Harry's son, and his companion on the Bench, Sir James Wellwood Moncreiff, 'Creefy', a fellow Whig, devout Evangelical and Free Churchman. The example of the Moncreiffs did much to reconcile Cockburn to Evangelicalism, with the proof that it could inspire congenial men of his own social class, and need not resort to vulgar emotionalism or fanaticism, both tendencies that he diagnosed and deplored in the movement. While he could smile at his friend and *Circuit Journeys* companion, 'whose piety and simplicity sometimes gives him odd views', he respected and admired the 'simple, pious and warm-hearted' Creefy as a judge and a man.

Personal friendships were an important element in shaping Cockburn's generally benign attitude to the public face of Evangelicalism, especially evident in his attitude to the Disruption. He was gratified to see his own preferences shared by men of rank and station who were prepared to go to the length of secession, for the Free Church was distinguished from earlier ruptures in the Kirk in that: 'its adherents are not almost entirely of the lower orders. They have already peers, baronets and knights, provosts, and sheriffs, and a long train of gentry', and he added, more lyrically, 'Theirs is the only Presbyterian battery which has as yet played upon the Church from aristocratic ground'. In reality the aristocratic ground was very narrow. It rested on the admittedly broad acres of John Campbell, 2nd Marquess of Breadalbane and a lavish patron of the Free Kirk. But unless one includes a future earl (Fox Maule, later 2nd Viscount Panmure and 11th Earl of Dalhousie, whose father, Lord Panmure, was bitterly opposed both to his eldest son and to the Free Kirk), he was the only great aristocrat to join the Free Church. Only a small minority of seventy-one landowners supported the new Church in 1843 either by joining it, or by signing an address to their fellow-landlords who were indulging in the discrimination of refusing sites for new churches, and the majority of those Free Kirk sympathisers were small lairds concentrated in the counties of Central Scotland. The Aberdeen Evangelical newspaper *Banner* was more accurate in identifying, in April 1842, a 'compact body of opposition' among lairds, and a 'majority of enemies' among the aristocracy.

Though Cockburn had exaggerated the quantity, he did make a valid point. The new secession was far more of a national movement than its eighteenth-century predecessors, embracing most of Gaelic Scotland as well as large numbers of active, middle class, urban congregations whose financial power alleviated the real privations suffered by many seceding rural ministers. Cockburn was glad to see Highland crofters and Lowland burghers proving that the new Church was popular, but it was the conjunction of populace and property in a national cause that appealed particularly to his Whig heart. This impression was sealed by the presence of so many legal friends in the Free Church. The group of what Cockburn's colleague, Lord Cuninghame, had once called the 'godly advocates' in Parliament House was strongly Whig, and most of them became Free Churchmen. The sight of so many legal, Whig friends like Lord Moncreiff and his son James, Alexander Dunlop, author of the Church's 'Claim of Right' of 1842, and Graham Speirs, Sheriff of Midlothian, in the van of the Disruption helped to remove many reservations about the event from Cockburn's mind

Thomas Chalmers also represented the Evangelical virtues to Cockburn though he was not unaware of his faults; as he said in *Memorials*, 'I have known him long and pretty well'. Cockburn regarded the evangelical conversion of Chalmers as the trigger which released his great energies: '. . . it was only on being elevated by the deep religious feelings which afterwards took possession of him that his powers were developed in their full force. From that moment he was a new creature; and devoted himself, as if with new faculties, to the moral and religious improvement of his countrymen.' In common with Jeffrey, Cockburn genuinely liked Chalmers, and he gives probably the best picture of a man whose human qualities were usually obscured by contemporary adulation and the atmosphere of near-hagiography that surrounded him as the founding father of the Free Church. Chalmers inclined temperamentally to Toryism. He clashed frequently from 1834 to 1840 with the Whig government, damaging the cause he was advocating passionately—the underwriting of his Church Extension scheme with state grants, which was anathema to the Dissenting allies of the Whigs in Scotland—by allowing himself to become identified with the Conservative opposition by his opponents. But though Cockburn was irritated by churchmen who allowed themselves to be used as political tools, he recognised the forces driving Chalmers into this position, regarding him as a 'natural-born Whig' deflected, by the imputation of French infidelity, from true allegiance to Whiggism, and to an apparently greater Tory support for the Kirk.

Chalmers also seems to have enjoyed Cockburn's company, overcoming his distaste for dining out by allowing himself to be enticed out to Bonaly from time to time, and Cockburn, himself a pleader of great skill, responded to the public oratory of Chalmers, pointing in *Memorials* to an effect on hearers, lost on the printed page:

> I have often hung upon his words with a beating heart and a tearful eye, without being brought to my senses till I read, next day, the very syllables that had moved me to such admiration, but which then seemed cold. The magic lies in the concentrated intensity which agitates every fibre of the man and brings out his meaning by words and emphasis of significant force, and rills his magnificent periods clearly and irresistibly along, and kindles the whole composition with living fire.

Cockburn's candid, but affectionate, appreciations of Chalmers are among his best character sketches. In his *Journal* obituary of 1847, he dwelt on the lack of personal arrogance in Chalmers, and: 'the quaint, picturesque oddity of his look, figure and manner; his self-coined diction and thick articulation; his taste for cumbrous jokes, and the merry twinkle of the eye, and the funny expression of the corners of the lips, which showed that graver cares had not quenched the frolicsomeness that had distinguished his youth'. These were human qualities that appealed to Cockburn and were probably drawn out of Chalmers by him; but he also pointed to his friend's sense of toleration:

> I hope posterity will be able to understand in the rare circumstance that, in these times, he was a liberal Churchman. A more thorough Calvinist there could not be; but he never questioned the possibility or the right of honest enquirers to find neither Presbytery nor Protestantism in the Bible; and, while adopting the principle of an

Establishment, there was no protection, short of
Establishment, which he did not concede to others. Even
as a polemic he desired no victory but what could be
gained by reason.

Cockburn speculated that 'the Free Church will not know how
useful he was until it shall experience the smaller men into whose
hands it has fallen', and hoped (against what he saw as an
opposite trend), that the Free Church would be inspired by 'the
love of those tolerant virtues of which his heart was the sanctuary'.

An earlier, private version of Cockburn's eloquent appreciation
of Chalmers was written to Mrs Sophia Rutherfurd on 1st June
1847, little more than a day after the latter's death, and is a
shorter, less studied, but more fluent reaction to the news:

Who was a greater living Scotchman? . . . And his walks
have been so varied.—Not confined to the common place,
technical, salvation of souls, he has enriched and enobled
this pursuit by striking discussions on every kindred moral
and political subject; and often leaves us to ask whether
his pen or his tongue be the most powerful. He never
wasted himself on little objects, nor tried to reach his ends
in a little way; but aimed high, and sought no conquests
but those that reason and enthusiasm, operating on the
minds of masses, could achieve. That concentration of the
mind on the object of present interest, which zeal always
implies, sometimes made him forget what was due to other
men or matters, and has exposed him to the only doubt,—
that of inconsistency—to which he has ever been supposed
to be liable. But this partiality of vehemence never made
him long, or seriously, unjust. And thro'out a life of ardent
practical conflict, he was uniformly simple, affectionate and
true. . . . His name was a tower. His voice a thunderbolt.
. . . How thankful I am that I was often within the flames
of his eloquent enthusiasm; and that I was familiar with the
honest smile, and the quaint, picturesque, oddities, of this
most loveable original.

As well as being an affectionate farewell to Chalmers, this eulogy
indicates the virtues of Evangelicalism that Cockburn saw represented by him. The Evangelicals were also called at various times
the 'Popular' or 'Orthodox' party, and the 'Wild' or 'Wildmen',
and for Cockburn these various terms represented facets of their
attitudes. For the popular aspect Cockburn had every sympathy,

as it represented, in the Veto Act form devised by Chalmers and Lord Moncreiff in 1834, the kind of compromise between popular demand and the traditional rights of property (and a barrier against more radical demands), similar to the Whig reforms of 1832 in secular politics. He saw an ideal blend of conservatism and popularity in Chalmers, with the latter's ability to harness the 'minds of masses' through reasoned oratory and zeal, and for these virtues he forgave Chalmers his vacillations, errors of judgement and political blunders.

Cockburn was also a supporter of the social views of Chalmers, who believed that 'pauperism' was finite, and a moral disease which the Church could eradicate by intensive combination of religious and social effort in each parish to remove the contagion of compulsory poor rates and return to a pure voluntary system. This 'Christian and Civic Economy' as it was called in Chalmers's book on his Glasgow experiment of 1818–1823, had a particular appeal to Scottish Whigs. It was partly based on the new political economy they admired, and Cockburn was a strong disciple, writing enthusiastically of Chalmers's schemes in the *Edinburgh Review* of October 1824. His declaration that Chalmers tried to widen the horizons of the Church from an over-concentration on counting of souls to the exclusion of men's material condition is an interesting comment on the evangelicalism of his age often echoed today. But Cockburn did not reveal that many Evangelicals, and the Kirk as a whole, greeted Chalmers's Glasgow scheme with scepticism and rejected its general applicability. It was the organisation that Chalmers evolved, and the prototype social casework of his agents, that inspired later admiration and imitation, while his theories were too easily adapted to give a blanket moral stigma to poverty.

The orthodox aspect of Evangelicalism was accepted by Cockburn in a man like Chalmers, who was reluctant to push it over the line marking it off from intolerance and zealotry, predelictions which Cockburn genuinely abhorred, and which he believed that Chalmers had restrained by his own example. There is little doubt that many aspects of contemporary Evangelicalism, in its wider non-party sense, repelled Cockburn. He certainly expressed distaste for Calvinism, a reflex usually activated by contemplation of ruinous medieval church buildings and kirk-yards like Beauly Priory, whose condition was ascribed in *Circuit Journeys* to the state of mind induced by 'Scotch Calvinism, which holds spirit to be everything and matter nothing'. But like many later zealots on this theme he forebore to mention that church fabrics were controlled by the local property-owners (heritors), not the church courts, and collapse of ancient buildings was often due to the practical parsimony of rate-avoiding heritors, rather than to metaphysical malevolence.

Karl Miller has discovered, and described in *Cockburn's Millennium*, a streak of pantheism in his subject which he illustrates so well from Cockburn's surviving poetry, and there are certainly some indications of heterodox impulses in Henry Cockburn. About 1806 he wrote to his friend, John Richardson, that he had '... dined with Dr Davidson who deplored that I had given up even my religious *profession*'. But twenty-five years later he had certainly resumed formal membership of the Kirk, when the Kirk Session of Broughton in Peeblesshire ordained Mr Solicitor-General Cockburn as an elder of the parish. There is little doubt, however, that this non-resident elder was ordained by the minister and session—the patron of the parish was a Whig, James Oswald of Auchencruive—for the purpose of returning him as a commissioner to the General Assembly, where Cockburn sat as an elder during most of his Solicitor-Generalship (1831–1833) as a watchdog of the government. He also admired David Hume, regarded as the arch-infidel by ardent Evangelicals, and wrote warmly in March, 1846 to Hume's biographer, John Hill Burton, that: 'those who cannot be religious without being intolerant will never forgive you for being fair. And let them to their worst. The humane piety of David's life, and the almost divine tranquillity of his death have done more in favour of true religion, than all his speculative doubts have ever done against it. The real question is, whether *religion and his speculations being properly understood*, these two be at all inconsistent.'

Among other aspects of 'Wild' Evangelicalism, Cockburn also disliked the growth of a new public Sabbatarianism in mid nineteenth-century Scotland, complaining in *Circuit Journeys* that the judges were, by 1838, deprived of a military band preceding them to the kirk on Sunday and 'the pious have, within these six or eight years, taken his music even from his Majesty's Commissioner to the General Assembly'; and in 1842 he can be found stigmatising the 'Calvinistic grimness' of a Sabbath in Perth. This clear growth of Sabbatarianism was defined correctly as new, Cockburn having earlier noted in *Memorials* that:

I could mention many practices of our old pious which would horrify modern zealots. The principles and feelings of the persons commonly called evangelical were the same then that they are now; the external acts . . . were materially different. Hearing what is often confidently prescribed now as the only proper mode of keeping the Christian Sabbath, and then recollecting how it was recently kept by Christian men, ought to teach us charity in the enforcement of observances which, to a certain extent, are necessarily matters of opinion.

Cockburn the judge saw all too much human frailty in his courts, and was drawn to contrast zealous Sabbatarian activity with the stark fact that the Sabbath was 'sacred . . . to whisky and brutality' in the most destitute, crime-ridden alleys of industrial cities like Glasgow. He had put his finger on an area where eminently respectable contemporary Evangelicalism often failed to make a serious impact.

Cockburn was also dismayed at the quality of the preaching he sometimes endured on circuit, relieving his frustration with typically pungent comments. In 1839 he suffered in Inverness under 'a worthy fanatic', Dr Clarke who roared out 'two and a quarter hours of *sheer absolute nonsense*'. Inveraray provided him with a long, dreary sermon in 1843 and he departed with the comment, 'God help the natives, both for the quality and the quantity'. Perth, a black Sabbath spot for Cockburn, furnished a sermon in 1845 from a young minister, Mr Anderson, 'who if he does not soon get more sense and less ambition, will settle into an eloquent ass', and on his return to the Fair City in 1848 he heard the same 'mouthy declaimer' whose 'fancy goods are of a bad pattern, and want body', These comments reveal the sharp, irreverent Henry Cockburn, all the more cutting because he had a high conception of the vocation of a minister of religion, and disliked what he saw as bluster and declamation. Cockburn appreciated fire and emotion in a preacher, but only, as with his favourite, the great Free Church preacher and philanthropist Thomas Guthrie, who did not, in his view, pander to 'vulgar popularity by fanaticism or any other unbecoming art'.

Most of Cockburn's sharp comments about ministers are reserved for those he detected as guilty of sectarian intolerance, particularly when this involved interference in political processes. In this respect he was alienated by the attitudes of the mainly

Presbyterian 'Seceders' and other allied Dissenters outside the
Church, a dislike probably based on a Whig distaste for the leading
personalities of the anti-Establishment 'Voluntary' movement, led
by the Radical Edinburgh draper, Duncan McLaren, whose
'Central Board of Dissenters' led the battle against the Church.

The rancorous feud between Churchmen and Voluntaries was
worst in Edinburgh, where it thoroughly disrupted Whig management of city politics. Cockburn showed political and social
prejudice in his views of the Radical Edinburgh Dissenters, who
were drawn largely from the ranks of small manufacturers and
traders, and the 'labour aristocracy' of independent craftsmen,
groups that had little in common with a mandarin like Cockburn.
However, he did define their role in the decade up to the Disruption of 1843, over-censoriously but not inaccurately, as
essentially a negative one:

> The tone was bad: not so much joy at their own growth,
> as dislike of the growth of the Church, from which they
> differ so little that their object used to be, and ought to be,
> to remove its errors and to reunite with it, instead of
> aiming at its overthrow in order that they may triumph in
> its place ... the selfish jealousy of sectarians, at the very
> moment they were boasting of their independence of the
> State Act.

Voluntary Dissent was strong and well-organised politically in
Edinburgh, Glasgow and many of the larger towns, and Cockburn
probably feared the challenge of its radical brand of Liberalism to
his conservative Parliament House Whiggery.

It was in the field of education, however, that Cockburn appears
to have displayed most anticlerical and secularist feeling. The
parish school system was patently failing to keep up with the
pressures of demographic, educational and religious change in mid
nineteenth-century Scotland, and, in common with many intellectual Whigs, Cockburn was impatient to sweep away the
legislative obstacles presented by the Established Church's monopoly of management of the parish schools, in order to create a new
non-denominational system of national education. In November
1846, he wrote to a fellow-enthusiast, Professor John Stuart
Blackie: 'If I had as much power as his Majesty of Prussia I would
clearly compel my subjects to have the *Secular* system; and let them
lean on the rule of three without imbibing the Trinity at the same
time.' Mere tinkering with a parish system still controlled by

Established Kirk sessions and heritors would '. . . only aggravate the Drone-age, of the Laird-named, and Priest directed . . . Education will be right, exactly in proportion as secular sense and vigour are allowed to supersede clerical ignorance and intolerance.'

But, as often with Cockburn, indulgence in such ringing phrases and anticlerical zeal had more specific than general application, in this case to the post-Disruption Established Church, which he regarded politically as a reactionary rump, drained of its best blood (he did not live long enough to see clear signs of its revival), and unworthy to retain a monopoly of official education. In 1854, following the establishment in Edinburgh of an association to press for national education, he wrote more soberly:

> Popular education . . . is involved in no material difficulty
> *in itself.* Its difficulties arise, almost entirely, from religious
> repulsions. It is clear to my mind that keeping the popular
> education any longer in the hands of the [Established]
> Church is nonsense . . . and now, when the Church is the
> minority . . . giving it the control is just excluding the
> majority from being taught. The expediency of chemically
> combining religious and secular education is not so clear.
> I am rather inclined to approve of it—*if it can be done*; and
> that on two grounds. One is, that as religion must be
> taught, and as it is a great public safeguard, it is wise to
> interweave it with people's earliest feelings and ideas; the
> other, that at least this being the opinion of almost our
> whole population, it is in vain to attempt any other system.
> The baffling difficulty is how to get this principle carried
> into operation. Each sect thinking every other sect
> religiously wrong, nobody has yet shown *how* all sects can
> be taught religion at the same school.

Cockburn's secularising zeal had cooled since 1846, and he had abandoned in favour of more sober analysis the temptation to mint vivid catch-phrases. Not only was religion in schools a means of social control it would be dangerous to remove, but religion itself had to be taught, and where could it be imparted to children effectively but in schools? Above all, no satisfactory inter-denominational system was in being, or even in view, and native caution restrained his libertarian instincts. In fact, Cockburn's anti-clericalism was more a function of his Whig devotion to libertarian causes like Catholic Emancipation, and later, the related issue of State grants

for Roman Catholic education at Maynooth College, and of his
genuine aversion to denominational intolerance, than of any
doctrinal devotion to secularist ideas. 'Union or dis-union', he
wrote in the *Journal* in 1847, 'the ear listens in vain, amidst these
movements of religious parties, for a whisper of toleration.'

But more often than he willingly revealed, Cockburn attacked
churchmen or Dissenters simply for mixing religion and politics,
especially when this frustrated Whig policies or politicians. In May
1833, Cockburn, as Solicitor-General, had been unable to restrain
the General Assembly from passing a resolution against the Whigs'
Irish Education Bill (regarded as compromising with Popery and
diluting the Bible), and wrote angrily to Jeffrey about his first
defeat at clerical hands (he had forestalled an earlier attempt in
1832) sending on perforce 'a Petition to Parliament by which it
last night pleased about 160 beasts in the Venerable [Assembly] to
signalise their folly in opposition to about 50 wise men ... the
majority was composed of the more rancorous Tories and the more
bigotted evangelists'.

Cockburn identified this same alliance of Tories and Evangelicals formed to harry the Whig administrations of Lord
Melbourne from 1834 on the issue of state endowment for the new
extension parishes of the Kirk, grants which the Whigs were restrained from conceding by their partial dependence on the
powerful new Dissenting political interest. The Scottish Whigs
were tormented by this issue for four years, but the Auchterarder
case, as Cockburn noted with grim relish in June 1838, provided
nemesis for the Tories, and an object lesson of how dangerous and
unpredictable playing the Church card could be:

> When this feeling arose the Tories hailed and encouraged
> it. Their best weapon all over the empire has been the
> Church; and in Scotland their cry was, Whigs and Popery!
> Conservatives and Extension! In thus using the pious as a
> political tool, they were destined to have the very same
> fate with their political rivals. It was necessary that they
> should inflame the religious with extravagant notions of the
> importance of the Church, of its irresistible power, and of
> the absolute necessity of calling all its thunders forth. This
> is an invocation which is never made in vain to churchmen.
> Accordingly, for four years, our churchmen have taken
> their new friends at their word, and have acted so
> thoroughly on the assumption of the Church's omnipotence

that they have almost thrown off their allegiance to the
State, and are at present in disdainful hostility to the timid
and astonished Conservatives. . . .

Of course, Cockburn forebore to mention that Chalmers had
put the Church extenders' case first to the Whigs, and that the
Prime Minister, Lord Melbourne, had half-promised action and
then recanted; therefore the actions of churchmen were not merely
'fanatical', but quite understandable, had Cockburn not seen them
through Whig spectacles. However, he was saved from greater bias
by his own view of toleration and his belief in the historical
legitimacy of the Evangelical leadership of the Kirk, while con-
firming his own belief that religion and politics were a fundamentally unstable mix: 'It is no reason for being unjust to the
Catholics or the Jews that we don't like their tenets. It is equally
foolish to attempt to suppress the claims of the Church of Scotland
because we think them strange or fanatical. The mere critic of
manners or opinions may be allowed to sneer; but the statesman
is bound to manage a people in reference to their hereditary
feelings.' The only 'highly satisfactory' result was that: 'It has
made it clear that no political party can be comfortable in using
our Church as a political ally. It won't work with the Radicals,
who are attached to the Dissenters. It is at fierce war with the
Whigs, who won't drain the public purse, and persecute other
sects, to please it. And it has now thrown off the Tories, who
support patronage, and attempt to make the Church surrender
its spiritual supremacy.'

The anticlericalism of Cockburn was largely political. He feared
the solvent effects of a 'devout Presbyterianism', superseding
all other allegiances, on established political loyalties. After all,
the Evangelical or Wild Party had been traditionally thought
Whiggish and the Whigs had given them patronage on their
return to office in 1830. But Cockburn held that zealotry had
overcome gratitude as the party turned on the Whigs over issues
like the Irish Education Bill and Church Extension. The Kirk had
historic claims and legitimate rights, but in politics it intervened
as an anarchic force, and Cockburn, an increasingly conservative
Whig, feared its potential to disrupt and remake the political
system of Scotland which he had helped to create in 1832, and ever
afterwards looked on with proprietorial pride.

The formation of the Free Church in an atmosphere of bitter
hostility to a Conservative government went far to ensure the

former's adhesion to Liberalism and removed the more general threat of Evangelicalism to the Whigs. But in the Edinburgh context Cockburn continued to dislike the religious dimension which permeated city politics to the detriment of a Whig luminary, T. B. Macaulay, the historian, who lost the city seat in 1847. Cockburn was well aware that many of Macaulay's troubles were self-inflicted and that the historian had paid the penalty for perfunctory attention to constituency business, but he found the alliance of Radicals and Evangelicals which unseated Macaulay as ominous as the earlier coalition of Evangelicals and Tories and deplored that 'the great rise and the profound folly of many of those who choose to describe themselves as exclusively Evangelical, have made them fancy it is their duty, and in their power, to introduce their peculiar views into the secular business of the State; and that, in order to hasten this millennium, all that is requisite is that they should get the House of Commons stuffed with people like themselves'. However, in this context Cockburn spoke as the representative of the threatened Whig establishment of the city, and many of his anti-Evangelical remarks at this time have to be read in that light.

Despite his admiration of Hume, which hints at heterodoxy, the rather scanty evidence available on Cockburn's personal religious views does not reflect any fundamental scepticism, and his self-deprecating description of himself in *Circuit Journeys* as an 'ordinarily pious man', unmoved by perfervid religiosity but dutiful in his religious observance and attendance, is probably nearer actuality. Karl Miller has quoted Cockburn's encouraging and suitably devout letter of 1809 to his diffident friend, the poet James Grahame, who had forsaken the Scottish bar for an Anglican parish, and the praise accorded in it to the unique and sacred tie of a minister of religion to his people is repeated in letters to his other close clerical friend, Charles Anderson, minister of Closeburn. Cockburn had written to Grahame of the tie of a minister to his people as one 'which strengthens while every other decays, at last consigns his bones to the hallowed respect that becomes the death-given exaltation of his Soul', and a similar motif recurs in his description to Charles Anderson in February 1826, of the elderly Sir Harry Moncreiff 'preaching every fortnight with all the pleasing vigour of a powerful dogmatist, mellowed by Time, and exalted by the approaching prospect of eternity'.

Even allowing for a natural desire to please two friends by

writing respectfully of their vocation, these are not isolated instances of Cockburn's admiration for lives of exemplary devotion. In common with his pictures of the Moncreiffs and Chalmers, he praised the testimony provided by the conduct of other devout legal friends like Graham Speirs, Sheriff of Midlothian, who combined pious *gravitas* with 'reasonableness and toleration', having 'put on a new nature' and abjured youthful irregularities after Evangelical conversion. As always, Cockburn's damnation of the unco guid was reserved for those who mixed their piety with sectarian intolerance or political meddling. Certainly —as the Grahame and Anderson letters indicate—his reading of Hume does not appear to have tempted him to reject either immortality or redemption of the soul, and his fine consolatory letter to Cornelia Dick Lauder on the death of his friend, Sir Thomas, in June 1848, underlines this more explicitly. In this emotional and obviously sincere tribute he confessed to her daughter that he felt unworthy to offer consolation to a woman of 'sense and piety' like Lady Dick Lauder: she knew 'that the severed will meet again. . . . She knows that it is God's doing; and she knows what this implies.'

Cockburn also reacted strongly to any suggestion that his closest friend, Francis Jeffrey, was a sceptic, and in this matter, given their close identity of views, it is possible that he was speaking for himself as well. Chalmers, who was friendly with Jeffrey, had been troubled by the latter's conversation (and a letter) which he felt indicated 'infidelity'. Cockburn refers briefly to the episode in his *Journal* eulogy of Chalmers, merely using it to construct a tribute to his departed friend's Christian charity. But it was also the subject of correspondence, and probably conversation, with Chalmers's minister sons-in-law, John Mackenzie and William Hanna (the biographer). Cockburn wrote in strong and firm terms to the Rev. John Mackenzie in May 1850, on receiving an enquiry as to Jeffrey's views:

> *If* Jeffrey professed infidelity to Chalmers, nothing can ever convince me that he did so as a sincere expression of his true opinions. Because tho' he was not a religious man, or rather not what is commonly considered so, *most unquestionably* he was not an infidel. He must have been trying an experiment on Chalmers's charity or forbearance; or, possibly, protecting himself from the imputation, to his own mind and the mind of his friend, of courting Chalmers

by the profession of those religious feelings by which he
knew that he was most easily attracted, and which, in the
Doctor's sense, Jeffrey did not possess. But he might have
wanted these and not been an infidel.

However, I am glad that any letter bearing such a
construction, is destroyed.

This may appear to be rather elaborate special pleading, but
Cockburn knew Jeffrey's mind better than any man, and the
latter's propensity for drawing-room teasing could have extended
easily into irreverent musings which created alarm and dismay
in Chalmers. Certainly Cockburn, a more conventional man,
would have been horrified at any personal imputation of
religious infidelity, and he defended his dead friend's reputation
vigorously.

However, orthodoxy, in the sense that a strict Evangelical
Presbyterian of his own age would have understood the term, was
another matter. Cockburn is on record in the *Journal* and *Circuit
Journeys* expressing clear dislike of Calvinism. But it would appear
that his distaste for his native brand of theology (based on the
Westminster Confession of Faith of 1643, the 'chief subordinate
standard', below the Bible, of the Church) was for its metaphysical
influence and aspects of its operation as a social gospel rather than
for its particular theological tenets. As was discussed earlier, his
attack was on the aesthetic inadequacies of contemporary Presbyterian worship, and particularly the neglect of the Church's
medieval heritage in buildings and monuments, and on a new,
rigorous Sabbatarianism, enforced alike on the willing and the
reluctant: matters of ecclesiastical polity and attitude of mind
rather than great issues of basic doctrine. Cockburn was certainly
out of sympathy with the prevailing ecclesiastical ethos of his age,
and particularly that of his later years. But there is little evidence
that he thought long or hard on theological matters, and his autobiographical writings make no mention of the stir created by the
celebrated Assembly heresy trials of John Macleod Campbell
(1831) and Edward Irving (1833) for infringement of the
Westminster Standards. His view of the Church was social and
political rather than theological, but there is no real evidence to
contradict his own affirmation of temperate piety, or to indicate
any radical disagreement with fundamental Christian beliefs.

Cockburn's practical experience, as a junior Government
minister, of the management of Church affairs, was a basic

influence on his attitude to the Kirk, and on his viewpoint in the legal battles of 1838–1843, which he had, reluctantly, to consider as a judge. Cockburn entered on his Solicitor-Generalship with high hopes, writing in the last paragraph of *Memorials*: 'We have come upon the public stage in a splendid, but perilous scene. I trust that we shall do our duty. If we do, we cannot fail to do some good to Scotland. In the abuses of our representative and municipal systems alone, our predecessors have left us fields in which patriotism may exhaust itself.' The last sentence was more prophetic than Cockburn could have realised, for while parliamentary and municipal reform acts were carried in 1832 and 1833 they proved to be far from perfect instruments to attain the Whig millennium. The basic drafting of the Reform Bill (Scotland) was Cockburn's; and though the Whig M.P., T. F. Kennedy of Dunure, had been involved in earlier discussions in 1830, Cockburn declared in the *Journal* in April 1831 that: 'The Scotch bill was originally drawn by me, but in doing so I had no experience of popular elections, and had got only a few general directions; and I was prohibited from consulting any mortal except Jeffrey, who was in London.'

The result of this work in a vacuum, with Cockburn and Jeffrey's main external guide being the principles of the English Act, expecially implementation of clauses regarding £10 freeholders in the counties, was predictable. As Dr William Ferguson has pointed out, muddled drafting on English principles, and a dismissive attitude to Scots feudal law, created ample opportunity for the creation of faggot votes in the counties based on old, but valid, feudal principles, judgement in the registration courts being left to sheriffs, who were themselves political appointees. Burgh reform was less beset with legal problems. Cockburn, fearing Radical town councils, admitted that 'I tremble for the first burgh election', and was pleasantly surprised that the new electors had chosen more moderate people of higher social station than he expected. But he was less enthusiastic about the growing amount of local political power captured by Dissenters: 'For the Church the composition is not so good; dissenters often form the majority. The effect of this on Parliament and on the General Assembly will soon be seen.'

Cockburn was to become increasingly depressed by the sectarianism in local politics exemplified by his own city of Edinburgh. The royal burghs returned sixty-seven commissioners to the

G

General Assembly and his prediction about Voluntary Dissenters using their local power to obstruct Evangelical policies was also fulfilled. By May 1841 the Evangelical Glasgow newspaper, the *Scottish Guardian*, estimated that the Evangelicals had lost fifteen burgh votes through Voluntary intervention either by active returns of Moderates, or deliberate failure to send an elder to Assembly. The political nation, in its parliamentary and local spheres, was genuinely extended, and Cockburn continued to regard his and Jeffrey's creations with pride, despite their flaws. But the fruits of reform did not prove so sweet as he expected, and by the summer of 1833 he was expressing considerable disillusion to Jeffrey at the paralysis of Scottish government caused by ignorance and indifference towards Scottish business at Westminster:

> It is plainly necessary—nothing short of necessary—that some high person should be made Secretary for Scotland, and that it should be understood that Government is to support him. Nothing can be more shameful than that great measures such as Burghs, Patronage etc. should be left to swelter and flounder on as they may . . . and that Government does not feel its existence, character or comfort at all involved in the result, but leaves the Lord Advocate to be abused for everything —even for those things which they force him to do, or prevent his doing.

Clearly Cockburn had found that reform of government, substituting the more systematic management of Home Office and Treasury for the old informal system of individual managers, had not eradicated the problem of metropolitan neglect of Scottish affairs. Fortunately, he saved the letters from Jeffrey cataloguing their official frustrations from the burning of his papers in 1845. He overcame the problem of his friend's execrable handwriting by having the letters copied into four folio volumes sprinkled with his own salty and near-contemporary comments, and preserved only a selection of the original autograph letters. This correspondence provides considerable insight into the difficulties of Jeffrey and Cockburn with their political superiors.

The Grey administration in which Cockburn and Jeffrey served as ministers outside the Cabinet was a government united only in the great cause of Reform but otherwise riven by conflicts created by strong and temperamental personalities, notably by the immense dissension caused by the wayward and capricious Lord

Chancellor, Henry Brougham, Jeffrey's old *Edinburgh Review* collaborator, and by the proud and touchy Lord Durham, Grey's son-in-law. Jeffrey, overwhelmed by uncongenial work, immense correspondence, and indifferent health exacerbated by the anxieties of office, was a disappointing Lord Advocate, and he and Cockburn, who were basically trial counsel, proved to be poor legal draftsmen. But some allowance must be made for their weak position on the fringes of the government, and their dependence on making representations through cabinet ministers like Brougham, who considered himself well qualified to solve the patronage problem but never produced any coherent scheme, and Lord Melbourne, who, as Grey's Home Secretary and later as Prime minister, treated Scottish affairs in general and Church problems in particular with a languid and bored indifference relieved only by a shrewd appreciation of the political pitfalls in the way of action.

The Whigs toyed in 1833 with various proposed bills to give parliamentary sanction to a congregational voice in patronage through an effective 'call' to the presentee. Jeffrey, as Lord Advocate, claimed the support of a majority of Scottish M.P.s for a Patronage Reform bill. But, as his letters to Cockburn clearly show, the political will was never strong enough at Cabinet level. The process seems to have begun in March 1833, Jeffrey reporting to Cockburn on 12 March that: 'The Chancellor [Brougham] is in great vigour, and I think will bring out his patronage scheme very speedily. The plan now is rather to have a *standing committee* of delegates for the communicants, whom, with certain of the Elders the selection from the Government list is to be left.' This scheme, apparently for the one third of church patronages in Scotland held by the Crown, was disliked by Cockburn and Lord Moncreiff, the former commenting in a note that it would not satisfy popular demand and merely create 'a contemptible body of parochial jobbers'.

In fact Scottish Whigs were in a considerable state of anxiety in 1833 over the political implications of demands for the reform, and even the abolition, of patronage. Cockburn wrote to T. F. Kennedy on 28 January that the anti-patronage agitation terrified him 'particularly in reference to future elections', and Jeffrey commented on 23 March, in reply to Cockburn's papers on the issue, that: '. . . when nearly one third of the whole Presbyterian body [the secession churches] is actually exercising popular election of its pastors, can you wonder that the other two-thirds should clamour ferociously and confidently for the same privilege? My own opinion is that we cannot resist this clamour; and that no man who resists it *in toto* will ever be returned again by any popular constituency in Scotland.'

As the General Assembly of May 1833 approached, Jeffrey and Cockburn showed considerably more consistent judgement than their Cabinet masters. The former seems to have persuaded Melbourne to allow him to write a letter to Cockburn, dated 7 May, to serve as an 'Informal Message' to the Assembly encouraging it to prepare legislation to give effect to the principle 'that no presentee should be forced on a parish against the serious and earnest reclamation of a decided majority . . . of the people', and warning that, if the Church did not create clear legislation to achieve this end, the government would 'find it impossible to avoid (or long delay) bringing in a legislative enactment' even without the 'light and encouragement' of the Assembly.

However, contradictory instructions soon followed, as Brougham intervened. 'I have seen both Lord M[elbourne] and the Chancellor', wrote an exasperated Jeffrey to Cockburn on 23 May 1833,

> all I can learn is that a letter was written to Lord
> Moncreiff by the latter recommending a Committee of
> Assembly to consider the whole matter, and report next
> year. Lord M[elbourne], who saw the letter, says it urged
> this peremptorily, and protested *against the veto*, while the
> Author himself says he recommended nothing except *salve
> jure* of any communications we had made, or arrangements
> we had concluded, with other parties. I fear the first
> edition is the most correct, and that we shall all suffer for
> this rash and sudden interference   . . . The Chancellor has
> a most erroneous notion that the excitement of Patronage
> is going down, and that this reference to a committee will
> let it die an easy death, instead of raising it to new life,
> as it certainly will if carried.

Cockburn complained, in a footnote, of his bewildering situation, saying that 'down to the last day [before the Assembly] inconsistent instructions came; one saying give the people a veto—another stick by Patronage. Lord Moncreiff and I stuck to both: got Chalmers to move the Veto.' However, Cockburn's note, obviously written rather later, confuses the narrow failure of Chalmers's veto motion in 1833 with its success in the 1834

Assembly, making it doubtful to which year he refers; but the general picture of vacillation and drift is accurate enough. Brougham was reported by Jeffrey, on 30 May 1833, to be moving into 'a growing dread of the *liberum veto* in the parish', a portent of his later ultra-erastian position as a judge of the Auchterarder case in the House of Lords; and on 17 June Jeffrey concluded accurately that: 'The Government, I think, is *quite* determined to *do* nothing this year, and, if possible, to *say* nothing either'.

It is probable that the Grey government found justification for their inertia in the discordant demands of the patronage reformers, some Evangelicals cautiously advocating a collegiate selection of presentees by Kirk sessions and heritors, others favouring the veto solution of Chalmers and Lord Moncreiff, and the most radical demanding total abolition, by repeal of the contentious Patronage Act of 1712. It was the radicals, lead in Parliament by Sir George Sinclair of Caithness and the ultra-Evangelical Fife M.P. Andrew Johnston, who troubled Jeffrey most, and his lack of political muscle became painfully obvious. This was not entirely personal: the office of Lord Advocate, as Cockburn warned a late holder, Andrew Rutherfurd, in 1839, was an unenviable one whose occupant 'walks on hot cinders and sits on gun powder', and as contemporary Advocates no longer commanded phalanx-like obedience from a bloc of Scottish M.P.s, as in the days of Henry Dundas, their political stock had slumped, and the Cabinet tended to use them as figureheads or as decoys to deflect awkward Scottish questions. Their political power and patronage was circumscribed by the Home Office, and it was only in the legal field that they enjoyed any real independent initiative.

Therefore Jeffrey was compelled to proceed by lobbying the uncertain Brougham, and reported a typical discussion to Cockburn on 18 February 1834: 'I was two hours with the chancellor yesterday. . . . He put me off after all about *patronage*, though Sinclair brings in his motion on the 27th and we *must* express some purpose or opinion by that time'; and Cockburn, in a note dated 16 July 1835, sourly commented, 'Not expressed yet'. A week later, on 24 February 1834, Jeffrey detailed the typically confused Cabinet response: 'The Cabinet decided yesterday that they would (ultimately) legislate in aid (or instead) of the Venerable [Assembly] in making the principle of Chalmers's motion the Law . . . but they seem disinclined to any specific *public* pledge either *in favour* of it or *against* popular election, wishing not to provoke specific objections or angry demands, and to go into Committee with the appearance at least of everything being left open. I doubt a little as to the prudence of this.'

In fact the only action taken by the Whig government was to buy off Sinclair with a Select Committee which produced an inconclusive and fruitless report. It is significant that Cockburn took care to record this entire episode in such detail, and it must have been a severe shock to his Whig complacency for he appended a remarkably strong, almost vituperative, note to the copy of one of Jeffrey's letters (5 June 1833):

> There was never such an instance of the habitual ignorance
> and indifference of Government (all governments) to
> Scotch affairs as in this of patronage:—a deep, vital and
> pressing question—kindred to others in the English and
> Irish churches, and in which one plain course was clearly
> pointed out by responsible and consulted Scotch advisers;
> yet because it was *as yet* merely Scotch, and conducted
> without turbulent agitation, it was impossible to get *any*
> *line whatever* adopted by ministers. This has long been the
> established system for managing this part of the empire.

This statement is stronger than Cockburn's other proto-nationalist outbursts in the *Journal*. Whether the legal advice on patronage offered to the government was as strong or consistent as he indicated is a matter that would repay further examination. But his point is clear enough: Scottish business was bottom of the scale of priorities in Parliament, far below the claims of England and Wales, and overshadowed by the problems of governing Ireland, and his Scotch gorge rose at this neglect, even to the extent of attacking (privately) fellow-Whigs. Therefore, however irritated Cockburn became later at the actions of the Church, he was always very conscious of his belief that a Whig government of which he had been a junior member had treated the Kirk shabbily in 1833 and subsequently, and that the ultimate Disruption was as much a product of political ignorance and evasion as of the intransigence of churchmen. As he said after the event in the *Journal* for June 1843:

> . . . the truth is that, notwithstanding a world of professions,
> Government was never duly anxious to compose these
> differences. The Whigs in general had no love of Churches.
> and it was only for its patronage and for the politics of the
> Moderate party that the Tories in general loved the Church

of Scotland. Neither Government understood the subject, and both trembled for Church of England questions and for the Dissenters. Their ignorance, which no doubt has all along been profound, is but a poor apology for their infatuation.

Political experiences, as well as personal predilections and individual historical interpretation, could not fail to influence Cockburn's judicial attitudes to the series of Church cases from 1838 and 1843. In fact, faced with the oldest and most insoluble of politico-legal problems: the clash of jurisdiction between a Church, claiming Divine sanction for its government and a consequent independence in its pastoral regulation, and the rights of the State which paid and maintained that pastorate to regulate its material structure. It was almost inevitable that the individual personal, religious and political biases of the thirteen judges of the Court of Session could not be kept out of their judgements.

Cockburn had feared any recourse to a civil court, given the absence of any Act of Parliament to buttress the Kirk's veto, and wrote in the *Journal* of June 1834 that: 'If the Courts of Law should overrule what the Assembly has done, Parliament must interfere; otherwise there will be an indecent collision between the civil and the ecclesiastical power, in which the churchmen will probably stick to their point, even though the spiritual cure should go to one presentee and the temporal benefice to another.' Cockburn was already making a distinction between the temporalities and spiritualities of a parish charge, but this was a distinction which erastian lawyers would not countenance. As Dr Hugh Watt has pointed out, John Hope deliberately altered the form of appeal in the Auchterarder case from one expressing simple concern for possession of the parish stipend to a wider declarator for the interdiction of the Presbytery of Auchterarder on the grounds that they were bound to receive and admit the presentee (a spiritual act, in the eyes of the Church) if he was qualified according to existing Statute law, the Kirk's own Veto being 'illegal and injurious to the patrimonial rights of the pursuer'. This move opened out the whole case from being merely a parish lawsuit into a challenge to the Church's right to regulate the spiritualities of the charge if they were not combined in the same person as the holder of the presentation and stipend as judged by a civil court: a distinct extension of erastian control on the Church, and the very problem that Cockburn had feared would arise.

Predictably, Cockburn rejected Hope's extension of the issue, objecting in his Auchterarder judgement of 1838 at being compelled to give an opinion on the 'abstract proposition' of the pursuers which they had no proved interest to maintain, especially as the principles of the case involved 'the subsistence of the General Assembly as a supreme and independent ecclesiastical authority'. He could not condemn the action of the defenders (the Presbytery) because they were acting within their jurisdiction, even though wrong, adding that: 'I acknowledge the great principle that the Church, as an establishment, has no power but what the State has conferred on it. But I cannot infer from this that all power is to be withheld from the Church for which no express clause can be produced in any act of Parliament. Scarely any old institution could stand upon this rule for a single hour.'

Cockburn's arguments were largely pragmatic rather than legal though he did consider that a Scots Act of 1567 c. 7 did give the Church rights of collation broad enough to cover the Veto. But what he chiefly feared was a damaging and ultimately sterile collision of Court and Church in which the former's dignity 'must necessarily be put in jeopardy by its exposing itself to a conflict in which it cannot explain how it is to prevail'. His opinion as one of the minority was in line with his earlier opinions, and in fact this applied to most of the Bench. A majority against the Presbytery was equally likely, given the strong and old-established Moderate views of the senior judges Lord President Charles Hope and Lord Justice-Clerk Boyle, who had opposed the Veto Act in the Assembly, and the Tory erastianism of Lord Meadowbank and Lord Medwyn, a devout Episcopalian. But Whigs on the Bench also opposed the Church's case, led by the elderly Lord Gillies, and including Lord Cuninghame, Cockburn's successor as Solicitor-General, who as a member of the 'Whig Clique' of Edinburgh had been influenced strongly by the arguments of Voluntary Dissenters against the Church.

In view of the judges' political and ecclesiastical antecedents, guarded language and actions were desirable, as Cockburn hinted in his speech. But Lord President Hope was not a man to restrain himself. Cockburn, who rather liked him and generally respected his judicial dignity, had commented also in *Memorials* on his 'hot temperament not cooled by a sound head'. The Church issue brought out these defects in Hope, who gave immense offence to Evangelicals by his ultra-erastian judgement, particularly the passage in which he declared that while the Saviour was Head of the Church in the proper, theological sense, '. . . that our Saviour is the Head of the Kirk of Scotland in any temporal or legislature or judicial sense, is a position which I can dignify by no other name than absurdity. The Parliament is the temporal head of the Church.' The old Whig, Lord Gillies, added fuel to the flames by equating the Kirk to a mere corporation: 'it is said that the General Assembly is a legislative body. So is every corporation.'

In the light of such naked erastianism from the majority of the Court, the Church majority also raised its terms of reference in the Assembly of 1838, taking up its position on the broader and more emotive issue of 'Spiritual Independence' from the 'aggression' of the Court, which was compounded by that of the House of Lords in 1839, where Lord Brougham gave particular offence by a prejudiced and superficial judgement, parading his Moderate antecedents through relationship with William Robertson, and representing his rejection of the Kirk's 'pretensions' as the surrogate judgement of his illustrious relative. Cockburn also commented on Brougham's Anglocentric tone, saying in the *Journal* that 'It irritated and justified the people of Scotland in believing that their Church was sacrificed to English prejudice.'

Cockburn's fears of the effects of Auchterarder rapidly proved to be all too accurate. The Church openly challenged, and showed itself willing to defy, the Court of Session, and further clashes were inevitable. The Auchterarder decision enabled Thomas Clark, a candidate for the vacant crown parish of Lethendy rejected under the Veto procedure by the Presbytery of Dunkeld, to obtain an interdict against his rival presentee, Andrew Kessen, which the Presbytery of Dunkeld refused to recognise, ordaining and inducting Kessen to the Spiritual charge of the parish. The result of this action was their summons to the Court of Session in June, 1839, and the censure and levying of costs against the Presbytery and Kessen. Cockburn reluctantly felt obliged to join the majority in finding the breach of interdict proven, but joined with a narrow majority of the Court to defeat a potentially disastrous imposition of jail sentences on the ministers:

> Gillies, Meadowbank, and Mackenzie where clear for
> imprisonment; and Medwyn had no objection to it.
> Moncreiff, Jeffrey, Fullerton, Cuninghame, and myself
> were for finding them liable in expenses; but for also
> finding that, in consequence of the difficulty and novelty of

their situation, it was unnecessary to proceed further. The
President, the Justice-Clerk and Murray were rather for
the jail; but at last the Justice-Clerk proposed a mere
censure and costs. . . . Our moderation, though it surprised
most people at first, is already felt to have been wise. It is
received as the strongest proof of our conviction of the
ministers' helplessness, and it disappoints some of them who
are ambitious of martyrdom. It was a strange exhibition.

Cockburn's remarks reflect his real unease at the implications of
the Court's actions. As he had warned over Auchterarder, the
Court could not impose its will on a defiant Church majority without loss of dignity. Stern corrective action would only create
martyrs by imprisoning recalcitrant ministers, and fertilize a
massive campaign of civil disobedience. The ingredients for a more
serious clash than Lethendy were present already with the decision
of the Assembly of May 1839 to form a 'Non-Intrusion Committee'
headed by Chalmers, to rouse the country and fight all future
'intrusions' on the Auchterarder pattern, compounded in December
by the results of the Marnoch or Strathbogie case. In this instance
the majority of the presbytery concerned (Strathbogie) opted to
obey the Court interdict rather than the Assembly, provoking the
Commission [standing committee] of the latter to suspend them
from the exercise of ministerial duties.

The Evangelical majority of the Church were becoming isolated
rapidly, as normally discordant political interests combined to
oppose their claims. By December 1838, the Conservatives were
disengaging themselves already from their former close support of
the Kirk's extension and endowment campaigns, Lord Aberdeen
warning John Hope in December of the bad effect of Lethendy on
Anglican opinion, and dismissing any attempt to get endowments
for the Kirk: 'in prudence we ought not to attempt it . . . Failure I
think is certain.' A year later on 30th December, 1839, Sir James
Graham was explicitly warning Chalmers that if the Kirk wished
to fight 'the good old cause' of Spiritual Independence to the
finish, it 'contemplates with complacency the severance of the Kirk
from the State, and the maintenance of the officiating pastors by
Voluntary aids'.

Jeffrey and Cockburn had speculated even earlier on this
possibility, the former writing to his friend from London in April
1838, that if all the Kirk's claims were rejected, 'Then we shall
have a new secession by and bye'. But they were now passive

spectators of the impasse into which the Church was drifting, as Cockburn journalised in May 1839:

I cannot blame them for trying to assert what until lately no man doubted was their right, and what seems essential to their existence as a Church.

But they will fail. They have appointed a committee to confer with Government with a view to legalise the Veto Act. If it be a Whig Government the answer must be—'You boast of your hatred to us, and wish us to renew the persecution of Dissenters; we won't run our heads against an English and Irish post to please you.' If it be a Tory one, the answer will be—'You are against patronage and the law; get you gone.' If it be a Radical—'We hate the Church; your ruin rejoices us.'

Cockburn's Court of Session efforts were now concentrated on restraining his more warlike colleagues. In February 1840 Lord President Hope considered that a Non-Intrusion meeting at Huntly had passed resolutions insulting to the Court, and called two meetings to consider recommending prosecution of the offenders. As Cockburn reported privately to the Lord Advocate, Rutherfurd, on 3rd March, the resolution was abandoned: 'And so we escaped a horrid scrape; but not without a meeting made painful by some irritation'. With Church and Court both obdurate, Cockburn saw the best way out of the impasse through an act of Parliament 'to legalise *the* Veto or *a* Veto, and thus reconcile the People by softening patronage without destroying it'. But various attempts in 1840 to devise bills acceptable to the Assembly failed to satisfy.

Lord Aberdeen's bill came nearest success, but foundered on his refusal to accept an unrestricted congregational Veto, and Lord Advocate Rutherfurd, bitterly conscious of being, as he said to Cockburn, 'in place, but without power', drafted a rival bill to Aberdeen's which was shelved by the Cabinet when the latter's attempt failed. The 'melancholy game' continued, and contemporary cartoons depicted choleric judges and ministers belabouring and abusing each other. If Cockburn had appeared in the Lethendy case to waver from his firm view of the independence of the Church in regulation of spiritualities, he was brought back sharply to his old position by the actions of most of his colleagues in the First Division of the Court in January 1840, when they extended their interdict in Strathbogie to prohibit all ministers,

other than the seven suspended by the Church for obeying the
Court, from carrying out any pastoral duties in the parishes of the
seven 'rebels'. Cockburn was appalled:

> No calm lawyer can approve of this proceeding. It implies
> that suspension of a clergyman from his clerical functions
> is not the exclusive privilege of the Church . . . that the
> illegality of the spiritual grounds on which the Church
> suspends is a legal reason for the civil court defeating its
> sentence, and that it is competent for the civil court to
> enforce its own view by not only encouraging suspended
> ministers to set their ecclesiastical superiors at defiance . . .
> but by excluding every other Established clergyman from
> preaching within a large district, though the right of doing
> so is left open to everybody else, including Catholics and
> Dissenters.

He deplored again the intemperate tone of Hope and Gillies to
the detriment of 'the weight of the Bench': 'The President [Hope]
accused the clergy of fraudulent manoeuvring, and Gillies asserted
that they had violated their oath of allegience and committed
perjury!' The predictable result was ostentatious defiance by
churchmen: 'Ministers, and generally the most eminent ones,
defying martyrdom, have been preaching within the forbidden
ground almost constantly. Hitherto no attempt has been made to
drevent or punish this, because it is seen that fining or imprisoning
the clergy would do no good—another proof of the imprudence of
granting an interdict which cannot be enforced.'

As Cockburn realised, the Court was also caught in an impasse,
producing futile interdicts which only served to raise the tem-
perature of the dispute. Subsequently he adhered firmly to his
declaration in March 1840, that however much he disliked aspects
of the Church and of Evangelicalism, and that 'there would
probably be no Established Church in our Utopia', he and Jeffrey
were 'immovably certain that the Church has the law on its side'.
He was able to find mitigating reasons for the final deposition of
the seven Strathbogie ministers in rebellion against the Church by
the Assembly of May 1841, pointing out that high courts of law
(the Assembly being one in its own sphere) had clashed acrimoni-
ously from time to time, witnessed by a contemporary clash
between the House of Commons and Court of Queen's Bench.
While regarding the depositions as unnecessary and impolitic, he
was not prepared to declare them to be beyond the Church's

powers. The Church would have improved its case by suspending operation of its Veto legislation, but he believed the Court of Session was guilty of as great an aggression by attempting to: 'compel the Church *to withhold ordination or to grant it* . . . not merely to the effect of giving the suspended or deposed man all the *temporalities* of the benefice, but of recognising him as the holder of *the spiritual cure*'. The Stewarton case of January 1843, the penultimate 'effective slash' of the Court at the Church, served, as Karl Miller has pointed out, as a platform for Cockburn to re-emphasise strongly his position among the minority judges, and to renounce his partial, Lethendy case inconsistencies. The decision, as Cockburn appreciated, effectively froze the physical structure of the Kirk, and he again stressed its effect in depriving it of another aspect of its independence. It also deprived over two hundred ministers of representation in their Church's own courts and set its constitutional structure back to the status of 1833, making an already projected Disruption almost inevitable. The final, and most erastian decision of the Court—'it is not easy to go beyond this', commented Cockburn—was that of March 1843, with Disruption imminent, to revoke the sentence of deposition passed by the Assembly on the Strathbogie ministers. As Cockburn added, the next logical step was the absurd one of the civil court actually creating its own ministers, and he correctly predicted that 'all these judgements will be retreated from'.

Therefore, given the inaction of Parliament, whose amending legislation was the only solution Cockburn saw to the crises, the Disruption was almost a welcome relief. The majority of Evangelicals, and a large minority of the Church, retreated with their principles intact, and the Court of Session was saved from further loss of dignity. Cockburn gave his judicial colleagues credit for sincerity of motive, 'but passion sometimes invades the Bench', and whatever sound legal principles lay behind the majority verdicts, 'they soon got rabid, insomuch that there seemed to be no feeling except that of pleasure at winging Wild-Churchmen. . . . Where two supreme authorities clash, they cannot be both obeyed.'

The welcome Cockburn accorded to the Disruption was not only a product of his romantic nationalism, or of clannish ties with many of its leaders, though, as Karl Miller has rightly said, his piety often looks like patriotism. His support was also political and pragmatic, for he saw the issue of patronage reform as one that

Whigs could have satisfied with safety, and was disillusioned and shamed during his years of political office and later by their failure to grasp the problem. Reformers had been proved fallible, and political guilt was probably an element in Cockburn's sympathy for the Kirk's case. He was glad to see that the Free Church 'has more Whiggism in it than Toryism', but this was no thanks to many leading Scottish Whigs, especially those of the managing Edinburgh 'Clique' who had been led by political expediency to support the Dissenting interest against the Church. But Cockburn could claim at least that, though he had no real dislike of patronage, he had remained reasonably consistent in his support for its reform. In the court cases Cockburn had left the detailed constitutional arguments in favour of the Kirk's case to Lord Moncreiff, but he outlined his own view of the co-ordinate juris-dictions of Church and State lucidly, and did all he could to point to, and check the effects of, his majority colleagues' provocative language and actions.

In Church matters Cockburn liked to think of himself as a 'wise middle man', but, as it is hoped this essay has brought out, he was not always granted an omniscient view, and the verve and vivacity of his skilled pleader's arguments should not blind the reader to his areas of bias and blindness. Given these reservations, Cockburn was still in many respects a detached observer in the middle ground of Kirk politics, and his rather stronger attachment to the public tenets of Evangelicalism was no bad thing for the chronicler of an age when Evangelicals dominated the Church and shaped her politics. His picture of the Church was a metropolitan one, with all the distortion produced by looking at an institution from the centre. But in policy matters the Kirk was a remarkably centralised body, with corporate action flowing from its Assembly, a body which he had known, as he said in *Memorials*, since pleading his first case there in May 1807. Cockburn could not avoid immersing himself in the workings of an institution so deeply rooted in Scottish nationality and politics; and however repelled he was by its more uncompromising radicalism and zealotry, he always recognised its national claims, and defended them. It is hard to imagine having to write on the Church of Scotland in Cockburn's age without his sharp and incisive analysis, vivid and apt phrases, and eloquent descriptions of the events he lived and recorded so well.

A NOTE ON SOURCES

Cockburn's autobiographical writings and printed correspondence are quoted from Harry A. Cockburn's edition of *Memorials of His Time* (Edinburgh 1909); the *Journal* (2 vols, Edinburgh 1874); *Circuit Journeys* (Edinburgh 1888); and *Letters Chiefly Connected with the Affairs of Scotland* (London 1874). Reference is also made to C. Robertson, *Report of the Auchterarder Case* (2 vols, Edinburgh 1838), and to A. L. Drummond and J. Bulloch, *The Scottish Church 1688–1843* (Edinburgh 1973); Karl Miller, *Cockburn's Millennium* (London 1975) and his introduction to the Chicago 1974 edition of *Memorials*; also to W. Ferguson's article, 'The Reform Act (Scotland) of 1832: Intention and Effect', *Scottish Historical Review* xiv (1966), pp. 105–114. My recent dissertation. 'The General Assembly of the Church, the State, and Society in Scotland: Some Aspects of Their Relationships, 1815–1843' (University of Edinburgh, M.Litt., 1977) deals with related subjects in greater detail.

Manuscript material in the National Library of Scotland has been drawn on for Cockburn's letters to Charles Anderson (MS. 3546), John Stuart Blackie (MS. 2622), Cornelia Dick Lauder (MS.Acc.6433), James Grahame (MS.Acc.2515), Francis Jeffrey, Cornelia Dick Lauder and John Richardson (MS.Dep.235), and Andrew and Sophia Rutherfurd (MSS. 9687–8); and for Jeffrey's letters to Cockburn (Adv.MSS. 9.1.1–10) and George Cook's letter to Lord Melville (MS.Acc. 5106). Other sources used include Lord Aberdeen's letter to John Hope, 1838 (British Library, Add.MS. 43202); Cockburn's letter to Jeffrey, 1833, now in the Brougham papers (University College London, MS. 43905); Sir James Graham to Thomas Chalmers, 1839 (New College Library, Edinburgh); and Cockburn to John Mackenzie, 1850 (Mrs A. Frackleton, Edinburgh). Grateful acknowledgement is made to the authorities concerned for permission to use original documents in their keeping.

Cockburn and the Law

JOHN M. PINKERTON

N O ONE has ever claimed for Henry Cockburn any distinguished place as a lawyer, whether as an advocate at the Scottish bar or as a Senator of the College of Justice and Lord Commissioner of Justiciary. Had he confined his activities to the narrow places of Parliament House in Edinburgh, and left behind no writings, or even just his life of his friend Francis Jeffrey, he would be as forgotten as the majority of those who have sat on the bench of the Court of Session. He was called to the bar at a time when Edinburgh lawyers of the Enlightenment, Kames, Monboddo, Hailes and several others of almost equal reputation internationally, had departed from the Court of Session leaving behind successors more familiar with the details of multures and entails than those of contemporary philosophy and belles-lettres. Into the new circle he was received as a fair lawyer, an ingenious pleader before a jury, and a charming and informative companion.

Having undergone the necessary trials of public and private examination Cockburn was admitted to the Faculty of Advocates in December 1800. Then, as now, the Faculty placed no limit upon the numbers of those who might be admitted to the bar, and any young man above the age of twenty-one who had successfully completed the examinations, a task which was not unduly taxing, and paid the necessary entry money to the Faculty, was duly admitted. As far as the Faculty was concerned the more who joined the better, for the sole income of the Faculty was derived from the payment of entry money, which was largely used in the maintenance of the Advocates' Library which continued until 1925 to be the principal library in Scotland available to the public. But unlike so many others Cockburn arrived in the Faculty with every advantage of birth and family connection. For these reasons alone, said Brougham, he was 'certain of professional advancement'. Whatever claims he may have advanced in later years, it was most unlikely he would have gone the way of many others, into obscurity and away from Parliament House. Not only was his father a judge of the Court of Exchequer in Scotland, but his father's cousin, Henry Dundas, Viscount Melville, exercised power and dispensed offices in a manner which even the most recent Secretary of State for Scotland could not hope to emulate.

Yet it was not only the large numbers of advocates at the bar at this time which made life precarious for those without family connections, but also the manner in which the Court of Session conducted its business. Advocates were primarily practitioners before the Supreme Courts, the civil Court of Session, the criminal High Court of Justiciary, and the fiscal Court of Exchequer. The business was chiefly done by the first, for before the second the accused was seldom able to pay a fee and the advocates provided their services, as had been done for centuries before, largely gratuitously. In the Court of Session the litigation was mainly concerned with questions of heritable property in one form or another, disputes about boundaries, defective conveyances, entails, feudal obligations, mills, rivers, fishings, and the like. Heritage was the principal and safest form of investment before the invention of the limited liability company; it was not liable to sink like a ship, or to be destroyed by fire, like a warehouse, or stolen, like corporeal moveables. The Court of Session had exclusive jurisdiction to deal with all disputes relating to heritage.

The Court consisted of fifteen Senators, some of whom were also Lords Commissioners of Justiciary, and they normally all met together in Court, like a rather cumbersome committee. Cases were mainly conducted in writing, each side being obliged to have printed the voluminous writings which contained the statements of fact and arguments on law upon which the case depended. Each Senator received a copy of each of the writings, and the oral debate in Court was short and not the most important part of the proceedings. The Court then decided the case, each Senator casting a vote if there were division, and issued a brief interlocutor incorporating the decision of the Court. In general the judges issued no written opinions, and hence the law reports only contained a summary of the written arguments and the interlocutor.

In such a system it was inevitable that those young advocates most closely connected with the landed classes were most likely to succeed. And any advocate who had the double advantage of family connections, and an ability to state in writing arguments

H

based upon the arcane mysteries of Scottish feudal conveyancing and law of land ownership was certain of a substantial practice. Cockburn enjoyed the first advantage but not the second, and hence it may be assumed that an initial flow of work from the friends of his father and Dundas, relating largely to heritable disputes, was not maintained when it transpired that he was not adept in these fields of the law.

Had Cockburn been surer of success in the Court of Session it is unlikely that he would have made the mistake of accepting from the hands of the Tories the office of Advocate-Depute. At that time the Lord Advocate was not only the principal law officer of the Crown in Scotland, but also responsible for a wide field of government in Scotland. The appointment was invariably political, and the holder of the office resigned with the Government. In 1807 the Tories were returned to power and Melville appointed Archibald Colquhoun of Killermont as Lord Advocate. The Lord Advocate was not asked to choose his own deputies. Melville selected them for him, choosing William Erskine, later Lord Kinedder, who had been an advocate for seventeen years, Alexander Maconochie, second Lord Meadowbank, and son of the first Lord Meadowbank, who had been an advocate for eight years, and Cockburn. For Melville the appointment was a typical one, as Cockburn had the qualifications of family connection and some skill before the criminal courts. But it is difficult to see why Cockburn accepted the office, and it appears from the *Memorials* that he lived to regret the decision. While the holding of the office was entirely inconsistent with the Whig principles which he was to champion so ably, it should be remembered that an advocate-depute was not called upon to assist the Lord Advocate with his political work, but only as a prosecutor in the High Court where politics were not normally involved. It will also be appreciated that while defence work produced little or no remuneration, the advocate-depute received a good salary. If Cockburn's initial successes derived from family connection were by 1807 not growing as hoped for, it is the easier then to understand his over-hasty acceptance of the office. In any event he resigned in 1810 and thereafter remained faithful to the Whig cause.

The next seven years were to be the most difficult of Cockburn's professional career. His practice in the civil courts was small. In the criminal courts he was limited to appearances for the defence, where the variety was slight, the work poorly compensated financially, and the possibilities of advancement few. In the same years his energies were also deprived of a political outlet. But his knowledge of Scottish criminal law was substantial and it was in these years that he developed that skill with juries which was to be not only his chief professional asset but also he foundation of a good public reputation. Contemporaries of both parties are united in praise of his ability before a jury. 'He had a finely modulated voice, an unlimited choice of happy and concise expressions, and a command of the human passions in all their phases altogether peculiar to himself.' 'As every truly pathetic speaker must be Mr Cockburn is a homely speaker; but he carries his homeliness to a length which I do not remember ever to have heard any other truly great speaker venture upon.' His harshest critics said that his only ability was the power to persuade a jury, and his skill at identifying himself with the prejudices and feelings of his hearers. 'He put the case in a way so simple that the jurymen could not misunderstand it.' It was inevitable that speeches designed to create an effect by their simplicity do not appear so felicitous in print.

The best account of Cockburn's professional life seems to be that of Sir Archibald Alison, Bart. Though younger than Cockburn he was an advocate-depute from 1823 and frequently his opponent in the High Court. While Alison was a Tory, nevertheless, in accordance with the tradition of the Scottish bar, he was one of the convivial circle of friends who resorted for entertainment to Bonaly. He was a successful author, and latterly as Sheriff of Lanark from 1834 to 1867 his popularity was extraordinary. This is what he said:

> Mr Henry Cockburn, afterwards Lord Cockburn, was as great a contrast to John Clerk as it was possible to conceive. He had not the intellectual power of that great lawyer, nor the occasional force and intensity of his expression; but he was gifted with far greater oratorical powers. He had the soul of genius in his composition. No one was so capable, in Scotland at least, of moving the feelings of his auditors, or by a happily turned expression or epithet of thrilling the heart. On this account his influence was unbounded with juries, especially in criminal causes; and he very frequently could thus 'make the worse appear the better cause'. I often experienced that in criminal cases, especially those involving the life of the

108   JOHN M. PINKERTON

> prisoner, which I conducted on the circuits, and he was
> generally the leading counsel on the other side, he seldom
> failed on such occasions to so move the jury that in the
> face of the clearest evidence they brought in the verdict
> 'By plurality not proven'. He was indolent, and averse to
> *continued* labour, though none by fits and starts could make
> greater efforts; on this account his general practice was not
> so considerable as it otherwise would have been.

Just as the procedure if the Court of Session has changed so
mightily since the first quarter of the nineteenth century, so has
that in the High Court. The crimes committed were relatively few
in number and simple in character. The most serious were tried by
judges on circuit but the sittings of the Court were brief and the
cases very short. The accused had normally made a declaration
immediately after arrest, and the prosecutor merely demonstrated
that the declaration was false. The danger to a defence now
represented by a demonstrably false special defence of alibi was
then represented by a false declaration. Once a criminal case was
begun it could not be adjourned, and hence in the more complex
cases prosecution and defence were not anxious to extend the
duration of the case through the night. On many occasions the
defence would not exercise the right to address the jury at the
conclusion of the evidence. In consequence the normal circuit
would deal with many cases each day, and the scope for extensive
rhetoric by the defence was limited. Furthermore the property
qualification of jurors was substantial, so that they resembled more
the magistrates in a District Court than a modern jury. The jurors,
who frequently had extensive local knowledge, were not only
entitled to ask questions but frequently exercised the right.

It is inevitably difficult to capture the precise reasons for
Cockburn's success in the criminal courts. So much depends upon
the atmosphere of the occasion and so many cases are long forgotten, no record having been kept of the speeches. It is possible
to examine two occasions when Cockburn's addresses to juries
have been preserved. In a duel in 1821 James Stuart of Dunearn
shot Sir Alexander Boswell. The duel had been conducted strictly
in accordance with the accepted gentlemanly code for such
occasions, and Stuart had tried to avoid the confrontation. At his
trial for murder Cockburn was one of the six advocates for the
defence, pleading before a jury mainly of landed proprietors including several baronets. The sympathies of Cockburn were en-

tirely with the accused, and he adopted the unusual procedure of addressing the jury before the Crown had started to lead the evidence. His language was indeed simple, but the construction of the sentences was carefully contrived: 'Now he who had borne all his intolerable injuries with a degree of courage far more heroic than that of braving present danger in the field; he, who, during his own personal danger, had behaved as if he had not been the novice in such matters that he was, no sooner found himself un-expectedly the survivor, and saw his antagonist at his feet, than he was instantly dissolved in all the tenderness of an infant.' Stuart was acquitted despite the law against duelling, and Cockburn's reputation was enhanced by his success on this occasion.

The second speech of which a record survives was that made on behalf of Helen McDougal who was charged with her lover Burke, the body-snatcher. It was an occasion which aroused great public concern because of the connection between Burke and the University of Edinburgh. Helen McDougal was likely to be con-victed by a jury drawn from the richer classes of society, who had become apprehensive that the bodies of their relatives might be removed from the graveyards. In these circumstances Cockburn devised a common defence, inviting the jury to put from their minds all matters of prejudice, in the hope that they would also put from their minds the weight of evidence against his client. 'But what she is endangered by is the cry of the public for a victim. I need scarcely remind you, that this is a cry to which you, who are set apart from the prejudices of the public, and are sworn to look at the legal evidence alone, must be completely deaf. Let the public rage as it pleases. It is the duty, and the glory, of juries always to hold the balance the more steadily, the more that the storm of prejudice is up. The time will come when these prejudices will die away. In that hour, you will have to recollect whether you this day yielded to them or not.' The jury returned a verdict of not proven.

Cockburn's professional practice grew rapidly with the establish-ment of the Jury Court in 1816. Before that date questions of fact had been decided within the Court of Session by the judges, though the system of resolving disputes of fact was entirely un-satisfactory. In England there were civil juries, but not in Scotland, and there had long been pressure for a change. Curiously, civil juries were introduced from England to Scotland at a time when they were being less used in England, and now they have almost ceased to be used in Scotland as well. The Jury Court was at first separate from the Court of Session but its jurisdiction was limited to answering issues on questions of fact. Having regard to the limited classes who were qualified for jury service it is difficult to see why the bias and prejudices of jurors were different from those of the judges. It was not as though fifteen widows from Dalkeith were to try actions for damages against coalmasters. While Cockburn was delighted with the reform, he never explains what in his view were the peculiar virtues of jurors that were not possessed by judges. From his own point of view the introduction of civil juries meant that he was now for the first time well re-munerated for appearing before juries. The older practitioners in the civil courts had never addressed a jury, and accordingly were not employed before the new court.

Cockburn's attitude towards juries seems to have been ambiva-lent, and in none of his writings does he attempt to give a reasoned justification of their use. In the *Sedition Trials* his distrust of juries is apparent: 'At last the verdict expresses little else than the jurymen's previous creed'. The problems in the criminal courts he considered to be the power of the sheriff to select the forty-five names on the jury list, and the unchallengeable discretion of the judge to select the fifteen jurors from the lists. In the 1820s a right of peremptory challenge and a right of ballot were introduced and thus these particular problems were solved. But why should this mean the jury no longer brought in a verdict which only comprised 'the jurymen's previous creed'? The criticism of juries made in the *Sedition Trials* applies to all juries, and particularly to those of one sex and class in society, but Cockburn does not appear to have recognised this weakness. It is the more surprising as he was so familiar with this field of the law, but perhaps he was too close to the system of juries to appreciate its fundamental defects. Indeed his final verdict, when he was himself a judge and engaged on circuit journeys was that 'the qualification of the whole had better, perhaps, be raised'. The development of juries since 1844 has, of course, been in precisely the opposite direction.

In 1834, after a successful career at the bar, latterly as Solicitor-General for Scotland, Cockburn was raised to the bench with judicial title of Lord Cockburn. Three years later he was appointed as one of the Lords Commissioners of Justiciary. By this time the Court of Session had twice been reformed and the old fifteen had been divided into two Inner House divisions each of four judges, with the remaining Senators sitting singly in the Outer House as Lords Ordinary. There was a right of appeal to the Inner from the Outer House, and from the Inner House to the House of Lords. Within the High Court of Justiciary there was no right of appeal, though in the more important cases more than one judge sat. In the Outer House the judges now attached notes to their interlocutors, explaining their reasons for their decisions, and cases might also be reported from the Outer House to the Inner for decision. In the most important cases the judges of one division would consult the other judges so that the views of all could be obtained. As the cases of Lord Cockburn were reported in the Law Reports it is possible to form an accurate view of his abilities as a judge.

By far the most important case before the Court while Cockburn was a judge was the Auchterarder Case when the Court of Session had to decide whether in the Church of Scotland the parishioners had the right to refuse to accept the presentee chosen by the patron. The Court held that they had not, and thereby made inevitable the Secession. On this occasion Cockburn dissented, for he considered that the Court of Session had no jurisdiction to interfere in ecclesiastical matters. 'No doubt it is our duty to declare the law, and the duty of all to obey it, both from inclination and necessity. But it is also the duty of a Supreme Court to avoid every collision through which it cannot see its way.' His approach was therefore a pragmatic one, and perhaps if others had followed his example the Secession might have been avoided. But there is nothing in his opinion upon the substantive matter of dispute. It is rather the opinion of a lawyer seeking a lawyer's way out of a constitutional problem.

Curiously the same solution adopted by Cockburn in another important constitutional case produced a very different result. This was the case of Pryde v. The Kirk Session of Ceres. The pursuer was a penniless widow dependent for her own support and that of her eight children upon the funds of the Parish of Ceres. The parochial funds were administered by the Kirk Session though obtained from the heritors. It was in the interests of both Kirk Session and heritors that the payments for the poor should be reduced to a minimum, but in terms of the Act of the Scottish Parliament they were obliged to provide 'needful sustenation'. The pursuer was offered 3s.6d. per week by the Kirk Session, and she raised an action against the Kirk Session to have it declared by the Court of Session that this was insufficient for her 'needful sustenation'. It was argued by the Kirk Session that the Court had no jurisdiction to entertain the action, the matter being wholly within their discretion. All the judges were consulted, and the majority held that the Court had jurisdiction and could direct the Kirk Session to provide what was necessary. Lord Cockburn again dissented. 'It is agreed that they have a legal right to "needful sustenation". But this is a mistake. They have only a right to such sustenation as certain persons, called heritors or members of kirk-session, shall, in their conscientious discretion, think needful.' The reasoning is very similar to that in the Auchterarder case, that is that the Court of Session had no power to supervise the Kirk Sessions. In neither case does Lord Cockburn apply his mind to the real matter in issue, with the consequence, at any rate in the Ceres case, that he arrived at the wrong decision. It is difficult to believe that Cockburn would have found in favour of the Kirk Session of Ceres if he had started from a consideration of the best method of relieving the destitution of the pursuer.

It might have been expected that Cockburn with his long experience of jury trials would have been successful in their conduct as a judge. This however was by no means always the case. In Collins v. Hamilton the pursuer was the proprietor of a paper mill who sued the owner of dye-works situated upstream for damage to his paper caused by the discharge of dye into the river. It was a type of case which was relatively common at a time when the increasing use of chemicals in industry had led to the gradual pollution of rivers. This case was tried by Lord Cockburn and a jury on five days and the pursuer's experts were examined concerning the chemicals which had contaminated the paper. The defender's counsel did not cross-examine the pursuer's experts upon the analysis of the chemicals and did not put to them the possibility that they were derived from somewhere other than the defender's dye-works. But the defenders were allowed to lead evidence of these matters. In his charge Lord Cockburn directed the jury. 'In my opinion the pursuer has not made out his case. . . . Now I have never seen a pursuer in an action of damages do so little to show direct loss as has been done here.' The jury having returned a verdict for the defender, the pursuer enrolled a motion for a new trial before the Inner House. The Inner House had little difficulty in allowing a new trial, for it was the clearest case of a defender being allowed to lead evidence without laying a foundation in cross-examination. But Lord Cockburn was so incensed at the proceedings in the Inner House that he had printed a pamphlet justifying his conduct at the trial, and complaining that he was not asked to sit with the Division upon the motion for a new trial. It is not an occasion which reflects well on Cockburn's abilities either as a lawyer or as a judge.

One critic said of him after his death that his short judgements were frequently right in fact though wrong in law, and there were certainly occasions when his opinions were reversed in the Inner House but adhered to in the House of Lords. The knowledge of Scots Law disclosed by the House of Lords at this time was generally not great. Lord Cockburn's cases tended to be 'impatiently heard and imperfectly understood'. This is the impression conveyed by Cockburn's *Circuit Journeys*. There are very few occasions on which any account of the cases is given, and it appears that Cockburn was more interested in people and places than legal business on circuit. Autumn 1838: 'We had 81 cases to try. And this took six entire days. The great majority of the cases were thefts, and, including the whole, I don't think I ever saw so many cases so devoid of interest.' Autumn 1842: 'We had exactly 98 cases to dispose of. There was no capital case, and the whole batch was utterly uninteresting, the great majority being commonplace theft. The exile of about 60 of our fellow-creatures is upon our souls.' Autumn 1845: 'The cases were mere dirt; thirty-nine, of which above thirty were thefts. Such common-places might almost be tried by steam.'

He was far more interested in the trappings of a judge's power, and the respect due to the office. The judges he thought should have official lodgings like the English judges. 'At present they get a room in the King's Arms, or Blue Boar, and may be seen struggling with their own macers in the stable yard, for the use of a key with a horn at the end of it. This indecency is prevented in England.' 'Judges should never expose themselves unnecessarily —their dignity is on the bench', and hence badly managed public processions were particularly disliked by him. 'The whole defended by a poor iron mace, and advancing each with a different step, to the sound of two cracked trumpets, ill-blown by a couple of drunken royal trumpeters, the spectators all laughing.' Equally the courthouses required to be dignified, the new building in Glasgow designed by William Stark in 1810 being criticised as there was only one door for 'counsel, agents, jurymen, and most coming

and going'. A good court required a separate access 'for each
class of the members of the Court, judges, counsel, agents, jurors,
witnesses, and distinguished spectators'.

At the first opportunity, he, like the other advocates and judges,
was away from Parliament House to enjoy the delights of vacation,
for it was no part of his philosophy of life that a judge should never
be seen off the bench. The dignity of the judges did not require a
withdrawal from all other forms of public life—on the contrary
their reputations would be enhanced by other activities. In 1836
there was a slight reduction in the length of the vacations and
while Cockburn welcomed the improvement in the administration
of justice consequent upon the reduction of delays, he regretted
the intrusion into that part of the year set aside for other activities:

> People talk of the surcease of justice—what a mercy for
> suitors. It is this abstraction from legal business that has
> given Scotland the greater part of the literature that has
> adorned her. The lawyers have been the most intellectual
> class in the country. The society of the Outer House has
> given them every possible incitement, and the Advocates'
> Library has furnished them with the means and the
> temptation to read. What a proportion of our eminent
> men have been trained in this scene. But had they been
> worked out by nearly constant professional toil or
> expectations, or vulgarised by law being the chief object
> of their lives, they would have contributed no more to the
> glory of Edinburgh or of Scotland than any other body of
> legal practitioners. The dispensation of justice, however,
> cannot be sacrificed to considerations which the public do
> not understand; and so we must submit to our fate.

Cockburn goes on to explain that he really worked long hours,
doing a fifty-hour week for twenty-six weeks of the year. It does
not look as though there was ever a real risk that he would become
'vulgarised by law being the chief object' of his life. On the other
hand he preserved that remarkable devotion to the Faculty of
Advocates which has persisted through many generations, ascrib-
ing to that institution not merely dominance in the law, but also
in the intellectual life of Scotland.

It followed in Cockburn's view that sheriffs should reside in
Edinburgh with the other members of the Faculty of Advocates:

> The judge, who is generally resident at a distance from the
> Supreme Courts, to a certainty loses his law. He loses

what is of far more consequence, his sense of strict judicial delicacy of principle. He comes to consider the judgement of his own district practitioners, or of his servants, or of his own conceit, as the only check on his ignorance or dishonesty. The fact is, almost without an exception, that the resident sheriffs are blockheads. All the good ones breathe the legal atmosphere of the Supreme Court.

No exception should be made in the case of Glasgow, although there was sufficient business there to give full employment to a sheriff. 'To be sure, if they wish to make him a mere police officer, his residence near theirs may be proper. But this is the business of his substitute.' From this outburst it may be concluded that Cockburn both as advocate and judge relied much upon the advice of his colleagues, but while the subject of residence of sheriffs remains one of debate it is clear that many sheriffs resident furth of Edinburgh have discharged their functions with distinction. One of the Sheriffs of Lanarkshire, with his 'residence near thieves' at Possil, was Sir Archibald Alison, who was the equal of any lawyer in Edinburgh, not only as author of a reliable textbook on criminal law, but also as historian of Europe.

In Cockburn's time there were many distinguished lawyers in Parliament House from whom informal advice could be sought by the fireside in the Outer House. Of them the greatest was Professor George Joseph Bell, whose contemporary reputation seems to have been equal to his later high regard. Cockburn considered that Bell's *Commentaries* 'will do more for the fame of the law of Scotland in foreign countries than has been done by all our other law books put together'. By the time that Cockburn wrote Jeffrey's life, nine years after the death of Bell, his *Commentaries* had already become 'an institutional work of the very highest excellence, which has guided the judicial deliberations of his own country for nearly fifty years, and has had its value acknowledged in the strongest terms by no less jurists than Story and Kent'. Cockburn did not have the same view of Hume's *Criminal Commentaries*. He himself having strong, and frequently erroneous, views on the law of sedition, assumed that Hume had composed his work 'in a great manner for the purpose of vindicating the proceedings of the Criminal Court in the recent cases of sedition'. As Hume was a Tory Cockburn considered 'his delineation of Principle superficial, his views on all matters of expediency or reason narrow, indeed monastic'. Whatever a monastic view on a matter of reason in the context of Scots criminal law was supposed to be, Cockburn's evaluation of Hume's work has not stood the test of time, any more than much of the rest of his writing on the criminal law of Scotland.

Cockburn's *Examination of the Trials for Sedition which have hitherto occurred in Scotland* was published in 1888 and the long introduction provides the fullest account of Cockburn's views on the criminal law, particularly that relating to the crime of sedition. Considering how closely involved Cockburn was with the criminal law, and particularly with trials for this crime, it is remarkable how little understanding he had either of the dilemma of the Government in 1794, or of the attitude of the judges, or of the historic principles of Scots Law which were applied by the judges. For Cockburn it was all so simply a matter of party politics, the Whigs always right and the Tories wrong, and though he himself had not been directly involved in the events of that year, being a boy of fifteen, and he had revised his account of the trials nearly sixty years after the events, he was unable to clear his head of party polemicals and war-cries.

The definition of sedition caused little difficulty—'the publication of any sentiment intended and calculated materially and speedily to obstruct or weaken the legal authority of the State'. It was the application of this principle, and in particular the determination of what was admissible as evidence for the Crown to prove the crime, that caused disagreement. Cockburn accepted that the prosecutor might attempt to demonstrate the unsoundness of the opinions published by the accused, and also accepted that the Court had 'to assume the truth of all the principles of the Constitution'. Where his analysis breaks down is where he fails to state what are 'all the principles of the Constitution' in a state without any written constitution. Clearly Melville and Cockburn would not have agreed as to the principles of the constitution, but it was for Cockburn to state what he considered to be the principles if he was to attack the conduct of the judges in upholding what they regarded as the principles. Cockburn only states that the monarchy and the truth of Christianity were amongst the agreed principles. But he never explains what principles of the constitution were to be detected in the existing system of parliamentary government. To what classes should the franchise be extended; is there a need for a second chamber; by whom should the judges be appointed; is the Act of Union capable of repeal? These are a few of the fundamental questions to which he never turns. He was a characteristically moderate lawyer, with sufficient conscience to press for reforms in jury trials, in the procedures of the Court of Session, in the manner of electing town councils, and in dozens of other fields of legal procedure and rules, but he lacked the vision of a leading reformer to question the foundations of the legal system. It followed that he failed to grasp the principles of those who had been encouraged by the French Revolution to press for changes in the structure of society, any more than he truly appreciated the position of the Tories and their judges who were determined that the miseries of France in turmoil would not be repeated in Scotland.

In the field of law reform Cockburn's views were often sound, and he was instrumental in procuring certain important changes. Looking back in 1834, Cockburn felt that the Scottish system of criminal law was the best in the world. The only defects he could detect as remaining were that in political cases the weight of the Crown pressed too heavily on the accused, and the manner of the Court was 'not yet what it ought to be'. He acknowledged that neither of these defects was readily capable of solution, and indeed he might have realised that advocates of every generation regard the manner of the Court as not what it ought to be. While Cockburn himself was most pleasant to appear before, at the end of a case most lawyers prefer to have appeared before a judge who has done justice to the parties by applying the law rather than one who has only been polite to those appearing.

Cockburn displayed on the bench a refreshing disregard for unnecessary forms. He records a circuit to Ayr in 1851 at which the Clerk of Court had failed to bring any of the official papers upon which the cases proceeded—indictments, declarations and the like. Cockburn explained to counsel that if they asked for adjournment their clients would merely stay in prison until the next circuit, and the trials were then conducted exactly as though all had been in order. He was opposed to those technical rules of evidence which stated that spouses and children could not give evidence against their spouses and parents, rightly concluding that these, coupled with the rules as to corroboration, merely enabled families to commit crimes in concert. In 1840 he recorded wrathfully the reply of a man who had had the option explained to him, 'Odd! A' like that hoption, ma Lord!' Another reform, which he adopted from Romilly, was the proposal that the Court should 'be entitled to award costs to the unjustly accused against the prosecutor'. It would seem obvious that if a citizen has incurred expense in his defence, and has been acquitted by a jury through a verdict of not guilty, that he should be able to recover that expense from the prosecutor. To hold otherwise would be to concede that the prosecutor had some justification in his proceeding which would be contrary to the presumption of innocence. Yet this reform has not been introduced. In practice, in Cockburn's time, as now, relatively few of those prosecuted in the High Court have to bear the cost of the defence.

Cockburn appears in a less attractive light when trying one of the cases arising out of the Highland clearances in 1849. The whole population of Solas in North Uist, amounting to about sixty families, had been ejected from their townships. No houses were provided for them, no poor-house, no ship. They had only the beach to lie down upon. Four of those ejected had made slight resistance to the Sheriff's officers. They were charged with rioting and deforcement of officers of the Court. Cockburn considered the clearance odious but necessary, though he does not explain why. He 'was afraid of an acquittal, which would have been unjust and mischievous', but the jury convicted and he imposed sentence of four months' imprisonment. It is difficult to see why if the clearance were odious a verdict of not guilty would be inappropriate, and why in the circumstances any period of imprisonment was necessary. Only the jury distinguished themselves, by giving in a written verdict recommending the utmost leniency in consideration of the cruel proceedings in ejecting the whole people of Solas 'without the prospect of shelter or a footing in their fatherland, or even the means of expatriating them to a foreign one'.

Likewise in the Court of Session most of the reforms advocated by Cockburn related to matters of procedure, and his proposals were generally accepted in his lifetime. On one matter of substantive law, the law of entails, he had conflicting views. He did not favour the abolition of entails though he could appreciate the argument for this. 'The mind of the age is favourable to freedom in the commerce of land. Capital is clamorous for earth. Nothing can justify the eternising of individual caprice over the fixed national property.' Nor did he favour the contemporary movement towards the granting of additional powers to the heir in possession, as this was 'burdening those to come'. Yet he came down finally in favour of entails as a mode of shoring up a decaying nobility. 'It is of great importance to a public that likes nobility by birth that nobles should not be beggars. A mendicant peer is very unmonarchical.' Assuming this reasoning was seriously intended, and it looks as if it was, it sounds rather strange in the mouth of a leading Whig. It is all the more remarkable as having been written the year before statutory reform of entails effectively brought the whole system to an end. The young radical had by 1847 become the old reactionary.

Major changes in the structure of the Court of Session took place between 1808 and 1825, these in turn involving the almost total reconstruction of Parliament House. Only Parliament Hall now remains to remind us of the Scottish Parliament and of the eighteenth-century Court. Even there nothing remains unaltered but the roof. The old Inner House was at the south-east corner of the Hall, small, dark, brown-painted and dominated by an unclean fireplace behind the bench. In 1808 the judges were split into two Divisions, and this involved the rebuilding of the Court, the new First Division being built somewhat to the east of the old Inner House, and the Second Division occupying what has become the Law Room of the Advocates' Library. This reform was actually introduced by the Tories though it had been proposed by the previous Whig administration.

The first major change was the introduction of jury trial before the Jury Court, presided over by the benign Chief Commissioner Adam. For practitioners other than those like Cockburn, who were chiefly instructed in jury trials, the greatest change of all came in 1825, when extensive procedural reforms were introduced, changes which brought in the system still used by the Court of Session to this day. The chief new weapon was the record, a printed document recording in brief and concise form the contentions of the pursuer and answers of the defender. The pursuer is required to state first the remedy which he seeks from the Court, using the terminology which he hopes that the Court will use in its decree, then a statement of the facts upon which he founds, and finally logical propositions showing why the facts averred entitle him to a legal remedy. The defender replies with answers to the statement of facts, admitting or denying the pursuer's averments, and concluding with his propositions on the law. The new system was much less cumbersome than the old, but as the argument on the law was reduced to a few propositions the Court had to introduce a system of formal debates on the law, and oral pleading became common. In practice the Act of 1825 was most successful, and the constitution of the Commission which unanimously advocated the reforms is not without interest. It contained no laymen, public officials or representatives of interested outsiders, but merely the holders of the nine highest legal offices in Scotland assisted by four leading English barristers. The final round of changes took place in 1830 when several legal offices were abolished as unnecessary and the jurisdictions of the Admiralty, Exchequer and Jury Courts were incorporated into the Court of Session. But that was the end of innovation and the curious forms of those three Courts, which died nearly one hundred and fifty years ago, are still to be detected in the rules of the Court of Session.

Down to 1825 there were 'whole tribes of silent and laborious' advocates who did nothing but prepare written pleadings. 'Many of them produced a quarto volume every day. They actually fed themselves and married, and reared families, and left successions, upon it.' Yet the improvements of 1825 did not produce an increase in the volume of litigation. On the contrary, by 1848 the number of cases had declined, and Cockburn looked back with a touch of regret to the old days when not only were cases more numerous, but also the law and lawyers extended current business to interminable lengths. The fact is that the introduction of legal reforms, the simplification of legal procedures, the reduction of legal expenses, and the ready availability of legal advice do not inevitably create an increase of legal business. The volume of litigation depends much more closely on social and economic factors than on anything which lawyers or reformers may do. Certain societies are naturally litigious, each man disputing with his neighbour every infringement of territorial rights, every suspected slight, and every occasion of injured pride, and others take such matters in their stride. The Scottish have always tended to the latter course.

Another cause of the decline of the business of the Court of Session was said by Cockburn to be the improvement in the quality of the Sheriff Courts: 'The absence of counsel generally, and of Court of Session fees, makes them cheaper than the Court of Session'. He was well aware of the danger inherent in the decline of the Court of Session: 'What would Scotland have been since the Union without the Court of Session? The Parliament House has been the great active scene for Scottish ability and learning, and speaking and patriotism. Even already there is a chill shade over this once splendid Temple of Justice.' The solution he saw, even in 1848, to be yet further reforms of procedure. This was not so. The problem was more fundamental. For historical reasons no proper consideration has ever been given to the scope of the jurisdiction of the Court. The ancient provision whereby the Court had exclusive jurisdiction in questions of heritage and status was only relevant when heritage was the only sound investment, and status the most important matter in family law. Social patterns had changed leaving the Court of Session to conserve the foundation of a historic ruin. More basic questions needed to be asked. Should the Court have both original and appellate jurisdiction? If the former, how far should it extend? To these matters Cockburn does not seem to have turned his attention, being too closely involved in the reform of procedure.

On the subject of criminal penalties Cockburn had determined views. The most salutary punishment he believed to be capital, and he regretted that its use was so rare, and that juries were reluctant to return verdicts which justified that result. 'The truth is that the suppression of the gallows deprives modern Courts of half their charm', he wrote in 1844. The alternative of imprisonment he treated with contempt. Those whom he sent to prison seemed to return to the Court again. 'Out of twenty thieves, I have no doubt that at least twelve had been formerly convicted in the Justiciary, and had all laughed at long imprisonment. So far as thieves are concerned, it plainly won't do.' In 1842 he inspected Perth Prison which had just been opened for long-term prisoners. It was intended that long sentences should take the place of transportation:

> But with the true, regular, professional, middle-aged
> criminal, who requires a change of nature—reformation—
> I don't expect much from comfortable living, though in
> confinement, nor from steady occupation, even though
> combined with considerable solitude. I fear that such
> criminals must be given over, and that, after all, there is
> nothing for it but to get rid of them by exportation.

Clearly Perth Prison was considered too comfortable. It was also 'far too small. The 400 cells, being all that are now built, will be full next year.'

Transportation was the penalty preferred by Cockburn to

I

imprisonment, and he believed it desirable to vary the periods of transportation according to the seriousness of the crime. In 1853 he regretted the introduction of 'penal servitude' in place of short transportations, and until that date the majority of those convicted in the High Court were transported. 'I am clear for getting them out of this country in as great numbers as possible.' Hanging and transportation were the only certain ways of disposing of hardened criminals. 'If there be a thoroughly reformed, twice-convicted thief, I would rather pay a shilling to see him than to see any other wonder in any living show.' Eventually Cockburn came to regard imprisonment as 'the first stage of the transporting process'.

He also entertained a characteristic judicial contempt for pleas of insanity: 'He will get his sentence commuted on the score of his mental weakness, which is now the ground always taken up by the pious and benevolent, and it is far too often successful. . . . There are very few acts of criminal malice that are not helped on by the idea that this defence may be successful in the time of need.' The complaint is one familiar to practitioners in the criminal courts, but he does not attempt to give any definition of insanity for criminal purposes.

Whatever else his virtues in public life, Cockburn's record as a lawyer can be shown to have been an imperfect one. As a young lawyer he did not acquire sufficient grasp of the principles of Scots Law to enable him to rise in the customary manner at the bar. He turned instead to a political career which destroyed the advantage of family connection which he enjoyed. As a Whig politician he was involved extensively in the promotion of law reform, but those reforms, however necessary, largely concerned matters of procedure and detail not touching upon the fundamental principles of the system. When forced to consider the substantive law, such as entails, his inability to appreciate either the structure of the law or the whole background left him unable to see the obvious necessity for change. His most serious legal writing, on the Sedition Trials, is riddled with inconsistency arising from a failure to analyse the British constitution of his time. Finally as a judge he turns from the liberal aspirations of his youth to express the reactionary views of advancing age.

On the other hand his skill as an orator before a jury, whether civil or criminal, was undoubted. The homely expressions, simple language, and calculated delivery charmed all who heard his speeches. To the traditions of the Faculty of Advocates, and the

COCKBURN AND THE LAW

customs of Parliament House he was most loyal, more particularly during the years when his practice consisted largely of gratuitous services for poor criminals. As an advocate he was fearless and effective, as a judge he was courteous and kindly, and as an example to lawyers he was one who could be wisely followed.

Cockburn, Nature and Romance

KARL MILLER

1798 is remembered, in 1978, as the wonderful year when the *Lyrical Ballads* were published. In the same year, the poet Thomas Campbell revisited scenes of his youth at Cathcart in the West of Scotland, and wrote a poem on the subject. And in that year, too, the Miss Hills, Isabella and Helen, came to live at Woodhall, just below the Pentland Hills, on the way down to Edinburgh. Wordsworth and Coleridge, and their *Lyrical Ballads*, have been under discussion ever since. Campbell was famous once, a *Golden Treasury* staple who was quite widely held, during his lifetime, to be among the most wonderful of contemporary poets. As for the Miss Hills, they were never famous.

These three events have in common that they made a difference to Henry Cockburn's activities as an amateur poet, and to the entry into romantic poetry of the romantic Pentland Hills. In 1798, Cockburn was nineteen years old. He was starting on a period of his life when he and his friends can seem on occasion to be saying what Wordsworth had said of a time before: that it was bliss to be alive, and heaven to be young.

Four years ago, I published a book about him, *Cockburn's Millennium*, which paid attention to the previously neglected subject of this historian's interest in poetry. Having had access to new information, I would like to present some afterthoughts on this subject, and on the relationship between the literary outlook of Cockburn and his friends, several of whom wrote for the *Edinburgh Review*, and that of the leading writers of Romanticism, in its early days or dawn. The progress of taste from Sensibility to Romanticism, as it is sometimes described, was formerly pictured in terms of the crossing of a ditch or divide, with Edinburgh Reviewers, among others, failing to make the leap and falling into the condition of reactionaries. The texts I shall look at, some of them unfamiliar, may possibly, or so I hope, impart new reasons for setting that picture aside, with its overtones of revolution, and salvation, its hint of Moses, the Red Sea and the flight from Egypt. What we see in these texts instead is a slow process of change. We see the young Wordsworth thinking what was often thought, and learning from poets who were often acknowledged at the time as leading practitioners of the later eighteenth century. This process depended on the steady persistence of a concern with ideas of deliverance from the ordinary life of the society: literature had already taken a turn towards nature, and towards childhood, towards simplicity, kindness and calm, and towards ideas of extinction, and, in this area, no new turn was forthcoming. If we consult the long run which lands us in the Victorian age, we may agree that an alteration in taste had occurred by then: the heroic couplet, and certain masters of the remoter eighteenth century, had fallen from favour, and so on. But it cannot be claimed that this change caused, or was caused by, an indifference to the eighteenth century's imaginary escapes.

Cockburn's Millennium printed the texts of five poems which had been attributed to Cockburn, while expressing doubts as to the authorship of one of them. Some had been preserved as a result of his friendship with John Richardson, and form part of the Richardson family manuscript holdings in the National Library of Scotland. Others passed to the Library from the surviving Cockburn connection, on the death of a great-grandson, while my book was being written. The first of the poems, as they figure in an appendix to the book, is given in two versions, which correspond to two drafts in Cockburn's handwriting. This is 'The Linn'. In a preamble to the first draft, the Cockburn holograph explains that the poem is his, and dates it 18 July 1809. The second draft, which derives from the Richardson family, has a coda which comes after the text of an epitaph and which consists of a requiem for a 'desolate stranger'. This stranger I found to be a Frenchman who was killed in captivity near Edinburgh during the Napoleonic Wars.

Apart from their respective drafts of 'The Linn', the Cockburn family had kept 'Relugas' and 'On losing a staff', and the Richardson family had kept 'How solemn the close' and 'The Holy Grove, or, Geraldine'. Three of the five poems belong to the later years of the first decade of the nineteenth century, while 'Relugas' is dated 1828 by Cockburn, and 'On losing a staff', which exists—contrary to an implication in my book—in a late nineteenth-century copy, is annotated by the transcriber as 'written before 1826?'.[1] Of the two poems whose manuscripts are not entirely in Cockburn's hand, 'Geraldine' was regarded in the book as a special case, and a puzzle. Was it, in fact, by Cockburn? In a teasing letter of 1808 to the poet James Grahame,[2] Cockburn mires the issue in references to eighteenth-century and Renaissance literature, links the poem with the departure of a niece, and makes out that it is both modernised Shakespeare and 'Dick's own'. Geraldine is the name of the lady sung by the Tudor poet, the Earl of Surrey, and sung again by Scott in 1805, in *The Lay of the Last Minstrel*; the name is also used in Coleridge's 'Christabel', which still remained unpublished in 1808. I now have reason to think that the poem should not be assigned to Cockburn but to someone else, and that the someone else was a reader of Coleridge.

I tried to show in my book that while the *Edinburgh Review* could misjudge poetic innovation, Cockburn, who wrote for the journal on legal and political questions, was capable of responding to controversial poets whom it tended to condemn, and that his verse not only imitates Scott's anapaestic 'Helvellyn' but also exhibits a certain affinity with the poetry of the Lake school, and with that of Wordsworth in particular. Long notorious for his hostility to the new romantic poetry, Cockburn's friend Francis Jeffrey, editor of the *Review*, was less hostile to it, less coxcombically deaf to its appeal, than romantic poets and, in time, romantic scholars were apt to allege. He liked a lot of it, and these friends were in due course to disagree over Keats and Shelley, with Cockburn remarking: 'He had always a foolish passion for these two'.[3] If Cockburn's own poems do not disclose a foolish passion for Wordsworth, they are at least those of a more 'Lakeish' person than eventual despisers of the *Edinburgh Review* might have expected to meet with in its vicinity. So much was said in the book, and I have come across further material which seems to say the same thing. The urbane and witty author of Cockburn's *Memorials*, of the journals and letters, hard-headedly hostile to Germanism in matters of culture, was also earnest and ecstatic in his feeling for the countryside, for mavises, dahlias, sunsets, and for the lovely scenes of his youth, and hardly likely to sneer at 'Tintern Abbey'. There can have been no intention to mock on the occasion when, as I now find, he copied out three of its most distinctive passages.

Cockburn's poetic hat is stuck with other men's flowers, as are the hats of many poets and of most amateur poets. In my book, I concentrated on 'Helvellyn' as a source for the mood and language of 'The Linn', but I have since noticed another source in

Campbell's nostalgic 'Lines on Leaving the River Cart', a poem to which I have already referred, as among the events of 1798. All three poems move to the same metre, which was very much a music of the new time, so far as it is right to talk of a new time. Perhaps the buoyancy of these poems, their anapaestic swaying and tripping, is some persuasion to talk in this way. The Campbell is one of many poems of the period, and of many romantic poems, which deal with a return to childhood, or to the scenes of a childhood. It reads:

> O scenes of my childhood, and dear to my heart,
> Ye green-waving woods on the banks of the Cart!
> How oft in the morning of life I have strayed
> By the stream of the vale and the grass-covered glade!
> Then, then, every rapture was young and sincere,
> Ere the sunshine of life had been dimmed by a tear;
> And a sweeter delight every scene seemed to lend—
> That the mansion of peace was the home of a friend.
>
> Now the scenes of my childhood, and dear to my heart,
> All pensive I visit, and sigh to depart;
> Their flowers seem to languish, their beauty to cease,
> For a stranger inhabits the mansion of peace!
> But hushed be the sigh that untimely complains
> While friendship with all its enchantment remains—
> While it blooms like the flower of a winterless clime,
> Untainted by change, unabated by time![4]

I have also since noticed, for 'Geraldine', a dependence on Coleridge's poem, 'Love' ('My Hope, my Joy, my Genevieve!'), added to the 1800 edition of the *Lyrical Ballads*. Having noticed this, I went on to examine a commonplace-book—a manuscript anthology of favourite pieces of verse which was compiled by Cockburn and some friends, frequenters of the Pentlands, and which is now in the Osborn Collection, Yale University Library. I discovered that the Campbell and the Coleridge were both there, along with the extracts from 'Tintern Abbey' which I have mentioned. These extracts lead off the anthology.

It occupies 282 quarto sheets, watermarked 1805, and consists of over two hundred separate items: very few are identified by the transcribers, only one of whom is identified by name in relation to any single item. Some items are the work of the transcribers themselves. The first two, from 'Tintern Abbey', are dated 'Woodhall

Novr 15. 1807', and towards the end of the anthology the date 1809 crops up. It seems probable that the anthology was compiled over this period of two years. The last item, however, Scott's lines on Weirdlaw Hill, is a poem of dejection written during a sickness of 1817 which had robbed his Border vistas of their charm:

> Yet not the landscape to mine eye
> Bears those bright hues that once it bore.[5]

This item could have been added later as a suitable close to the celebrations of nature contained in, and constituted by, the anthology.

When Cockburn referred, as he once did, to 'romantic people',[6] he did not include himself among them, though he was prepared, on that occasion, to behave as they might behave. But it is clear that his anthology, produced at a time when the Romantic movement had recently declared itself, is touched by a sense of what the movement stood for. The French Revolution is held to have assisted the romantic revolution described by historians, and we have always known that Cockburn and his friends were excited, when they were young, by the events and portents of 1789 in France. We can now say with more confidence that they were also excited by literary events in Britain for which France is understood to bear a responsibility, though they would not have called them a revolution. So we may join together, for certain purposes at least, Wordsworth's bliss of earlier days and the happiness on their hills of Cockburn and his Scottish Whigs. He and his friends could not have known, of course, what sympathetic hindsight claims to know about Romanticism and its revolution, and would not have understood that 'Tintern Abbey' was French. The verse they gathered has a good deal to communicate about the behaviour of British poetry from Milton to Wordsworth, and very few talented living writers are ignored (Crabbe is surprisingly absent). To the historian who believes in ends and beginnings, however, or in revolutionary dawns and divisions, this is not the most useful of documents. The tears and tasteful landscapes of eighteenth-century 'sensibility' do not die out as the collection approaches 1807. It tells us, as it were, that an interest in solitude gave way to an interest in solitude.

Eighteenth-century publishing went in for Collections of Extracts, and Sensibility suggested that groups of friends, too, might collect moving passages of poetry, with an eye to fine lines, flights of fancy, the purple patch, to improving reflections and displays of bravura—might rear in company, or at any rate collectively, jolly cairns of verse in praise of loneliness and grief. Of the cairns so piled, or compiled, several were no doubt left to rot in muniment rooms and elsewhere, but Cockburn's golden treasury has survived, to render its account of the early days of romantic taste. Fifty years later, Palgrave piled—and, with some of the same stones, produced a monument to romantic taste at a high point of pride and success.

Those who joined with Cockburn in this act of homage to the muses were the Pentlands' aptly-named Miss Hills, Helen and Isabella, and their niece Elizabeth; John Richardson, who was to marry Elizabeth, and to become a prosperous London solicitor while retaining 'the impressible temperament of an orphan lad'; James Grahame, author of *The Sabbath*, which gained a sizable early popularity, and of other volumes of poetry, a sad man, who probably drank even more than was customary among the convivial males of his acquaintance, and who became an Anglican curate in 1808 and moved to Bath; and another 'Hill', so identified by Cockburn, with the rest, in a brief preface to 'this little volume', who may have been a brother of Helen and Isabella. This was a Whig *jeunesse*, and Cockburn was to be responsible, with Jeffrey, for the Scottish end of the Reform Bill of 1832. Their friendships were pursued in Edinburgh and its environs, a scene from which the high heart might soar to Arthur's Seat and to the Pentland Hills: physically and morally, these eminences were Edinburgh's higher plane. Richardson's impressibility was credited by a memoirist to his youthful acquaintance with 'the beautiful valley of the Esk, the woods of Melville, the smiling, sequestered village of Lasswade', and with 'classic Hawthornden', these fostering 'the love of reverie, or of the delights of indulged fancy which clung to him during life'.[7] The seventeenth-century poet Drummond retired to his romantic (rather than classic) house at Hawthornden in search of virtuous leisure, writing upon its wall: '*ut honesto otio quiesceret*'. He might have been reckoned a spiritual forefather of these transcribers: but none of his verse is transcribed. With the exception of two stanzas from *The Faerie Queene*, so far as I am aware, no poetry before Milton appears in this rather large little volume.

I would like to draw on the anthology in order to offer further discussion of Cockburn's literary background, and of the poems he wrote and relished amidst those 'friendships so true' to which 'The Linn' pays tribute. For this purpose, I need to furnish a chronology of relevant dates.

In 1798, as I have said, 'Tintern Abbey' was given to the public, Campbell revisited Cathcart and the Miss Hills settled in Edinburgh. Some two years later, Campbell visited Germany, and so did Richardson. The Harz Mountains thrilled to the note of Richardson's flute (recently auctioned for a respectable sum). The literature of Germany appealed to both these men, and Campbell was to form friendships there—with the critic August Schlegel, for instance—which put him in touch with new thinking of real value in philosophy and in the arts. He himself has very little of the air or temperament of an innovator, however, and contemporaries could think of him as both old and new, and as a kind of hybrid—a classical romantic. The assertion in his long poem, the immediately popular *Pleasures of Hope*, "Tis distance lends enchantment to the view',[8] was romantically treasured in later years, but his verse, martial and sentimental, exotic, plangent and polite, has been diminished, by distance, to a mannered competence. *The Pleasures of Hope* has this: 'On Erie's banks, where tigers steal along'.[9] Told of the factual error here, he stuck to his predators and reprinted the line. The following couplet[10] from the same work seems to have resounded in Edinburgh, on which he considered writing an epic poem:

> The world was sad! the garden was a wild!
> And man, the hermit, sighed—till woman smiled!

In aesthetic matters, he turned, as Cockburn did, to the Associationist principles of the Rev. Archibald Alison, a citizen of Edinburgh who argued, in the style of Hartley, that consciousness developed on a basis of association or connection, and that the links which fastened the individual to scenes of his childhood, or of past happiness, were of great importance. Much of the verse in the anthology is Alisonian in temper, and as such quite in keeping with the inaugural passages from 'Tintern Abbey'. In a letter of 4 September 1802, Campbell wrote:

> On my way to Minto I stopt to view the beautiful ruins of
> Melrose Abbey. Association (as the angel of taste—Alison

—has shown) is the foundation of our pleasure in
contemplating beauty and sublimity. My associations, I
confess, were picturesque and pleasant to a high degree in
looking, with 'a white, upturned, and wondering eye', to
those relics of fallen grandeur.[11]

What Campbell was to Melrose Abbey, Romeo was to Juliet.
That is to say, the white eye of wonder which is rolled by Campbell
is taken from the balcony scene of Shakespeare's play, where Juliet
enters, above, with a sigh, and Romeo, looking up, implores:

> O speak again, bright angel, for thou art
> As glorious to this night, being o'er my head,
> As is the wingèd messenger of heaven
> Unto the white-upturnèd wondering eyes
> Of mortals that fall back to gaze on him
> When he bestrides the lazy-passing clouds
> And sails upon the bosom of the air.

These lines seem to have prompted Campbell's description of
Alison as 'the angel of taste', and they may also be felt to lie behind
some other words in the letter. With their aerial perspective,
their above and below, they are lines which are bound to have
appealed to the aspiring Sensibility of the time, when a 'high
degree', as Campbell puts it here, of association could transport
the beholder to a sky with angels in it, and with Juliet in it, and
many a summit and spire. As a ruin, and as an arrangement,
therefore, of highs and lows, rises and falls, of tops and of toppled
towers, Melrose Abbey was, to the fine feelers who visited it,
especially vertiginous and strange, or so Campbell's language, in
its response to Shakespeare's, might suggest.

Ruins were a pleasure to the touring Campbell, for whom, as
his letter indicates, Gothic architecture was connected with 'wood-
land scenery'. In many of the pieces in the anthology, scenery is
joyfully connected with childhood—with a childhood recollected
amid the fallen grandeur of adult life. The pieces often talk about
pleasures, and it is past or first pleasures that are often meant—
those, alternately, of childhood and of youth. Three long poems
from which several extracts are taken have the word in their title:
The Pleasures of Hope, *The Pleasures of Imagination* and *The Pleasures
of Memory*, by Campbell, Akenside and Samuel Rogers respectively. And perhaps we can say that memory renewed the past for
Cockburn and his friends, and that the faculties of imagination

and hope could depict it as pleasant and permanent. We can also say that Wordsworth's Ode on 'Intimations of Immortality from Recollections of Early Childhood', published in 1807, would not have seemed outlandish to those impressed by such doctrines as Alison's.

There are, in the anthology, many texts which take pleasure in the world, and which speak of a time of pleasures—a long time, to whose later stages belong Wordsworth's revolutionary bliss and the happiness of Cockburn's Whigs, skipping like lambs, 'as to the tabor's sound', on the Pentland Hills. And yet these are also texts which speak of a wish to leave the world in which they take pleasure. This can sometimes appear to be a poetry of manic contrasts and extremes.

In 1803, a year after Campbell's vision on the road to Minto, Cockburn and his friends discovered their 'Linn'. 'Linn' is Scots for waterfall, and this waterfall was on higher ground to the west of Bonaly, in the Pentlands. At Bonaly, he was to plant his rural household gods, in a farmhouse which he was gradually to convert into a feudal tower. Down below Bonaly and towards Edinburgh the stream runs into Braid Burn, in a valley where Cockburn and Scott used to play as boys. On 5 October of the same year, Cockburn wrote to a friend, the Rev. Charles Anderson, telling him that Campbell had got married, and slyly adapting one of Campbell's resonant lines in order to do so. The letter belongs to the collection of Cockburn letters in the National Library, and the passage in question reads:

> Thos. Campbell is married. 'Tam the hermit sighed, till woman smiled.' Her name is Sinclair—from Liverpool—know nothing more about her. No money. This step I suspect to be more poetical than prudent. It will burden Pegasus with a wife and family—and we all know he is heavily loaded enough already. However it may have two great advantages—it will make Thos. more steady and laborious, second by making him less 'Peace-enamoured' it may preserve his health—though neither of these are quite certain as to poets.

This is a more worldly Cockburn than the one who wrote poems and collected them. Two months later, on 6 December,[12] he addressed the same man about troubles of his own, which might be a lesson to his correspondent. He felt that he had betrayed himself, at 24, by indulging in ambitious daydreams of a future greatness:

That poor man is unquestionably undone, who, if it be not corrected by a remarkably active and strong mind, encourages the habit of pleasing his imagination with very noble prospects of possible attainments. The delight he enjoys in resolving to be great is such a liberal rapture, that he mistakes it for, and is contented with it instead of, the exulting triumph of surveying from the watch tower of his ambition—actually reached—the surrounding subject country. Don't believe that when he discovers his error he can always push forward anew. He has wasted his time, he has acquired irrecoverable habits, his character is determined. He then spurns the humble walks of ordinary men; while the very discovery of his folly, instead of making spring to recover what he has lost, gives him up to gazing, with streaming eyes and a beating breast, towards a lovely scene, endeared by the memory of early hopes—from which he is now excluded for ever.

He is here using the language of his verse, and of the verse he liked, with its propensity for early and endearing 'lovely scenes', in order to decry the dreaming states, the pleasures of imagination, experienced in the poetry of the age, and of the previous age.

His circle of poetry-lovers, with access to the recently founded *Edinburgh Review* and to the immemorial Pentland Hills, was by now convened. Campbell was Elizabeth Hill's cousin, and her aunts were to be highly respected by Cockburn, Richardson and Grahame. Campbell himself did not write in the book which the others were to assemble, but his poems are no less prominent there than they are in Palgrave. Tam the Hermit went on to be one of the principal founders of the University of London, drawing on his German knowledge and connections, and to edit the *New Monthly Magazine* in London, breaking as he did so with the practice of journalistic anonymity and encouraging others to follow suit. He was a hermit, a solitary, only in his poems, and in one of the prevailing cultural styles, but his main public inter- ventions were postponed till the 1820s. By then, this Pentlands coterie was long dispersed, though Cockburn was never to want for friends, and was to wander the hills till very nearly the day of his death in 1854.

In August 1805, Scott and his wife set off on a tour of the Lakes, in the course of which, along with Wordsworth and Humphry Davy, he climbed Helvellyn. A young man had done this not long before, and had fallen and been killed. Scott and Wordsworth wrote poems on the subject: Scott's 'Helvellyn' was parodied by Richardson (and others including Jeffrey) in a poem about the colourful and miserable folk who hung about the Outer House of the Court of Session in Edinburgh, and it also supplied a model for Cockburn's 'The Linn'. So the poem of a friend and political opponent was echoed in the accents of Whig wit and of Whig romance.

The following year, 1806, Richardson sailed from Leith to London, to seek his fortune, but he did not forsake his native country. He kept up his Scottish connections, and, for honest leisure and for its fishing rights, acquired a Border estate, recommended to him by Scott; and when the anthology began in 1807, he took part in it, with poems of his own appearing among the items. In the same year, shot by a drunk militiaman at Glencorse Barracks on the south side of the Pentlands, a French prisoner-of-war was buried in a nearby kirkyard, and in that year, too, Wordsworth's 'Immortality' Ode was published in London, to be shot at in the *Edinburgh Review* by Jeffrey, whose esteem for Alison, the angel of taste, did not prevent him from calling it 'illegible and unintelligible'.[13]

According to Cockburn, 'The Linn' was written in 1809. It was written in praise of the past, of peace and seclusion, of 'nature and romance' (his words of a later date, in circumstances I shall explain later in this essay), and of the early friendships formed under the auspices of nature and romance. The anthology contains a text of the poem which corresponds to the second of the two versions printed in my book, except that it lacks both the words inscribed on the French prisoner's tombstone and the requiem for that desolate stranger. It seems that, after the commemorative 'Linn', the anthology did not have much longer to run, and Grahame did not have much longer to live: he died in 1811. In the same year, Cockburn and Richardson got married. Not to each other, to be sure, though Cockburn once observed that in their bachelor days Richardson 'used to be called my wife', and informed Grahame in 1811: 'You have heard, no doubt, of Richardson's intention to avail himself of my divorce and to marry again. Betsey is very well, an excellent girl, tapering away like the new-bursting poplar.'[14] The anthology can be read as reciting the pleasures of young people on the brink of marriage, chaperoned by a pair of estimable maiden aunts.

Cockburn was a classical romantic, like Campbell, and his own kind of religious believer. When young, he may for a while have come close to abandoning institutional religion, but in adult life he was devout, though also tolerant, and by no means sectarian. In old age, on the subject of Jeffrey's position in such matters, he thundered to a minister in another of the manuscript letters: '*most unquestionably* he was not an infidel'.[15] Cockburn, moreover, was quite enough of a Scottish patriot to be affected, in his patrician way, by the Presbyterian outlook of the country, where a new zeal was mustering which would eventually prove schismatic. If, therefore, like the Whig he was, he believed in civil and religious liberty, it was also the case that in the 1830s, at the time of the Disruption—the schism I refer to—the Presbyterian tradition could seem to him ancient and chivalrous and glamorous. On these and other matters, the contradictions in his position are pronounced.

If, in his capacity as poetry-lover, for instance, he was apt to sorrow over victims, he was able, in his capacity as Scottish Whig, to take a tough line in relation to those victims whose condition called for a reform of the poor laws: his was a line that favoured property and self-help. Another of his contradictions can be assessed as a tension between nature and romance, on the one hand, and right conduct, on the other. He once said that a taste for external nature could be set beside a taste for virtue as—in the language of evangelical eloquence—the 'second one thing needful'.[16] Such an idea of salvation would not have appeared strange to his companions on the Pentland Hills, and the anthology attests to a process by which sensibility was succeeded, or completed, by romanticism, under the supervision of a native piety. Under the influence of the French Revolution, Cockburn and his male friends tended to be, in youth, democratic, philanthropic and even sceptical: this outlook left its mark on the anthology, but in Cockburn's case, and Richardson's, as in the case of so many, including Wordsworth, it was soon restrained and revised.

I turn now in more detail to the content of the anthology. To do so is to be aware of an attempt to resolve the tension between the needfulness of virtue and that of nature. Time and again, these poems are poems of suffering and consolation, and the consolation is of a kind in which nature and virtue often meet. Solitude consoles. Scenery consoles. Virtue consoles. Childhood consoles. Early friendship consoles. All console, share in consoling, and open a way to another world. In Campbell's Cathcart lines, friendship is to compensate for the intrusion of a stranger into the 'mansion of peace' in which part of his youth has been spent. In Cockburn's 'Linn', youth plants seeds which may perpetuate the foliage of a lovely scene for the pleasure and instruction of future generations, and conduct them to 'the mansions of rest'. Time and again, and sometimes in so many words, the poems say: Hail, rural life! Hail, lovely scenes! Hail, solitude! Hail, childhood! Hail, friendship! 'Thou little spot! where first I suck'd the light,' says one line, and another says, in anapaests: 'The sole charm of my life is to live o'er the past'.[17]

'Domestic life in rural leisure pass'd' is a goal which is almost ubiquitous in the anthology, where these words are copied in one of a number of extracts from Cowper's *The Task*,[18] and it is a goal which is conveyed, in the main, by means of passages from the pastoral and meditative verse of the English eighteenth century. It was not a goal which could have been pursued without intermission except by those who were not only impressible but rich. It suggests holidays and country estates—the so-called 'paradises' of the age. It suggests second homes, as well as the 'second one thing needful'. And it suggests that to the contrast between nature and virtue should be added the further contrast between, in Cockburn's case, his activities as an advocate, judge and statesman and his quiet life, or Horatian *secretum iter*,[19] at Bonaly.

The tenor of the anthology can be studied with reference to passages selected for inclusion which can be shown, in two instances, to have caught the attention of other people, at other times. The first instance relates to Scott's account, in a letter of 1827,[20] of his meeting with Burns—sensible, rural, but his large dark eye 'literally *glowed*' with sensibility and passion—in an Edinburgh drawing-room in the winter of 1786: 'I may truly say, *Virgilium vidi tantum*'. Scott spoke of the effect produced on Burns by a print of Bunbury's, representing a soldier lying dead on the snow, his dog sitting in misery on the one side, on the other his widow, with a child in her arms. These lines were written beneath,—

Cold on Canadian hills, or Minden's plain,
Perhaps that parent wept her soldier slain;
Bent o'er her babe, her eye dissolved in dew,
The big drops, mingling with the milk he drew,
Gave the sad presage of his future years,
The child of misery baptized in tears.

Burns seemed much affected by the print, or rather the
ideas which it suggested to his mind. He actually shed
tears. He asked whose the lines were, and it chanced that
nobody but myself remembered that they occur in a
half-forgotten poem of Langhorne's, called by the
unpromising title of 'The Justice of the Peace'. I whispered
my information to a friend present, who mentioned it to
Burns, who rewarded me with a look and a word, which,
though of mere civility, I then received, and still recollect,
with very great pleasure.

Cockburn was a feeler and a weeper, as well as a hard head, and
it is more than possible that John Langhorne's lines reduced him,
as they had reduced Burns, to tears, the big drops mingling with
the ink when, twenty years on, he transcribed them for his little
volume. The volume has in it many unfortunates, many children
of misery. But none as violently moving, perhaps, as Langhorne's
blighted infant.

The second instance relates to a cento made by Wordsworth
and published by him in the collection *Yarrow Revisited* in 1835.[21]
A cento is a patchwork garment, or a piece of writing composed
of extracts from the writings of others—a kind of collage.
Wordsworth's cento was this:

Throned in the Sun's descending car
What Power unseen diffuses far
This tenderness of mind?
What Genius smiles on yonder flood?
What God in whispers from the wood
Bids every thought be kind?

O ever pleasing Solitude,
Companion of the wise and good,
Thy shades, thy silence, now be mine,
    Thy charms my only theme;
My haunt the hollow cliffs whose Pine

Waves o'er the gloomy stream;
Whence the scared Owl on pinions grey
Breaks from the rustling boughs,
And down the lone vale sails away
To more profound repose!

The poem is patched from Akenside's Ode 'Against Suspicion' (lines 1 to 6), James Thomson's 'Hymn on Solitude' (lines 7 and 8) and James Beattie's 'Retirement'. Wordsworth talked of 'a fine stanza of Akenside, connected with a still finer from Beattie, by a couplet from Thomson', and hoped that the result might prove 'a harmless source of *private* gratification'. This pleasure had, in fact, already been tasted, since all three of the passages appear in Cockburn's anthology—appear separately, it's true, but then the anthology is itself in the nature of a huge cento.

Wordsworth was willing, therefore, in 1835, to publish a 'poem' which had been put together thirty years before by a group of people in touch and in tune with the supposedly reactionary *Edinburgh Review*, and I don't believe that we can explain this by saying that he himself had become sufficient of a reactionary to concur with his old enemies. Beattie's 'more profound repose' is a phrase which occurs in Akenside's Ode 'To Sleep',[22] and 'profound repose' occurs in a second passage of Beattie chosen for the anthology.[23] An assimilation of the idea of nature to that of rest, and to that on occasion of some terminal sleep, is a feature of the kind of verse which appealed to Cockburn and company, and it is a feature of Wordsworth's cento, which, in this respect among others, may be thought to miniaturise the Pentlands patchwork.

The tenor of the anthology is determined by the idea of nature as counselling, consoling, uplifting, zestful, restful and terminal which is present in the poems transcribed. 'Kind Nature' is an expression that comes easily to the poetry the anthologists liked, and it is used in *The Seasons* by James Thomson, from whom a road runs, in the blank verse on this subject which was copied for the anthology, to Akenside, Cowper and Wordsworth. Of the patterns that can be perceived in the choice of extracts, this is one which a reader of the present time could scarcely miss. At the end of the road, but at some distance from it, are the lyric measures of Scott, Campbell and Tom Moore. Of the poets who precede Thomson in the selection Milton stands supreme, and perhaps the road can more accurately be perceived to run from *Paradise Lost*.

I shall now report the transcriptions that matter from this point of view. 'O Nature!' exclaims Thomson at the end of 'Autumn'. 'Snatch me to heaven . . .' Just before this, in Thomson's poem, appears a passage picked for the anthology:

> the man who, from the world escaped,
> In still retreats and flowery solitudes
> To Nature's voice attends from month to month,
> And day to day, through the revolving year.[24]

Immediately afterwards in the anthology appear parts of Thomson's 'Hymn on Solitude'. The opening line of the transcription, 'Hail, mildly pleasing Solitude', is that of a later version than the one used by Wordsworth, and the last lines given in the anthology are:

> Oh, let me pierce thy secret cell,
> And in thy deep recesses dwell!

Norwood's oaks, the poem says, can shield James Thomson from the crimes and griefs of London. A page earlier in the anthology appear these lines from earlier in 'Autumn':

> Then is the time
> For those whom wisdom and whom nature charm
> To steal themselves from the degenerate crowd,
> And soar above this little scene of things.[25]

In due season, that is to say, the sensitive man may steal and soar. In its figurative sense, the verb 'to steal' was to become widespread in romantic writing, and Thomson's frequent 'steals' may well have been influential here. This one is unusual in being reflexive: the sensitive man deprives society of his own commitment to it, and the theft is approved, the recourse to nature is approved, because society is at fault. There is never any doubt that nature teaches Thomson 'a moral song',

> as I steal along the sunny wall,
> Where Autumn basks, with fruit empurpled deep.[26]

To move towards nature is to move towards heaven, through scenes, on this occasion, of a Keatsian languor and lushness, and Thomson was the author of an ode, duly transcribed, in which he turns up the white and wondering eye of sensibility to a

> delightful world above
> Appointed for the happy dead.[27]

He was the author, too, of the long poem in Spenserian stanzas,
The Castle of Indolence, liked by Wordsworth, in which a battle is
fought between an active, soaring virtue and a state of sensual
sloth, where stolen pleasures, including those of the imagination,
may be enjoyed. Both of these opposing forces were to fascinate
readers on the Pentlands.

From Akenside were taken such passages as this, from his 'Hymn
to Cheerfulness':

> Is there in nature no kind power
> To soothe affliction's lonely hour?

And this, from *The Pleasures of Imagination*:

> Thus the men
> Whom Nature's works can charm, with God himself
> Hold converse; grow familiar, day by day,
> With his conceptions, act upon his plan,
> And form to his, the relish of their souls.[28]

From here we go to Cowper's *The Task*:[29]

> scenes that soothed
> Or charm'd me young, no longer young, I find
> Still soothing, and of power to charm me still.
> And witness, dear companion of my walks,
> Whose arm this twentieth winter I perceive
> Fast lock'd in mine, with pleasure such as love,
> Confirm'd by long experience of thy worth
> And well-tried virtues, could alone inspire—
> Witness a joy that thou hast doubled long.
> Thou know'st my praise of nature most sincere . . .

From here we go to 'Tintern Abbey',[30] where Cowper and Mrs
Unwin are Wordsworth and Dorothy. The first two pieces in the
volume, copied by Cockburn, are these:

> in after years,
> When these wild ecstasies shall be matured
> Into a sober pleasure; when thy mind
> Shall be a mansion for all lovely forms,
> Thy memory be as a dwelling-place

> For all sweet sounds and harmonies; oh! then,
> If solitude, or fear, or pain, or grief,
> Should be thy portion, with what healing thoughts
> Of tender joy wilt thou remember me,
> And these my exhortations!

The second piece is from earlier in the poem:

> These beauteous forms,
> Through a long absence, have not been to me
> As is a landscape to a blind man's eye:
> But oft, in lonely rooms, and 'mid the din
> Of towns and cities, I have owed to them,
> In hours of weariness, sensations sweet,
> Felt in the blood, and felt along the heart;
> And passing even into my purer mind,
> With tranquil restoration.

Well on in the volume a third piece from 'Tintern Abbey' is written out:

> Nature never did betray
> The heart that loved her; 'tis her privilege,
> Through all the years of this our life, to lead
> From joy to joy: for she can so inform
> The mind that is within us, so impress
> With quietness and beauty, and so feed
> With lofty thoughts, that neither evil tongues,
> Rash judgments, nor the sneers of selfish men,
> Nor greetings where no kindness is, nor all
> The dreary intercourse of daily life,
> Shall e'er prevail against us, or disturb
> Our cheerful faith, that all which we behold
> Is full of blessings.

This is a cheerfulness which comprehends the cheerfulness hymned by Akenside. The anthology is a context which directs us to think of the Cowper passage as adjacent to 'Tintern Abbey', and directs us away from those histories which used to say that there was a 'great gulf' between Cowper and Wordsworth.[31]

Immediately before the third of the 'Tintern Abbey' passages, and on the same page, are some unfamiliar lines which might

either look like evidence of poetry's progress towards an encounter
with the genius of Wordsworth, or appear to rank themselves
with the early impacts of his work: the effect of the anthology is
to approximate the possibilities in question, and to complicate
the notion of a missing link for the space that separates Cowper
and Wordsworth.

> Oh nature, nature! Thine the charm
> To raise the true-toned spirit and to warm!
> Thy face still changing with the changeful clime,
> Mild or romantic, beauteous or sublime,
> Can win the wond'ring sense to every scene
> From Kilda's shore to Yarrow's flow'ry green.
> Yes, I have felt thy power pervade my mind
> When every charm of life was left behind,
> When doom'd a listless, friendless guest to roam
> Far from the sports and nameless joys of home.
> Yet when the evening linnet sung to rest
> The day star wand'ring to the rosy west,
> I loved to trace the wave-worn shores and view
> Romantic nature in her wildest hue,
> When as I linger'd on the vaulted steep
> Iona's tow'rs toll'd mournful o'er the deep,
> Till all my bosom own'd a sacred mood
> And blest the wild delight of Solitude.

Burns has an impromptu which comes close to the wording of the
passage: 'Admiring Nature in her wildest grace'. But this is not
Burns. It comes from Campbell's 'Epistle to Three Ladies', one
of his liveliest poems, but one which he was never to publish.
The three ladies, free spirits of a new age, were Helen and
Isabella Hill and Grahame's sister Jean. Full of a recent visit to
the Hebrides, the epistle was written on the banks of the Cart
in 1797.[32]

As for the item immediately before these lines by Campbell, that
is a passage in which Akenside addresses his 'Northumbrian
shades', with their 'calm recesses'.[33] In Thomson, Norwood's
recesses are 'deep'. In the nature poetry of the time, deep is calm,
and those who sincerely recede from Wordsworth's 'dreary intercourse of daily life', or from Cockburn's 'humble walks of ordinary
men', in his letter of December 1803, are unanimously promised a
great but equivocal reward.

In 'Tintern Abbey', the mind is a 'mansion' for the 'lovely forms' of nature, while in Campbell's Cathcart lines of the same time a 'mansion of peace' is surrounded by lovely scenes, and in Cockburn's 'Linn' a bower conducts lovers of nature to 'the mansions of rest'. The poetry-lovers on the Pentlands cultivated a vocabulary and feelings which trench upon those of Wordsworth. In the 'Immortality' Ode, which gives thanks for 'first affections' and 'the thought of our past years', we read that 'Heaven lies about us in our infancy,' and that first landscapes are 'apparelled in celestial light', and we may tell ourselves that the same light shines in the world appointed for the happy dead. The Ode's last lines are these:

> To me the meanest flower that blows can give
> Thoughts that do often lie too deep for tears.

The anthology helps us to notice what has been noticed before, that the lines resume an effect of Gray's in the 'Ode on the Pleasure Arising from Vicissitude'. The passage in question is copied by Cockburn:

> The meanest flowret of the vale,
> The simplest note that swells the gale,
> The common sun, the air and skies,
> To him are opening paradise.

'Every one is by habit and familiarity strongly attached to the place of his birth, or to objects that recall the most pleasing and eventful circumstances of his life. But to the author of the *Lyrical Ballads* nature is a kind of home . . .' In these later words,[34] Hazlitt gives an Associationist's approval to what Wordsworth was up to, and in so doing resumes an opinion of Alison's: 'The view of the house where one was born', with its 'interesting associations' and 'images of past happiness and past affections', is 'indifferent to no man'.[35] We have seen how what Wordsworth was up to could be anticipated in the literary heritage available to his contemporaries. But the retreat to nature, and to a contemplation of childhood, and of a soothing immortality, could claim no clear sanction from the Presbyterian tradition, whose predestined rewards were to be achieved through strenuous good conduct of a kind more Roman than romantic. Cockburn and his friends had to reconcile two types of virtue: the virtues of retreat and the active virtue with which their compatriots were familiar.

The same contradiction is apparent in the literary heritage—in the poetry of Thomson, for instance. Soaring and sinking are contrasted in Thomson, but the recourse to nature can sometimes be seen as a combination of the two, which have in common— up and down being forms of away—an abdication from ordinary life. Thomson may be thought to meet the situation by means of sermons against sloth, and in favour of Britannic industry, and by strongly insisting that nature is his teacher: that insistence, too, was transmitted to the future. During the century that follows his death, nature teaches, and soaring and sinking are regularly contrasted in the recognition that to soar is to risk falls or dejections.

Cockburn knew what it was to soar, and to sink. He obeyed a code which kept him devout and made him a vigorous actor in public life. He built himself a castle in the heavens, and delighted, as 'one's own walls' went up at Bonaly, in their 'surgency'.[36] And in politics he was, though no insurgent, a tireless Reform Whig. At the same time, he was blamed in Scotland for his 'indolence' and 'love of enjoyment',[37] and late in life he fell deeply into debt. This history is perceptible in his choice for transcription of a poem in which the two orders of virtue are reconciled among the stars, in which soaring is pious and strenuous, and fatal:

> When I have seen thy snowy wing
> O'er the blue wave at evening spring,
> And give those scales, of silver white,
> So gaily to the eye of light,
> As if thy frame were form'd to rise,
> And live amid the glorious skies;
> Oh! it has made me proudly feel,
> How like thy wing's impatient zeal
> Is the pure soul, that scorns to rest
> Upon the world's ignoble breast,
> But takes the plume that God has given,
> And rises into light and heaven!
>
> But, when I see that wing, so bright,
> Grow languid with a moment's flight,
> Attempt the paths of air, in vain,
> And sink into the waves again;
> Alas! the flattering pride is o'er;
> Like thee, awhile, the soul may soar,

But erring man must blush to think,
Like thee, again, the soul may sink!

Oh Virtue! when thy clime I seek,
Let not my spirit's flight be weak:
Let me not, like this feeble thing,
With brine still dropping from its wing,
Just sparkle in the solar glow,
And plunge again to depths below;
But, when I leave the grosser throng
With whom my soul hath dwelt so long,
Let me, in that aspiring day,
Cast every lingering stain away,
And, panting for thy purer air,
Fly up at once and fix me there!

This is not a bad effort at soulful or prayerful flight on the part of
someone who had been charged by the *Edinburgh Review*, in 1806,
with immorality. The charge led to a Chekhovian duel at Chalk
Farm, with the critic, Jeffrey,[38] farcically confronting the author
of the poem, none other than Tom Moore, whose endearing
young charms were a fashionable and general pleasure of the
time. Whatever Jeffrey might think, the immortal part of Moore's
verse, as exhibited in his edifying strain, was relished on the
Pentlands: here was another disagreement within the ranks of the
Edinburgh Reviewers, and it is one which can be aligned with the
tensions I have attributed to the outlook of Cockburn and his
friends. The title of the present poem, 'To the Flying-Fish',
withheld by Cockburn, explains why Moore's airborne creature,
which soars only to sink, whose flight goes before a fall, is both
fish and fowl.

Cockburn does not copy the whole of the ode, and he mis-
copies a little. But he does not so much miscopy as strikingly alter
another edifying poem by Moore.[39] This, to the tune of 'Helvellyn',
reads:

A beam of tranquillity smil'd in the West,
    The storms of the morning pursued us no more,
And the wave, while it welcom'd the moment of rest,
    Still heav'd, as remembering ills that were o'er!

Serenely my heart took the hue of the hour,
    Its passions were sleeping, were mute as the dead,

And the spirit becalm'd but remember'd their power,
    As the billow the force of the gale that was fled!

I thought of the days, when to pleasure alone
    My heart ever granted a wish or a sigh;
When the saddest emotion my bosom had known,
    Was pity for those who were wiser than I!

I felt, how the pure, intellectual fire
    In luxury loses its heavenly ray;
How soon, in the lavishing cup of desire,
    The pearl of the soul may be melted away!

And I pray'd of that Spirit who lighted the flame,
    That pleasure no more might its purity dim;
And that sullied but little, or brightly the same,
    I might give back the gem I had borrow'd from him!

The thought was extatic! I felt as if Heaven
    Had already the wreath of eternity shown;
As if, passion all chasten'd and error forgiven,
    My heart had begun to be purely its own!

I look'd to the West, and the beautiful sky
    Which morning had clouded, was clouded no more—
'Oh! thus,' I exclaim'd, 'can a heavenly Eye
    Shed light on the soul that was darken'd before!'

It might be said of this poem that the white eye which sensibility
turns up to heaven has succeeded the glowing eye of passion. But
Cockburn transformed it when he wrote it out for the Pentlands
cento. The third, fourth and fifth stanzas are given as follows:

I thought of the days when to Virtue alone
My heart ever granted a wish or a sigh;
When the saddest emotion my bosom had known
Was envy for those who were better than I.

I felt how the pure intellectual fire
In indolence loses its heavenly ray,
And how soon when corrupted by baser desire
The pearl of the Soul may be melted away.

And I prayed of that Spirit who lighted the flame
That languor no more might its purity dim

And that sullied but little, or brightly the same,
I might give back the gem I had borrowed from him.

Moore's sexual meaning ('cup of desire') is amended to a general baseness; 'pity' is changed to 'envy', 'wiser' to 'better', 'luxury' to 'indolence'; 'pleasure' is changed to 'Virtue' on one occasion and to 'languor' on another. These last two changes might appear inconsistent, but can be accounted for if we suppose, as there is reason to do, that Moore's poem has been deliberately altered in order to bring it into accord with the feelings expressed by Cockburn in the letter of December 1803. In that letter he speaks of the days when, having resolved, in a 'liberal rapture', 'to be great', he had then frittered away, 'dreamed' away, his time without doing anything about it. What he now calls 'indolence' and 'languor' had defeated him. Cockburn has faced Moore's poem in the direction of his letter. 'Virtue' has taken over from 'greatness' in the motions of his self-reproach, but we may think that, for this man, the two had much in common.

Flight was a name, in the heritage, for the pure soul's passage to eternity. In Pope's ode 'The Dying Christian to his Soul', sinking is soaring, and 'seraphic': the Christian wants, 'trembling' with happiness and pain, to 'languish into life', while calling for wings in order to effect his escape. In Moore's ode 'To the Flying-Fish', there is a longing to be virtuous and a longing to die. The second of these desires comes and goes in the anthology in accordance with the temperament of transcriber and transcribed, but it is never wholly absent for long. In a poem which is, for once, ascribed to an author, dolorous James Grahame wishes to die, and be with a dead sister. Revisiting romantic Melrose, he is reminded of a time when he had gone there with this 'seraph':

> I marked the tear presageful fill her eye,
> And quivering say,—I am resigned to die.[40]

The Pentlands circle, however, was no suicide club, and the stress on soaring in the anthology is usually such as to represent it as an exercise of virtue—of Miltonic virtue, at times, as in the transcribed conclusion to 'Comus':

> Love Virtue, she alone is free,
> She can teach ye how to climb

Higher than the sphery chime;
Or if Virtue feeble were,
Heaven itself would stoop to her.[41]

Sinking, in the sense of sloth or sensuality, was harder to
represent as virtuous, but Cockburn's set can be said to have
considered the possibilities. Here again, the example of Thomson
was authoritative for these people. Indolence, in *The Castle of
Indolence*, is both deplorable and welcome, and the anthology has
the stanza which begins: 'A pleasing land of drowsyhed it was'.
It also puts a question from the same work: 'What, what is virtue
but repose of mind?'[42] Many of the varieties of repose have been
unsympathetic to Presbyterians, and we have observed how
Cockburn regretted his own indolence (though there was far less
of it to regret than there was in Thomson's case). At the same time,
within a busy Scotland, soon to burn with Evangelical zeal, he
and his friends were able to visit a pleasing land of pastoral
drowsyhed.

The romantic people of the early nineteenth century were
impressed by Thomson's indolence. Keats found in indolence a
virtue that could outclass the Wordsworthian (and, one might
add, Presbyterian) 'egotistical sublime', and all irritable reasoning: so that Thomson may be thought to have contributed to the
ideas summarised in the doctrine of 'negative capability', which
affirms that a sinker soars. Echoes of Thomson can be heard in the
poems of Keats: 'La Belle Dame sans Merci' can be shown to
have been preceded by, and 'The Eve of St Agnes' to have been
furnished from, *The Castle of Indolence*. Not that Thomson was
Keats's only source in this respect. The 'Ode to a Nightingale',
in which the poet soars and sinks, can be shown to have been
preceded by Akenside's Ode 'To Sleep', with its 'Lethaean rod'
and 'opiate airs', as well as by the same writer's Ode 'To the
Evening Star'. Cockburn's set did not go where Keats did in
reflecting on this subject, but it is evident that they gave thought
to the 'thoughtless slumber' induced by Thomson's poppy.[43]
Keats's reflections are the outcome of a long preoccupation, by
which the anthology is gripped, with the merits of silence and
stillness and sleep, of sensation and seclusion, and with the
chances which lay (for those who could afford it) with leisure.
For sentimentalists, nature was the pleasures of indolence, and—
where soaring and sinking, soaring and stealing, met—the

raptures of indolence; they revisited the lovely scenes of earlier days, and felt sorry for their servants, while believing, in some cases, as Jeffrey believed, that 'poverty makes men ridiculous'.[44] In Wordsworth, though, nature was not only a mother and a home, but a place where people worked, where, at the time of the anthology, Highland lasses reaped.

With this much said about the presence of the Lake school, and of its precursors, in the anthology, it is time to discuss a number of other features. If Thomson stands out in the selection, Milton stands out even more. Shakespeare and the Elizabethans are conspicuously absent (Jeffrey was attentive to the latter, while Campbell's seven-volume *Specimens of the British Poets* has very few specimens of Shakespeare). We would not expect Metaphysicals, and there aren't any. *Paradise Lost, Paradise Regained, Comus* and *Samson Agonistes* are frequently present; 'Lycidas', 'L'Allegro' and 'Il Penseroso' are transcribed. 'Hail, holy light' is treasured, and so, from the same poem, are Eden's marital joys ('With thee conversing I forgot all time'), and Satan's outcast state ('Me miserable! Which way shall I fly . . .').[45] Satan's rebellious self-assertion, which romantic people liked, is less obtrusive than Adam's:

> Did I request thee, Maker, from my clay
> To mould me man, did I solicit thee
> From darkness to promote me . . .[46]

Elsewhere, Akenside's Miltonic 'Say, why was man so eminently raised'[47] conveys that man was promoted to great things, to thoughts that soar 'beyond the limit of his frame'. Milton's own self-assertion and egotistical sublime are approved—the Milton agonistes who hoped he might 'fit audience find, though few'.[48] The glow of precious stones which he placed above his Paradise, and which Scott borrowed for a description of the Pentland Hills,[49] was caught, ten years before Scott's account, by these 'Pentlandisers', as Cockburn called them.

At the end of his life Cockburn urged a poetical friend: '*Be select.* Don't, as is so common, let your Life Boats, your imperishables, be sunk by heavier matter, of which most poets have an overstore. See what Collins, Gray, Goldsmith, and even Campbell, have gained by mere select paucity.' At the time of the anthology, he told Grahame that they were fundamentally in agreement about poetry: 'As to our "first principles", I don't believe you and I differ much, if at all. We are both satisfied that the worst fault that Poetry (the essence of purity) can have is Vulgarity, and differ only as to the application of this rule—i.e. what is vulgar'.[50] These are the views of a man who might have objected to the *Lyrical Ballads* on the grounds of their designed adherence to the language of ordinary speech, and Jeffrey, in fact, at the time of the anthology, referred to them as vulgar.[51] Cockburn's emphasis on purity, or gentility, is combined with what might seem like a Palgravian emphasis on lyric imperishability, and is compatible with the prominence among the chosen of Gray, Collins and Akenside.

Two rejected stanzas from Gray's 'Elegy' are restored, and the redbreast in one of them makes, perhaps, a sincerely flattering appearance in Cockburn's own 'How solemn the close', though the redbreast, like the linnet and the nightingale, was one of Sensibility's favourite fowls. Collins's 'Ode to Evening', 'How sleep the brave' and 'The Passions: an Ode for Music' are included, and are not surprising. The presence in strength of Cowper is not surprising either: the themes I have been examining require him, and he is pure enough. In copying his patriotic ode 'Boadicea', Cockburn appears to have altered the second line to read: 'Driven from her old abodes'. The wording, 'old abodes', was later to be applied to the heronry at Relugas, in his poem about that blissful country estate. There is a little, mainly epistolary, Pope in the anthology, and a little Dryden ('Alexander's Feast'). The only Ballad material is in the form of modern imitations (such as 'William and Margaret'), which has been attributed, and denied, to David Mallet.

Cockburn and his friends were not afraid of the vulgar Burns, who is richly present: 'To a Mouse', 'To a Mountain Daisy', a piece of 'The Cotter's Saturday Night' and of 'Tam o' Shanter' ('But pleasures are like poppies spread'—we are a long way from Akenside's pleasures here, as from Thomson's poppies). I was pleased to find that Cockburn had copied one of Burns's best poems, though not one of his best-known—'The Vision'. He omits the finest verse, which, for all its wit, might have served as the most authentic of the anthology's glimpses of distress:

> Had I to guid advice but harket,
> I might, by this, hae led a market,
> Or strutted in a Bank, and clarket
>   My Cash-Account:
> While here, half-mad, half-fed, half-sarket,
>   Is a' th'amount.

The 'rustic bard', 'stringin' blethers up in rhyme', is cheered by the arrival in his cottage of a sexually attractive Scottish muse:

> When click! the string the snick did draw;
> An' jee! the door gaed to the wa' ...

Then, with the last word providing the anthology's most delicate rhyme:

> I glowr'd as eerie's I'd been dusht
>   In some wild glen;
> When sweet, like modest worth, she blusht,
>   An' steppèd ben.

The girl's attractions are somewhat stinted in Cockburn's transcription. Her features have 'a hare-brain'd, sentimental trace', but the advice she brings him is not wild. He must know his place: he cannot learn to 'paint with Thomson's landscape-glow', cannot emulate the 'sweet harmonious Beattie's' 'Minstrel lays', or tear, with him, 'the sceptic's bays'. She also informs him, before binding his brow with holly:

> I saw thy pulse's maddening play
> Wild-send thee Pleasure's devious way,
> Misled by Fancy's meteor-ray,
>   By Passion driven;
> But yet the light that led astray,
>   Was light from Heaven.

By now the poem has moved from Scots into English, and into romantic rant and cant. Such passions are a long way from Collins's, and a short way from those regretted by the prayerful Moore. A prayer by Burns, also chosen for the anthology, supplements his assurance here, that his passions are heaven-sent, with this:

> If I have wander'd in those paths
>   Of life I ought to shun;

As something, loudly in my breast,
　Remonstrates I have done;

Thou know'st that Thou has formèd me
　With passions wild and strong;
And list'ning to their witching voice
　Has often led me wrong.

But God will take pleasure in forgiving him. Burns and Moore
shared the manliness which owns up loudly to its errors and
pleasures (Moore was a great user of the figurative and fugitive
'steal'), while sanctifying them with piety and fine feelings.[52]

Cockburn's copy of 'The Vision' leaves out a respectful allusion
to a West of Scotland estate inhabited by the judge Lord Craig,
who is mocked in a story told in Cockburn's *Circuit Journeys*.[53]
This is a small drama of sense and sensibility. Craig was 'driven
from the paradise of Barskimming where he had retreated for
nature and romance, by looking out on a dewy morning and
seeing the brute (as he called him) of a butcher killing a calf on
the lawn. "Would not you have fled too, Mr Sheriff Scott?"
"No, my Lord, I would have consoled myself by thinking of a good
veal cutlet." ' Cockburn is not writing here in the capacity of a
worshipper of nature and of suffering. This was a time when the
fatted calf was preferred to the stricken deer.

Mr Sheriff Scott, together with Burns and the expatriate
Thomson, is among the Scottish poets who are foremost in the
selection: the recently published *Lay of the Last Minstrel* and
Marmion were obvious quarries. Campbell was a Scots poet who
also laid firm claim to inclusion. Tam the Hermit was a friend of
these friends, and had already risen to eminence, though Cockburn
seems to have had doubts about his work ('and even Campbell',
runs a letter from which I have quoted). Parts of *The Pleasures of
Hope* were taken ('Like angel-visits, few and far between'[54]),
and so, among several other things, was his poem about the
battle of Hohenlinden, where Frank and Hun made 'dreadful
revelry'. The advertised compassion of Campbell and of Thomson
did not forbid enlistment in the ranks of the cheerers-on of that
bellicose Great Britain which was conquering the world in the
name of liberty. Thomson wrote a long poem of that name which
his biographer, Dr Johnson, 'desisted' from reading,[55] but which
was read on the Pentlands, and he wrote 'Rule, Britannia', which
says that Britons never will be slaves. This exponent of solitude

and affecting sights also enjoyed conversing with the elder Pitt. He held that Britannia should both rule and retire, advance and retreat, soar and steal.

Another North British bard, James Beattie of Aberdeen, praised by Burns in 'The Vision', has already been mentioned for his contribution to the anthology's concern with the theme of retirement—a retirement which may be soaring or recessive, active or regressive, which may run to the surgent four-stress line or to sensuous slow progresses learnt from Spenser. Beattie wrote a poem entitled 'Retirement', as Cowper did, and from his long poem in Spenserian stanzas, *The Minstrel*, which appeared in the course of the 1770s, just before Cockburn was born, the compilers took an expression of their master theme. The stanza they took follows the description of a pretty 'cultivated spot' in a wild valley: a Highland landscape, one might think, visited by a hero with an English name. 'Romantick visions swarm on Edwin's soul.' The sun is setting as the alexandrine approaches, and Edwin, distracted by his visions, does not hear the curfew bell: 'When slowly on his ear these moving accents stole'. The moving accents declare:

> Hail, awful scenes, that calm the troubled breast,
> And woo the weary to profound repose,
> Can passion's wildest uproar lay to rest,
> And whisper comfort to the man of woes!
> Here Innocence may wander, safe from foes,
> And Contemplation soar on seraph wings.
> O Solitude, the man who thee foregoes,
> When lucre lures him, or ambition stings,
> Shall never know the source whence real grandeur springs.[56]

Retirement here involves both a retreat from passions which bring to mind those of Burns, and a tendency to expire, seraphi-cally. This influential stanza, as we may think of it, given what we know of the language of later poems, is altered in transcription: 'awful scenes' becomes 'lovely scenes'. Beattie's anapaestic 'The Hermit', which may have influenced Cockburn's 'Linn', is entered elsewhere in the commonplace-book. It refers to a 'Kind Nature'.

Some of the pieces in the anthology are by the transcribers themselves, and one or two items which I have been unable to place may be theirs too. The verse of James Grahame, a North British bard in good standing at the time, is fairly copiously represented. From the author of *The Sabbath*, soon to be an Anglican priest, come Beattie-like lines in patriotic praise of the Covenanting field preacher:

> He by the gleam
> Of sheeted lightning oped the sacred book,
> And words of comfort spake: over their souls
> His accents soothing came. . . .[57]

Grahame's poetry was that of a humanitarian, who disliked blood sports, and who specialised in words of comfort. For Byron, he was 'sepulchral Grahame'. Cockburn said that this 'softest of human hearts' was enraged by 'what he held to be oppression, especially of animals or the poor, both of whom he took under his special protection'. Animals or the poor—these are the words of the man known to this essay as the Whig romantic. And the contradictions, the ups and downs, the soaring and stealing, which characterised these Scottish Whigs are nowhere better exemplified than in Grahame, and in Cockburn's language on the subject of his friend. To Grahame, we are told, 'nothing was a luxury that excluded the etherial calm of indolence. Yet his virtue was by no means passive. He was roused into a new nature by abhorrence of cruelty, and could submit to anything in the cause of duty.'[58]

John Richardson's work is also in the anthology. He wrote poems, some of them in admiration of Burns, and was spoken of as having to be dissuaded by Scott from neglecting the law as a result. One of his lyrics was sufficiently like Burns for Grahame, walking on Arthur's Seat with Richardson, Campbell and a party of ladies, to pretend to the ladies that it was by the half-sarket, heaven-taught Ayrshire ploughman. That walk on Arthur's Seat, where Campbell drew inspiration for *The Pleasures of Hope*, effected Richardson's introduction to his future wife, Elizabeth Hill.

Of the poems by Cockburn in the collection, which are in his own hand, 'How solemn the close' is given virtually as it stands in my book, where I say that the poem has to do with a lovely spot between the Braid and Blackford hills. In this glen, in the burn which runs through it, fed by his linn, Cockburn and some friends, when they were young, had piled up a pillar of stones—stones 'of lustre from the brook, in memory', as *Paradise Lost* puts it,[59] in words copied for the anthology. This pillar was meant to mark their departure from school, and is not the least, though it is the smallest, of the towers, ascents and surgencies for which he cared.

It is like the anthology itself—another pile of lustrous stones which commemorates the youth of Cockburn and his friends. As it happened, the pillar was washed away, and was replaced by a tin box with coins in it, including a new Glasgow halfpenny. The relic is hailed in the poem in words which might have been applied to the Whig Reform Bill: 'Thou Hope of the future and Pledge of the past!' When Cockburn's set used the word 'Lakeish', it was with a measure of disapproval, but it is Lakeish of the poem to say as it does: 'the vows of our childhood in Heaven are sealed'.

Cockburn's 'The Linn' is copied in a version which closely corresponds to the second published version, the one kept by the Richardson family, though, as I have said, the requiem for the murdered Frenchman is missing. In this poem, too, the magic of a spot, and the friendships associated with it, are at issue: both poems, together with Scott's 'Helvellyn' and Campbell's Cathcart lines, are examples of that anapaestic vein which was a favourite vehicle for the transports, regrets and revisitings of the period. A sense of the Scott and of the Campbell may have encouraged Cockburn, in 'The Linn', to add a lament for a dead stranger to the celebration of a beautiful place hallowed by the affections of youth: Scott's poem has a dead stranger, and the language of Cockburn's requiem often coincides with that of Campbell's poem. I say in my book that Cockburn's poem may also have been affected by a knowledge of Wordsworth and of Coleridge, but I am now inclined to discount the possibility of a debt to the latter. It is clear, though, that a sense of Coleridge went to the making of 'Geraldine', and the anthology makes this clearer still, with its inclusion of Coleridge's 'Love'. There is no text of 'Geraldine' in the anthology, but it contains another Geraldine poem which throws light on the first one, and suggests that the attribution to Cockburn should be cancelled.

Charles James Fox said that 'Love', whose author he did not know, was 'the most beautiful poem in the language'.[60] The judgement might seem to reveal an astonishing susceptibility to literary fashion on the part of a Whig romantic, and in treating 'Love' as a source for 'Geraldine', we may find ourselves thinking that one bad poem was to generate another. 'Love' was first published in the *Morning Post* of 21 December 1799. When the poem was admitted to the second edition of *Lyrical Ballads*, the Gothic atmosphere was mitigated, and a few stanzas were removed. In 'The Vision', Burns calls his passions heavenly: in the opening stanzas of this poem, as it appeared in *Lyrical Ballads*, Coleridge expresses, more majestically, an idea that is not dissimilar. These stanzas were copied for the anthology.

> All Thoughts, all Passions, all Delights,
> Whatever stirs this mortal Frame,
> All are but Ministers of Love,
>   And feed his sacred flame.
>
> Oft in my waking dreams do I
> Live o'er again that happy hour,
> When midway on the Mount I lay
>   Beside the Ruin'd Tower.
>
> The Moonshine stealing o'er the scene
> Had blended with the Lights of Eve;
> And she was there, my Hope, my Joy,
>   My own dear Genevieve!

As he lies on the mount beside his *tour abolie*, the poet sings a lay to which Genevieve listens with a blush, and which moves her to confess her feeling for him, forgetting her modesty to the extent of allowing him to feel 'the Swelling of her Heart'. She then becomes his bride.

The four-stress line, the woman's name, and the refrain in which it is repeated, link the two poems. There is some community of language, and the same hectic courtliness of address. But the dissembled eroticism of the Coleridge was not imitated by the Pentlands writer, who turns his attention to the 'lovely scenes' left desolate by Geraldine's departure. The Coleridge, moreover, affords not one drama but two: the lay tells the story of a knight who is scorned by his lady and goes mad. He is visited by an angel who is really a devil in disguise, as angels have often been during the long history of Gothic duality, and he then rescues the lady from a fate 'worse than death'. But there seems little doubt that 'Love' led the way for 'Geraldine', and its presence in the anthology, together, possibly, with the presence of a Geraldine in Coleridge's 'Christabel', might be taken to settle the point.

But who wrote 'Geraldine'? The poem bemoans the departure of a woman: in his letter of 1808 to Grahame, who might have been expected to be in the know, Cockburn, in treating the matter of its authorship as a joke, talks of the sad going away of a niece.

In the second Geraldine poem, copied for the anthology, the woman is back, and all is well. The poem has four verses, and the last two read:

> How sweet with Geraldine to walk
> Along the woodland's primrose way,
> And hail her favrite mossy thorn,
> Again in Spring's fresh cloathing gay,
>
> Again to trim the jessmine bower,
> The woodbine with the rose to twine,
> To welcome back the vernal year,
> And bless the day that made her mine.

In the Richardson family papers in the National Library of Scotland, there is another version of this poem, entitled 'The Budding Thorn'.[61] Geraldine's name is omitted, and the action transferred to 'Festiniog's lovely vale', but it is substantially the same poem. The last two verses read:

> How $\left\{ \begin{array}{l} \text{blest with thee at eve to walk} \\ \text{sweet, my Mary, now to walk} \end{array} \right.$
> By Tan y Builch's sweet woodland way,
> And hail thy fav'rite mossy thorn,
> Again in Spring's fresh clothing gay,
>
> Again to trim the Jasmine bower,
> The woodbine with the rose to twine,
> And prop the flower in winter fallen,
> And bless the day that made thee mine.

Not all the attributions for the large number of literary manuscripts included among these papers are correct, but it is probable that this one is, and that John Richardson also wrote the first of the Geraldine poems. Cockburn's letter of 1808 assigns it to a 'Dick': this could be a reference to Richardson. As for the talk of a niece, the Elizabeth or Betsey, the 'new-bursting poplar', who was to be made Dick's own was a niece of the Miss Hills.

At the time of the anthology, Edinburgh's upper crust inhabited a snug city, for all the anxieties occasioned by party conflict, a rising population, a run-down system of government, and the spread of 'French' political principles. Cockburn spoke of the ordinary happiness of their Edinburgh life,[62] which made

them slow to leave (though in 1823 they did) on a grand tour of
Europe—a Europe which turned out, on inspection, to resemble
Scotland. That Edinburgh life is implied in his lines about the
heronry at Relugas:

> Ye winged sages! Feathered Gods!
> How calm your social city rests;
> While ye, within your old abodes,
> Sagacious watch your solid nests.

The anthology shows a team of gentlefolk at play—in pursuit of
nature and romance—and these games formed part of their
ordinary happiness. But it could just as well be said that they
signified a desertion of that happiness, a desertion of their nests,
in search of the extraordinary happiness accessible on their hills,
and in the contemplation of distress, and of a poetry of refuge and
retirement.

The outlook of the people who played these games is not, of
course, to be equated with their victim-mongering moods, with
the affectation and sentimentality, the romantic chic, which is
apparent, and at times violent, in their choice of poems. If they
enjoyed grieving for the forlorn, they made efforts to help
them, though it is also the case, with Cockburn, that some of the
efforts of his statesmanship were liable to hurt them. Literature's
concern with the victim was not repudiated by the writers who
came forward in Britain during the remainder of Cockburn's life.
It was certainly not repudiated by Dickens, who made the
worldly Francis Jeffrey, his friend, cry over the death of little
Nell, and who was observed by Cockburn when he visited
Scotland: 'He with too bushy a scalp, but a very gentle, amiable,
sensible, man, with a soft bright eye, and clothes better even than
mine.'[63] Cockburn (an eccentric dresser) assigns to Dickens both
sense and sensibility: even in its impressible youth, Cockburn's
set wanted people to exhibit both qualities. We are, as we remain,
in a world in which it is possible to think that the same person
may have a hard head and a soft heart, and to think that these
two natures may at times be a trouble. No such trouble, however,
is suspected here.

Cockburn, then, was a man of feeling, a hermit, only by halves,
or at intervals, or on holiday, and his middle age was to prove
phenomenally active and successful. It may perhaps be significant
that the only two poems of his which appear to date from after

1809 are more urbane, more Augustan, than those that figure in the anthology. Of the late poems, 'Relugas', admittedly, stands in a possibly ambiguous relationship to the poetry of the eighteenth century. It is civic, as in the heronry passage, but it is also romantic: it uses that word in an affirmative way, and looks back on a lost paradise or playground. All the same, we are conscious, in the poem, of a community, of an Edinburgh, whereas, in 'The Linn', we are conscious of a few like minds, of a few fit friends, in flight.

The anthology has its share of blethers, and the blethers sometimes bear witness to an element of pretence, whereby lawyers pose as swains, refugees and broken hearts, and their ordinary happiness is presented as a misery from which they must escape, or as something ignoble. The most charmingly bletheracious item—a Cockburn word, this—are these anapaests, in which a romantic homecoming of a kind is experienced:

O Lurginclanbrazil, how sweet is thy sound
To my tender remembrance as love's sacred ground.
'Twas there my sweet Fannila first bless'd my sight
And filled my young heart with a fluttering delight.

When I thought her my own, ah! too short seem'd the day
For a trip to Downpatrick, or a sail on the sea.
To paint what I felt then all language were vain.
'Twas in truth what the Poets have studied to feign.

But too late I found that even she could deceive
And nothing was left but to sigh, weep and rave.
Distracted I flew from my dear native shore,
Resolv'd to see Lurginclanbrazil no more.

Yet still in some moments enchanted I find
A warm ray of her fondness beam soft on my mind.
While thus in blest Fancy my charmer I see,
All the world's a Lurginclanbrazil to me.

The poem is set in Ulster—in the Clanbrazil territory of Armagh. I am able to say of its authorship only that Scott has a poem which is in certain respects a replica. 'The Return to Ulster', written in 1811, not so long before the Weirdlaw Hill lines, is much the same metrically, and is set in the same place ('the pines of Clanbrassil'). Here again is a homecoming of a kind. A nostalgic revisiting of 'the scenes of my youth'—an 'Eden'

endeared to the speaker through its rapturous associations with
Celtic minstrelsy and the chase, and with a first love—has to
endure a disappointment: the scenes are not what they were. As
in the other poem, the speaker has 'learn'd the sad lesson, to love
and to part'. If Scott could smile at Sensibility's fuss over a fatted
calf, he was also able to yield to its sensations—to grieve for a
fallen climber, to return to Ulster. He was able to have his cutlet
and eat it too.

If there is nonsense in the anthology, however, many of its
pieces are fragrant and wholesome. Cockburn and company, in
their alertness to nature and misfortune, chose some of the strongest
verse that it was open to them to choose, and traced out the main
lines of development along which established themes were carried
forward into a future where these themes were made, and made
to appear, new, where the name and enchantment of romanticism
were lent to the later stages of that development. The anthology
is a memorial to a former taste, but it is a taste from which we
have yet to recover, and in which the taste of earlier times is
resumed. Its poems make the reader more aware of constancies
than of change; make him aware of how slowly a culture changes;
aware that, if we try to subtract what hindsight supplies, and what
distance supplies, from what we know of the past, we may come
to feel that change is an aspect of permanence. The choice
confirms what has been held in modern times about the dependence of romantic writers on their immediate predecessors. David
Nichol Smith was conscious of such a dependence when in 1926
he compiled his *Oxford Book of Eighteenth-Century Verse*, and it is
interesting that so many of the poems in that excellent anthology
should also appear in the Cockburn commonplace-book. Nichol
Smith has the components of Wordsworth's cento, Langhorne's
blighted infant, and Akenside's Northumbrian shades.

The flight from ordinary life was no new thing in 1807. What
was new, we may suppose, was an interest in the speech of the
ordinary life on which, for other purposes, these people turned,
and pretended to turn, their back, together with a more vivid
sense of the poet's individuality and idiosyncrasy. The old sense of
community was by no means gone: but in the poetry of recent
times, the individual, the exception, has started to speak to the
reader more intimately and more insistently. The old stress on
seclusion and departure persists. Meanwhile the idea of childhood,
and of a return to childhood, has taken on a deeper and more

sophisticated appeal: what had been the 'simple creed' of childhood, as it is called in the 'Immortality' Ode, was made, by
Wordsworth and others, less simple. It may be that in the opening
verse of Cockburn's best poem, 'Relugas', the intimate and in-
sistent voice of a new age can be distinguished:

> When wakeful in the night profound,
> The fearful pulses of my heart I hear,
> And long for some external sound,
> Relugas! be thy whispers near!

In writing about the pleasures and friendships of earlier days,
Cockburn begins by writing as if he were a child.

He has been seen, especially in Scotland, as comfortingly old-
fashioned, and as classical. The anthology does not enhance that
view of him. It has bits of French, Italian and Spanish verse, but
nothing in Latin, and not much from the poetry of high August-
anism. Coleridge is copied, and Cockburn's hand copies important
passages of Wordsworth. I gathered that there were those who
reckoned that my book, *Cockburn's Millennium*, was at fault for
describing him as having moved with the romantic times, and for
seeming to impose on him a double life in the Gothic mode. What
I meant to do was to relate his knowledge of that new mode to a
way of life that was, by turns, active and contemplative: I was
making him out to be a classical romantic, who could also behave
as a Whig romantic, and I was not making him out to be a
character in a Gothic novel. I am sure that, in matters of consequence to him, including literary matters, he did move with the
times. The anthology does not authorise every one of my arguments
in this area, but it does show him as responsive, much in the way
the book argues for, to the state of affairs in literature when he
came to manhood.

In one sense, romanticism was, for Cockburn, a false lead. If
some of his poems appear to turn their back on his society, on
Edinburgh, he himself can't be said to have done so. He was an
expert on Edinburgh, and wrote about it better than anyone else
has been able to write about it. And the weakness of his reclusive
or pastoral vein in poetry is a reminder of how much the literature
of romanticism has stood to lose as a result of its commitment to
departure. Romantic writers can't be blamed for the activities of
an amateur poet whose true muse was the muse of history, but
it is evident that the Cockburn who went in for romantic escape

is the least of the writers we recognise in his works, and that there is a cost to be counted when literature withdraws. Perhaps it is also possible to say that if there were English poets then who were relieved to have passed out of the Egypt of the eighteenth century, literature had come to think of human life as a kind of Egypt, and to transmit, more than it ever had before, a radical discontent. If it is right to regard this as a change, it is a change which has yet to be reversed.

His best pieces of poetry are in his annals, autobiographies and letters, and his letter about Tam the Hermit is a better poem than 'The Linn'. We do not look for humour in a poem like 'The Linn': the slightest spark would have sent the whole thing up in flames. And yet his most intelligent writing is frequently humorous. Not all of his poems lack wit: 'On losing a staff' has it, and his treatment of the Relugas herons has it. But even a joke retailed in his manuscripts can be turned into a better poem than 'The Linn'. One of his letters, for example, tells the story of an old Irishwoman who was giving evidence before the judge Lord Meadowbank, and who was being harassed by him. Eventually she felt she should explain: 'Me Lord, I'm no schollard, but just an ould wife like yoursell'.[64]

A similar claim could be made in respect of a single sentence in another letter: 'Better be the certain owner of a field of neeps, than the precarious expectant of a Venus'.[65] There are two languages here, to point the joke: a Johnsonian English, and a vernacular that calls a spade a spade and a turnip a neep. For Cockburn, the purity of poetry could not allow such an inter-action, and despite his feeling for Burns, and despite the fact that his deft, calm and colloquial, and not at all Johnsonian, narrative prose could move into Scots for direct speech, and on other occasions besides, he was capable of the thought that the man or woman of feeling should speak a correct English. Among the most recently discovered manuscript material is a letter of advice to a daughter in the South: 'Do observe their sweet and gentle English tongues, and try to take one of them out of their heads, and put it into your own—a tongue that cannot say Bawth.' Then: 'It is said, and I think truly, that the great superiority of *all* English manner to *all* Scotch, consists in the gentleness—the native and fixed habit of sweet-blooded gentleness—of the former. They can scarcely lay their hand upon you, or drop a word into your ear, but softly.'[66] In that advice, a note of prudence, of calculation, is undeniable: the sweet blood of gentle birth must be protected. But the soft heart of sensibility beats there too: the sensibility which wished to return to early scenes and early days, those of childhood and those of adolescence, which was sometimes disposed to take account of suggestions made in the early days of romantic duality, and which was compact of vicissitudes— ambitions, dejections and reposes, ups and downs.

'Geraldine' could be thought to have been written, in a correct English, by the precarious expectant of a Venus. It seems that the expectations were John Richardson's, and that they were fulfilled.

NOTES

The anthology compiled by Cockburn and his friends is to be found in the James M. and Marie Louise Osborn Collection, Yale University Library. Quotations from it are generally based, where published versions are conveniently available, on the published texts. The editions consulted are specified, so far as seemed necessary, in the notes. Errors or changes in transcription, on the part of the compilers, are mentioned only in so far as they have appeared to raise points of interest. I wish to thank colleagues at University College, London, who assisted me in the work of identifying the material. Mr Anthony Shipps, Librarian for English, Indiana University, advised me concerning Wordsworth's Cento in *Yarrow Revisited*, and I also received advice from my friends Christopher Ricks and Christopher Salvesen. I am grateful to the Curator of the Osborn Collection for permission to copy and to quote from the anthology. The abbreviations NLS, *ER* and *CM* refer respectively to the National Library of Scotland, to the *Edinburgh Review*, and to my book *Cockburn's Millennium*, published in 1975.

1. *CM*, p. 165.
2. Ibid., p. 159.
3. Ibid., p. 171.
4. *The Complete Poetical Works of Thomas Campbell*, ed. J. Logie Robertson (1907). The metrical character of the three poems is mainly anapaestic, with dactylic passages, it might be argued, intervening as a brake. That of 'The Linn' and of 'Helvellyn' is described as dactylic in my *CM*.
5. *The Poetical Works of Sir Walter Scott*, ed. J. Logie Robertson (1913).

6. *CM*, Preface, p. xi.

7. The account of Richardson's temperament and background is taken from an obituary article by Lord Moncreiff in the *North British Review* (November 1864).

8. Part I, l. 7.

9. Part I, l. 325.

10. Part II, ll. 37, 38.

11. The letter is printed in the *Life and Letters of Thomas Campbell* by William Beattie (3 vols, 1849), Vol. I, pp. 454, 455.

12. *CM*, p. 25.

13. *ER* (October 1807).

14. *CM*: Preface, p. xi, and p. 77.

15. To the Rev. John Mackenzie, 24 May 1850; MS. Mrs Frackleton, Edinburgh.

16. *CM*, Preface, p. xii.

17. Neither line has been identified. The first belongs to a passage whose language and sentiments are those of Samuel Rogers.

18. *The Task*, Book III, l. 292: *The Poetical Works of William Cowper*, ed. H. S. Milford, revised by Norma Russell (Oxford 1967), p. 170.

19. *CM*, p. 54.

20. As quoted in Lockhart's *Life* (2nd edition, 1839, 10 vols), Vol. I, pp. 185–187.

21. The cento is printed, together with Wordsworth's note on the subject, part of which is quoted here, in *The Poetical Works of William Wordsworth*, ed. Thomas Hutchinson (1928), p. 626. All three of the passages which compose the cento had already appeared, separately, in an anthology of Wordsworth's published in 1819—the ' Album' presented to Lady Mary Lowther.

22. Quotations from Akenside are drawn throughout from *The Poetical Works of Mark Akenside*, with a memoir by the Rev. Alexander Dyce (1894).

23. See p. 153 below.

24. See 'Autumn', l. 1304 to the end. Quotations from Thomson are taken from the Oxford Standard Authors edition of the *Poetical Works*, ed. J. Logie Robertson (1908).

25. 'Autumn', ll. 963–966.

26. 'Autumn', ll. 672–674.

27. 'Ode', Oxford edition, p. 423.

28. From *The Pleasures of Imagination* (1744), Book III, l. 629 to the end. Akenside's poem was redone, and retitled *The Pleasures of the Imagination* (1757). The anthology copies from both versions.

29. *The Task*, Book I, ll. 141–150.

30. The Wordsworth texts are taken from *The Selected Poetry and Prose of Wordsworth*, ed. Geoffrey Hartman, Signet Classics (1970). The three passages from 'Tintern Abbey' are, in order of transcription, ll. 137–146, ll. 22–30 and ll. 122–134.

31. That 'great gulf' comes from *A History of English Literature* by Emile Legouis and Louis Cazamian (revised edition, 1937), p. 931.

32. For the Burns impromptu, see *The Poems and Songs of Robert Burns*, ed. James Kinsley (1968), no. 169. The commonplace-book is followed for the text of the Campbell passage. A version of the epistle is given in Beattie's *Life and Letters*: see Vol. I, pp. 217–220.

33. *The Pleasures of the Imagination*, Book IV, ll. 38, 40.

34. *Selected Essays of William Hazlitt*, ed. Geoffrey Keynes (1930), pp. 742, 743.

35. *Essays on the Nature and Principles of Taste* (2nd ed., 2 vols, 1811), Vol. I, pp. 23, 24.

36. Cockburn letters, Advocates' Library, dated 30 August 1836, quoted with the kind permission of the Keeper.

37. *CM*, pp. 51, 248.

38. Jeffrey was reviewing (*ER*, July 1806) Moore's *Epistles, Odes, and Poems*, in which this poem appears.

39. From the same collection.

40. As copied for the anthology.

41. *The Poems of John Milton*, ed. John Carey and Alastair Fowler (1968).

42. Canto I, stanzas VI, XVI.

43. *The Castle of Indolence*, Canto I, stanza LIX.

44. *ER* (October 1802).

45. From *Paradise Lost*, Books III and IV.

46. Ibid., Books X, ll. 743–745.

47. *The Pleasures of Imagination*, Book I, l. 151.

48. *Paradise Lost*, Book VII, l. 31.

49. *CM*, p. 157.

50. Ibid., pp. 150, 151.

51. *ER* (October 1807).

52. *The Poems and Songs of Robert Burns*, nos. 62 and 13.

53. *Circuit Journeys* (1888), p. 54.

54. Part II, l. 378. The line is a cento of a kind: it appears to have been assembled from the memorable lines of earlier poets.

55. He admits this in his life of Thomson in *Lives of the Poets*.

56. *The Minstrel*, Book II (2nd edition, 1774), stanzas 9 and 10.

57. *The Sabbath* (1805), ll. 212–215.

58. Byron calls Grahame 'sepulchral' in 'English Bards and Scotch Reviewers', which also has the line: 'And godly Grahame chant a stupid stave'. Cockburn's description occurs in his *Life of Lord Jeffrey* (2 vols, 1852), Vol. I, p. 112.

59. Book XI, l. 325.

60. *Lyrical Ballads*, ed. R. L. Brett and A. R. Jones (1963), Notes, p. 298. The text is that of the original editions, and is followed here for quotations.

61. NLS MS 3991, f. 148.

62. *CM*, p. 81.

63. NLS: letter to Mrs Andrew Rutherfurd, 1 July 1841.

64. NLS: letter to Andrew Rutherfurd of 16 March 1840.

65. *CM*, p. 237.

66. NLS: from a letter of 1 February 1841 to his daughter Elizabeth ('Wifie').

The making of Cockburn's 'Memorials'

ALAN BELL

OF ALL THE MINOR SOURCES for the study of Lord Cockburn's life and works, none was more infuriating and archivally suggestive than the slim volume published in Edinburgh in 1932 over the name of his grandson Harry A. Cockburn, *Some Letters of Lord Cockburn, with passages omitted from the Memorials of his Time*. This prints extracts—sometimes tantalising extracts—from an unspecified quantity of letters which had come into the possession of Harry Archibald Cockburn, a London and Edinburgh wine merchant with literary aspirations. They were followed by parts—and what seemed to be only parts—of some supplementary *Memorials* material. But an appendix prints in full a long memorandum of 1887 and 1889 by Cockburn's son and last-surviving trustee, Francis Jeffrey Cockburn. In it this elder Frank Cockburn details the contents of a couple of boxes of literary and judicial papers, with some correspondence, which had been sent to him by the family lawyers for disposal. He clearly thought the whole task rather a bore—'those wretched papers are a bother', he wrote in a letter to a cousin—but he carried it out with a commendable, appalling, thoroughness. His record of what was done with the various bundles of his father's papers shows the destruction of most of them, and the presentation of a number of volumes (including, for example, Cockburn's much-cherished transcripts of Jeffrey's letters to himself, and various papers relating to legal cases in which Cockburn had appeared as counsel) to the Advocates' Library. F. J. Cockburn also recorded the retention of a few samples of his father's family and general correspondence from the lawyers' boxes, as relics for the next generation. The original manuscript of the *Memorials* (which we may deduce to be Cockburn's fair copy based on earlier texts previously destroyed), together with the printers' copy (as sent for publication by Cockburn's trustees), had been destroyed by Francis Jeffrey Cockburn, who felt that 'the *Memorials* has had its day'. Ichabod, Ichabod, one might feel on looking over this memorandum, the glory is departed.

It was clear from these appalling lists that little had survived, and that in the multiplicity of Cockburn descendants it might not be easy to trace the samples that had been preserved. Only two external sources of information were available to a scholar interested in the text of the *Memorials*. One was National Library of Scotland MS. 823, A. & C. Black's file copy of the *Memorials*, with many letters relating to the publication of the book laid in: most are concerned with illustrations and misprints, but some relate to Black's eager offer of £750 outright for the *Memorials*. There is also a somewhat disingenuous denial by Cockburn's trustees that any further manuscript existed—a first hint of the existence of the work subsequently published as the *Journal*. One gleaned from the Black correspondence the information that the first printing appears to have been of 3000 copies (of which Mudie's subscribed for 400), and that when a reprint was considered (an extra thousand was in mind) the trustees wondered whether they ought to attempt 'the replacement of some of the omitted characters from Jeffrey's Life' —this was the rearrangement of the text carried out when Harry A. Cockburn's well-known illustrated T. N. Foulis edition was published in 1909.

The other existing source for the history of Cockburn's papers was the large box of business papers deposited in the National Library by Messrs Lindsay, Howe & Co., W.S., of Edinburgh, in 1963. Some of these went back to Cockburn's own lifetime— minor accounts relating to circuit expenses, and a few business letters of his own including some important ones revealing the financial pressures to which he was subjected late in life. There were publishing agreements made by his trustees for the works; the sale to Black of the *Memorials* already mentioned; an agreement with Edmonston and Douglas in 1873 for a continuation (to be entitled *Journal*, as counsel felt there might be an infringement of Black's copyright if *Memorials* was used again in the title). Two thousand copies of the *Journal* were provided for, based on a manuscript to be prepared by the trustees (one of them was to dictate to a shorthand writer), to be published at two-thirds of profit to the trust. (The *Journal* cannot have been such a paying proposition, however, as 950 were still on hand at the end of 1875 and 943 a year after that.) There were also in the lawyers' deposited box agreements with David Douglas for 750 *Sedition Trials* and 1000 *Circuit Journeys*, both signed in 1887 at half-profits terms. Such relatively minor commercial facts obviously indicated a high degree of editorial control by Cockburn's son-in-law Thomas Cleghorn (Sheriff of Argyll from 1855) and his nephew Archibald Davidson, Sheriff then of Aberdeen and later of Midlothian.

The full extent of Cockburn's autobiographical manuscripts could be measured from an inventory of material found at the formal opening of his repositories soon after his death: four volumes of *loose* sheets of manuscript paginated to 1,747, with a last entry dated 17 April 1854, are recorded (this may have been an un-revised journal-form text of the *Memorials* plus what we know as the *Journal*); and also 533 pages, with the last page dated 30 April 1853, which superseded the first 584¼ pages of the larger manuscript just mentioned and are obviously the basis of the *Memorials* as printed. It is not just their bulk which makes one feel so annoyed with the successive generations of Cockburn's trustees for their destructions. It is even more infuriating when one knows of the very high store which Cockburn himself had set on his manu-scripts. A fine thing though the *Memorials* is, knowledge of facts like these could only make one wish for more, and curse those Victorian incendiarists. Ichabod indeed.

Autobiographising had long been a characteristic habit of Cockburn's mind, which always seems to have had a reminiscent bent. In 1806 (as seen above in chapter 2), he had written to his friend John Richardson of the memories of earlier life impressed upon him by re-reading an old commonplace book, 'which revived so many facts and strange old notions in me, notions that with all their absurdity I loved, that I began to lament I had never kept a minute diary of all the memorabilia of my days'. The written record on which the *Memorials* is based seem to date from 1821, when Cockburn began to sense (in the words of his preface) that it was 'a pity that no private account should be preserved of the distinguished men or important events that had marked the pro-gress of Scotland, or at least of Edinburgh, during my day'. Letters as well as diaries formed part of his memorial scheme, and have led almost accidentally to one piece of documentary preservation which has been notably beneficial to posterity. These transcripts of Jeffrey letters which were given to the Advocates' Library by Cockburn's son show the importance Cockburn attached to both writer and contents, but against this commendable piety towards an important private correspondence one must set Cockburn's own

Journal entry (of 3 February 1845) in which he announces the surely over-prudent cremation of most of his incoming correspondence.

No such incendiary feelings, however, seem to have been attached to Cockburn's 'Red Books', as he knew his autobiographical compilations. He became particularly interested in their future towards the end of his life, when the preparation of his *Life of Jeffrey* turned his thoughts to the publication of his own reminiscences. He had approached the task of writing about his friend with various reservations. One arose from their long intimacy. Then there was the uneventfulness of Jeffrey's life—'writing anonymous pamphlets (called Reviews) and bamboozling Courts' was not much of a framework. There was his own lack of literary expertise. 'No reputation to myself was ever in view', he wrote to Dr John Brown after the book was published: 'book making has never been within my craft, and living three score years and twelve abates the vanity of authorship, where that vanity has existed.' And there was also the disadvantage of a 'far too great nearness to modern times. Neither the living, nor the recently dead, can be freely talked of—and what a skeleton this leaves!'

Yet he was able to overcome each of these disadvantages. The *Life of Jeffrey*, followed by a cautiously selected volume of letters, is not a structurally tidy work. There are far too many digressions, but these fill out the comparatively uninteresting biography and are now the most valuable part of the book. They include Cockburn's description of the first impact of the *Edinburgh Review*, the twenty-page survey of the political state of Scotland when Jeffrey went to the bar in 1794, and many 'characters' for which Cockburn is famous elsewhere. These range from a phrase about his first seeing Jeffrey pleading before Braxfield, and being surprised 'at the vulgar overbearing coarseness of the judge' to longer sketches of the Bell brothers, John Macfarlan of Kirkton, Lord Glenlee, and a justifiably desiccated obituary of George Cranstoun, Lord Corehouse. The author of such characters, despite his maidenly protestations of inexperience, was no novice. The best parts of his *Life of Jeffrey*, with their lively and independent tone, come almost straight out of the 'Red Books'. Cockburn certainly knew what he was about when he consulted his friends about putting them into publishable form.

M

In the autumn of 1851 he wrote to John Richardson about the 'Red Books'. Even then the autobiographical journal was in two parts, dividing in 1830 as *Memorials* and *Journal* now divide; 'tho' I have eiked notes occasionally on passing occurrences, I have not read the volume you have for twenty years at the least', he remarked in offering Richardson a sight of later volumes for opinion. The following March he told Richardson that Mrs Andrew Rutherfurd had also been much diverted by the first volume—

> she has read it all, but is so charmed with old Esky that he half supersedes everything else. The sole question is, ought I to attempt to make a continuous history out of it, or ought I just to go on recording, and leave the mass to be put into shape by others after I shall be sodded? The chief objections to my doing this are 1st, that it would be done so near the persons and the events that it must be diluted into insipidity; 2nd, that an unbroken narrative necessarily loses the freshness of immediate memoranda. The objections to its being left to descendants are 1st, that it may be thought not worth meddling with, 2nd, that it may be selected and worked up ill. Perhaps a safe middle course would be for me to do it, but to leave it unknown and unseen till distance and my removal made its publication not indelicate. And there is another safe and simple course —present conflagration. By my settlement, as it at present stands, my trustees are *allowed* to do as they like with it— even to burn it—but are *advised* to be guided by you and Rutherfurd if you survive me.

Richardson's reply was prompt and enthusiastic:

> It is perfectly clear to me that you might make out of the red books two invaluable volumes of reminiscences. You have an overflow of materials in Esky and Hermand and the numerous other portraits . . . but nobody could put the whole together but yourself . . . I should lament that you did not in your living body enjoy the fruits. I am quite confident that two such volumes as you could make would bring you two thousand guineas. Therefore set about the labour as if it were to be forthwith perfected and put forth by yourself.

In April 1852 Cockburn signed the literary directions to his trustees which he had attended to as part of his Trust Disposition and Settlement. He noted Lord Rutherfurd's and John Richardson of Kirklands' special positions as recommended referees, as 'they are the only two persons to whom I have ever shewn a single line of my Volumes of Notes on Edinburgh'. He advised his trustees that:

> (First) a useful tho' not very saleable book could be made out of the account of our Sedition Trials. (Secondly) that perhaps an agreeable volume might be made out of my Circuit Journal. (Thirdly) that if well selected
> and edited a curious work might be made out of my Volumes of Edinburgh Events and recollections but this would require a very judicious hand. Lord Dundrennan would have done it well, but he being gone I cannot say who could be trusted next best. All I say is that if these Volumes had been written by another and I had had the editing of them I could have made a good book out of them.

And so matters stood, admirably arranged as to options to publish and opinions to be taken.

After Cockburn's death in 1854, Richardson wrote to Rutherfurd that 'I was anxious to talk to you about the Red Book which if you had a good gardener to prune and weed would—or ought to— sell for a couple of thousand pounds'. In August of that year Thomas Cleghorn wrote to Rutherfurd that he hoped it would be possible to retrieve the volume from London, 'as I know Davidson is very desirous to go over the Red Book more carefully than he had leisure for before, and I also wish to refer to some of the volumes'. The trustees apparently took the matter in hand themselves, a paid transcriber was appointed to copy the text which they had revised, a publisher bought the book for £750, and *Memorials of his Time* by Henry Lord Cockburn was published in 1856, with a preface dated May.

There matters rested, with a decent text prepared by the family receiving in due course the due honour of a steady popularity. Except for the permissible restoration to their probable original position of the passages borrowed by the author himself for the *Jeffrey*, the accepted text seems to offer few problems. Were it not for the publication in 1932 of the executor's private memorandum on the survival and subsequent destruction of supplementary manuscript material in 1887–1889, posterity need not have given the matter another thought. F. J. Cockburn recorded the existence of scribal copy of *Journal* and *Memorials* as sent to the printer, together with a set of *Memorials* proofs. There was, moreover, 'a large packet, containing the MS. of the *Memorials* in Lord Cockburn's own writing', and his son noted a number of passages (such as those on Erskine, the Speculative Society and George IV) which were not in the book as published. Francis Cockburn felt that the existence of these addenda did not necessitate the preservation of the whole manuscript: the editors had omitted them, and besides 'the *Memorials* has had its day and another edition is, to say the least, uncertain'.

Also included in the box in 1887 were some pages which seemed to have been separated from the rest, for some reason unstated. These included supplementary passages on *Blackwood's Magazine*, Braxfield and Brougham: Francis Cockburn felt that the fact of their separation may in some way have been important, but he saw little virtue in retaining them or in thinking of their publication in the future. In his memorandum of April 1887 he therefore decided to destroy the whole of Lord Cockburn's manuscript. In the supplementary memorandum two years later he reported that the printer's copy and proofs had been destroyed, together with the large packet of Cockburn's holograph; 'the separated pages [also] have been destroyed with the exception of a few pages which I have kept as curiosities for my own amusement'.

It was these reprieved pages which form the basis of 'passages omitted from the Memorials' in Harry Archie's *Some Letters* of 1932. These gave the pick of the rejected passages but *Some Letters* raises a number of points about the dating, placing and extent of these addenda which made a sight of the actual fragmentary manuscripts desirable for a close student of the texts. Fortunately the fragments descended to a Cockburn who was fully aware of their interest, and some sixty leaves of the *Memorials* manuscript (together with 150 Lord Cockburn letters deposited at the same time) came to the National Library of Scotland in 1975 from the family of the late Mr Francis Cockburn, a London solicitor who had taken a keen interest in the transfer (the acquisition is reported in the *Scotsman* of 17 January 1976).

The fragments tell us a good deal of the way in which the 'judicious hand' (to use Cockburn's phrase) of the trustees made 'a good book' out of the 'Memorials' material. It is not easy on the basis of their surviving pencilled annotation in similar hands to ascribe the adjustments either to Cleghorn or Davidson. Cleghorn seems from a memoir published after his death to have been a prig, but the executry papers suggest that it was Davidson who was principally responsible for the management of the literary estate. I shall refer to them indifferently as 'the trustees'.

The sixty foolscap leaves are all fluently written by Cockburn with the clarity and (usually) the accuracy which make his script such a pleasure to work with. They bear the heavy overscorings of errors in drafting which are also characteristic of his letters; their execution derives from his experience as a drafter of written pleadings when, as he told one of the projectors of the Speculative Society history in 1844, 'a hundred pages a day was then the common dose'. A few leaves have the watermarks J. WHATMAN 1838 or G. WILMOT 1839; most are watermarked SMITH & ALLNUTT 1849 or WHATMAN 1851 or ANSELL 1851. It is the two general chronological groupings rather than the individual marks which are important. Combined with the evidence of the unconsecutive page numbers we can see that those of 1838–1839 belong to the first batch of Red Book drafts paginated to 1,747 (as discovered and recorded after his death); 1849–1851 belong to the revised batch of 533 pages noted also after his death as having been completed in April 1853. The earlier group (which will be discussed later) seems to be from the original Red Book started in 1821, or part of a comprehensive revision of its earlier parts which had made good progress by the late thirties and was continued in unrevised form until the end of Cockburn's life; it was (at least in its later parts) probably akin to the *Journal*—a mixture of reflective and often retrospective memoranda, with occasional 'character' studies, undertaken from time to time but not forming a fully consecutive diary.

The group of later (1849–1851 watermarks) pages, much the larger part of the surviving fragments, represents the later revision of the manuscript undertaken by Cockburn with possible—or even probable—publication in mind. If revision was consecutive, as seems likely, and as some '1851' pages precede '1849s', terminal datings from the earliest watermarks must be discarded in favour of some time in 1851–1852. Perhaps he began the revision in a vacation after receiving Richardson's reply in March 1852 which urged him to revise for publication. The date 30 April 1853 noted by his executors as appearing on page 533 of the document found in his repositories (length and proportions may be inferred consistently with the printed text) shows the end of the job. Given

Cockburn's judicial concentration and a graphic fluency which was prolonged into old age, about a year for producing a revised manuscript of over 500 foolscap pages is not too short an estimate for a vigorous man in his early seventies. This concentrated revisal helps to explain the stylistic unity and narrative power of a text which draws on very disparate materials—memory as well as documents—for its sources. The trustees were certainly left with a neat as well as a pungent document for their attentions.

What did they do to tidy it up for publication? Using a hard pencil they made the usual minor sub-editorial adjustments of presentation, but went further than usual modern practice in improving the style to give it a more literary and less colloquial flavour. Some of the language was too robust for the susceptibilities of the period. The standards of a judge of Georgian upbringing were not those of a pair of circumspect Victorian sheriffs, who felt obliged to undertake omissions of potentially offensive words, phrases, and even whole pages of well-spiced character portrayals.

Minor adjustments included the avoidance of repetitions with permissible variations; spelling mistakes and inconsistencies were tidied up, all in a way a good publisher's reader would have done. But possibly colloquial terms are replaced—'youth' for 'lad' is characteristic. As well as improving the 'literary' presentation, as far as they understood it, they enforced a certain literary respectfulness on the text. Thus when Cockburn wrote of the fashion of imitating Lord Eskgrove in Parliament House, he said that 'Scott in those days was famous for little else'; 'Scott was famous for this particularly' is all the trustees allow him. Again on Scott, Cockburn wrote that at an early stage 'the fertility of his genius was to be its distinguishing wonder'; an adjustment to 'the fertility of his genius was to be its most wonderful distinction' is less happy and indeed ambiguous. There are plenty of minor tonings-down of language. Thus a remark in the passage on the *Beacon* row that Stuart of Dunearn 'was specially hated for the activity of his public spirit' becomes 'was specially disliked'. No wonder that with such dilutions the fact that Stuart 'thrashed Mr Stevenson the printer on the street' becomes 'caned the printer'. Many more examples of this sort of tampering could be adduced, in which words like 'contemptible', 'grossness', 'horrid' and 'wretch' may be seen pencilled away.

The larger omissions are of greater interest. A number of them are given (not accurately) in *Some Letters*, but there are additions to be made even to the portrait-gallery of the Bench. Take Braxfield and Eskgrove as examples: firstly, the *Memorials* as it is known on Braxfield:

> With this intellectual force, as applied to law, his merits, I fear, cease. Illiterate and without any taste for refined enjoyment, strength of understanding, which gave him power without cultivation, only encouraged him to a more contemptuous disdain of all natures less coarse than his own. Despising the growing improvement of manners, he shocked the feelings even of an age which, with more of the formality, had far less of the substance of decorum than our own.

This seems strong enough, finally and crushingly expressed, with a measure of social commentary to give weight to an *ad hominem* attack. But it was not what Cockburn wrote. Perpend:

> With this intellectual force, as applied to law, his merits I fear cease. For he had no other respectable power, or subject, and his habits were all gross. Ignorant, illiterate, and without any taste for any refined enjoyment, strength of understanding, which gave him power without cultivation, only encouraged him to a more contemptuous disdain of all natures less coarse than his own. Despising the growing improvement of manners, he gloried in his own cordial grossness; which was so audacious that it shocked the feelings of an age which, with more of the formality, had far less of the substance of decorum. Party politics, Scotch law, and obscenity, were the full range of his conversation, and of his thoughts. Every hour of his life not occupied by professional business was devoted to Claret, Whist, and less pure enjoyment.

That, more or less in the form in which he intended it, is Cockburn's more authentic assessment of a man of whom he wrote (in a sentence also omitted by the trustees), that 'the chief value of the bench to him was as a place for privileged brutality'.

Eskgrove, too, was not negligible as a lawyer, Cockburn admitted—'cunning in old Scotch law'. 'And here his excellence begins, and ends', remarks the manuscript. When we see that 'But a more ludicrous personage could not exist' was originally written 'for a more ludicrous or contemptible personage . . .' and that 'absurdity' was once 'absurd and despicable', our appetite is whetted by the promise of contempt and despite, and we are not disappointed by a passage which turns him from merely an ungainly fool into a ludicrous old lecher. (New matter is shown in italics in the passage following):

He seemed, in his old age, to be about the average height, but as he then stooped a good deal, he might have been taller in reality. His face varied, according to circumstances, from a scurfy red to a scurfy blue. His eyes were blue, and half cunning, half maudlin; the under lip enormous, and supported on a huge clumsy chin, which moved like the jaw of an exaggerated Dutch toy; his nose prodigious, *and absolutely purple with lust and liquor.* He walked with aslow, stealthy, sinister step, *as if conscious he was going to do what was wrong*—something between a walk and a hirple, and helped himself on by short movements of his elbows, backwards and forwards, like fins. *All this—the downcast, leering look, the red visage, indecent nose, sly edging walk, and a constant muttering motion of his lower lip—made him the very portrait of a superannuated Satyr.* The voice was low and mumbling, and on the bench was generally inaudible for some time after the movement of the lips showed that he had begun speaking; after which the first word that was let fairly out was generally the loudest of the whole discourse. *As to his mind, the intellectual part of it had been successfully applied to Scotch Law, and knew nothing else. The moral part of it was absorbed in three passions—libidousness (but is this a moral passion?), mean avarice, and a testy pride in upholding his judicial dignity. The thousand stories that are told of him all resolve into the exhibition of a supreme Judge, with an odious yet laughable appearance, under the influence of these vices.* It is unfortunate that without an idea of his voice and manner, mere narrative cannot describe his sayings and doings graphically.

We can see in a sustained passage like that the very different balance the author intended, and the scope and direction of the editors' busy pencil. Incidental details are added in later paragraphs on Eskgrove to confirm the view of Cockburn and the whole of the Parliament House that although 'he has been dead nearly fifty years, yet a story of Eskgrove is still preferred to all other stories'. This reminder of a lively and irreverent professional tradition rescues Cockburn from the charge of murmuring his predecessors by a spiteful embroidery of anecdote; it is a pity that we don't have the earlier draft to see how Cockburn first handled a judge who owes his immortality to the *Memorials*.

The trial of Alexander Richmond, the alleged government spy in the 1820s, has a number of adjustments in the drafting which may not be insignificant if examined in detail. Cockburn's manuscript contains a good deal about the *Beacon* row which was more severely critical of Scott's connection with the journal than the published text reveals; and preserves a whole long passage on the Royal Infirmary row of 1818 which the trustees felt it prudent to suppress nearly forty years later. These can be followed (allowing for a number of minor inaccuracies due to Harry Archie's carelessness or inexperience) in *Some Letters*. So too can the passages about George IV's visit in 1822. Here one pencil annotation has marked the whole passage 'out altogether?' and the answer 'yes' is given. This rejected passage included Cockburn's remarks on tartan mania:

> Hundreds who had never seen Heather had the folly to array themselves in Tartan. Nay, His Majesty himself received his loyal subjects at the Levee in a *kilt*!! Yes!—in August 1822 George the Fourth, aged about sixty, exhibited himself publicly in a *kilt*!!! Whether the Royal legs—the very skin of the legs—was displayed, or not, is *now* doubted, and I cannot say; for the agitation of kissing a king's hand for the first time generally disqualifies the kisser from examining other parts. But the kilt is certain. Bare or trousered the knees were undoubtedly philabegged. George the 4th held a Levee without breeches! Lady Jane H. Dalrymple of Bargany said that as he was showing himself to his Scotch subjects, he thought he could not let them see too much. Yet the tartaned clans—the most picturesquely dressed people in Europe—brighten every show.

> This glimpse of Royalty did neither good nor harm, and could not. The King was too unpopular to reconcile those who required it, if there were any, to monarchy, and what could such a man do to reconcile any body to himself.

That independent assessment was clearly unacceptable in Queen Victoria's 1856, and three quarters of a century had to pass before it was revealed.

Longer passages like this show something of the quantity of the variations between manuscript and print, but Cockburn's sprightliness comes through in shorter phrases, incidents, and character sketches. His eye for a characteristic anecdote is always acute. Thus here is a remark on Maconochie, Lord Meadowbank: 'There was a good deal of character in the outset of his written judgement sustaining the power of the Scotch court to dissolve English marriages. "The Lord ordinary *having been unsuccessful in pursuit of a doubt*".' Or on Adam Ferguson regretting his inability to attend the Speculative Society jubilee dinner in 1814, by saying, ' "I have lived long enough to be my own monument".' 'And so he had', Cockburn added; 'I have never seen anything more monumental, or more interesting, than that old man's milk white hair, antediluvian dress, scraggy throat, sepulchral voice, blind eyes, and strong intellectual spirit.' These are some good quiet recollections to set against the full-blooded arraignments of his notorious predecessors on the bench. And these are neat phrases: of Meadowbank's voice, 'Lord Affleck [said] that it was like the tones of a cracked hautboy; but someone else was happier in likening it to that of an obstreperous hen'. Archibald Fletcher, the veteran reformer, is mentioned as dying at the age of eighty-eight: 'He was a Celt; and in colour and consistency, very like a bit of dry cork'. That has the ring of Cockburn at his best—an unusual image clearly and confidently expressed.

Having said so much about the trustees as editors, it is interesting to see how in one passage Cockburn has edited himself. This means going back to some of the few drafts bearing an 1838 watermark. One of them contains material which was worked over for a text with an 1849 watermark. The preservation of both versions is probably accidental but is certainly fortunate. The passages concern the antipathetic John Hope, son of Lord President Charles Hope (Lord Granton), who in 1822 became a very young Solicitor-General; John Hope was later Dean and Lord Justice-Clerk and outlived Cockburn by four years. Here is a part of a long description of him written on '1838' paper referring to his appointment in 1822:

> It is perhaps premature to form any decided opinion of one so young, though he who leads in politics and holds the position of Solicitor-General can scarcely claim an exemption from criticism on the score of youth; but whatever fruit the tree may hereafter bear, its present condition is this. Tall and thin, with a forbidding countenance, and an air of stiff though gentlemanlike

formality—there is nothing attractive in his appearance. His manner is far from agreeable—measured without dignity, grave without weight, and cold apparently on system, as if he thought repulsiveness respectable.

Now see how Cockburn himself adjusted the passage to deal with a man who was now a colleague, on '1849' paper:

I did not know him well (if I have ever done so) till a later period, and can only tell what was his general reputation and style. At this time he was tall and thin, with a forbidding countenance, and an air of stiff, though gentlemanlike, formality. No young man could have less external attraction. His manner was measured without dignity, grave without weight, and cold, if not sour, apparently upon system, as if he had thought repulsiveness respectable.

The passage has been much altered, but the changes are changes of tense and not of tone. It is not just a reluctance to give up a good phrase, but a feeling too that first thoughts were best. The antipathy is fully confirmed by Cockburn's letters over a long period. The basically unapologetic and misleadingly antedated tone of the concluding part of '1849' scarcely helps to make the reflection any more acceptable: 'Such was the green bay tree, planted fast by the river of success. The fruits that it bore will be seen in their season. The violences of the day were not favourable to either the formation or the appreciation of character...' That did not dispel the obvious misgivings of Messrs Cleghorn and Davidson, and for one of the versions of the John Hope passage we must go to *Some Letters*; for both, of course, to the manuscripts.

There is more to the Hope pages than the fact of their suppression. Both versions refer to events of 1822, and it is clear from a close reading of the whole of '1838' that it is a partly-revised transcription of some sort of diary, journal or memorandum prepared more or less contemporaneously with Hope's appointment to the Solicitorship, that is, towards the start of Cockburn's self-recorded period of memorialising. This very first version was the copy text for a revision carried out in or after 1838; and a further rewriting, probably between spring 1852 and spring 1853, then took place. The preliminary memoranda are lost, probably destroyed in Cockburn's lifetime; with a very few exceptions, the 'Red Books' (or first revision), and the *Memorials* (or fair copy), were destroyed by his son. We must be grateful for the accidental preservation of a few samples, for their later publication by his grandson and particularly for his great-grandson's making them available for study in the national collection.

This mixture of biography and bibliography may seem at times to have come near to Peter Peebles's phrase (which Cockburn himself used of tiresome pleaders) of counsel spinning a long thread out of a sma' tait o' woo'. Cockburn's autobiographical inclinations and testamentary intentions for his writings, and the redraftings of his *Memorials* which produced the textual anomalies which have puzzled students of his works, all have their significance in the study of his life. Above all they confirm the importance of *Memorials of his Time* and its sister works, both as history and as literature.

Cockburn's Account of The Friday Club

with an introductory note by

ALAN BELL

OF ALL COCKBURN's lesser writings, his 'Account of the Friday Club' is perhaps the least known. It is also in its way one of the most characteristic. Unlike other essays of comparable length, such as the continental travel journal (see pp. 30-38; and Miller, *Cockburn's Millennium*, chapter 5), or the *Circuit Journeys* commentary on Parliament House figures in Richardson's Helvellyn parody (*Millennium*, pp. 307-315), the main Friday Club essay belongs to the period in which Cockburn was beginning to set his psychological as well as his documentary archives in order and to formalise his Memorials as such. Thus in addition to the recording which to his mind such a high-spirited fraternity deserved, there was a more pious necrological purpose —'it is gratifying', as he wrote, 'to see the names of those whose society we once enjoyed'. The actual documents preserved in the album in which the *Account* is written—fixture billets, tavern bills, and the like—are relatively disappointing, and do not convey the interest that Cockburn held would 'come at last to attach to any memorial, however slight, which recalls, or suggests, the private hours of conspicuous men, especially when they also happen to be mutual friends in times gone by'. It is the friendship rather than the eminence that is commemorated here, in a way in which Cockburn was particularly skilled.

He was never one to leave unblown the trumpets of his various sodalities, and his strongly-pressed claims of Friday Club distinction almost rival the high-flown estimates of Speculative eminence elsewhere in his works. From the time of the attempt to capture Galen's head from outside an apothecary's George Street shop to the anticipatory eulogy of Andrew Rutherfurd, there is an agreeably exaggerated element in the narrative which gives it a Cockburnian flavour. One of the Galen party, Sydney Smith, left

Edinburgh so soon—a mere two months—after the foundation of the Friday Club that the story, which is at least *ben trovato*, might be assigned to another, earlier manifestation of this Club; and the Rutherfurd passages are closely parelleled by several references in Cockburn's letters at the time his younger friend achieved the various upward steps in the legal hierarchy.

Cockburn himself published a brief account of the Friday Club in the first volume of his *Life of Jeffrey* (pp. 147-152), in which the membership list for 1803–1833 is prefaced by extracts from some of Jeffrey's letters (which incidentally, ascribe the idea of clubbing to Sir Walter Scott) to explain the 'private institution . . . upon which so much of [Jeffrey's] social happiness, and that of many of his best friends depended for nearly forty years'. The transformation from a weekly supper gathering to a monthly dinner club is elegantly explained. 'And here were many of the best social evenings of some of our best men passed', Cockburn concluded in words which have their counterpart in his *Account*: 'The professional art of show conversation was held in no esteem. Colloquial ambition would have been so entirely out of place, that there was never even an indication of its approach. The charm was in having such men in their natural condition, during their "careless and cordial hours". . . . Death, sickness, and age, having extinguished its lights, it has been wisely allowed to pass away', he wrote in 1852.

After Cockburn's death, the Friday Club volume was preserved by his trustees, and was one of the papers examined in 1887–1889 by his son Francis Jeffrey Cockburn, who felt that 'The History is, I fear too small to print by itself, and is too good to be destroyed': it therefore fortunately escaped the holocaust in which so many of Cockburn's papers were destroyed. The manuscript survived to be printed by Harry A. Cockburn, the author's grandson, in *Book of the Old Edinburgh Club* III (1910), pp. 105-178, where the text reprinted in a revised version below occupies pp. 108-125 of a longer article on Edinburgh clubs.

Harry A. Cockburn was not the most reliable of transcribers, and it is fortunate that in 1973 the manuscript was presented to the National Library of Scotland (MS. 15943) by the late Mrs Avise Cockburn. The text given below varies somewhat from that previously printed. Minor adjustments of punctuation have been made; a number of Cockburn's idiosyncrasies have however been passed over: abbreviations like *Edinr* and *tho'* are expanded;

sollicitor, nostrills, grattification, chearful, existance, and even an accidental *beveridge* have been normalised; a *Scotchman,* one of his lordship's shibboleths, has been restored. Spellings of proper names have been corrected. The opportunity has been taken to remove a number of misreadings—*hot water* for a *lot of water* in a recipe for punch; a *devout* substituted for *cleverest;* the *conversation* of James Keay of Snaigow, the token bore of the brotherhood, can now be seen as a *conservatism* tolerated by his Whig friends. Harry Cockburn omitted James Watt's urological warnings to the assembled company, and a number of telling phrases, notably that about Scott's cutting of Lord Holland (see p. 195) being so very unlike himself, 'except perhaps weeping over the Form of Process'. The allusion here is to Sir Walter's distress displayed in his speech at a Faculty of Advocates' meeting in Spring 1807 to discuss proposed changes in the administration of justice in Scotland: 'Little by little,' he had told Jeffrey and another Whig afterwards, 'whatever your wishes may be, you will destroy and undermine, until nothing of what makes Scotland Scotland shall remain.' Scott's public display of emotion—Jeffrey saw tears rolling down his cheeks as they walked down the Mound —was as uncharacteristic as his petulant cut of Lord Holland.

Just like his casual reference years later to Lockhart's biography having surprisingly revealed that Lady Scott had once been an agreeable woman, Cockburn's aside about the Form of Process has a penetrating quality which might lead one to doubt the sincerity of Cockburn's respect for Scott. Political differences not unnaturally gave something of an edge to a relationship founded on genuine affection, but they were never allowed to obtrude unduly. Scott's attitude to Cockburn and his Whig friends is best recorded in his *Journal* for 8–9 December 1826 after enjoying 'capital good cheer and excellent wine—much laugh and fun' not at a Friday Club but privately with John Archibald Murray and a bunch of kindred spirits: 'I do not know why it is that when I am with a party of my Opposition friends the day is often merrier than when with our own set. Is it because they are cleverer? Jeffrey and Harry Cockburn are to be sure very extraordinary men, yet it is not owing to that entirely. I believe both parties meet with the feeling of something like novelty—we have not worn out our jests in daily contact. There is also a disposition on such occasions to be courteous, and of course to be pleased.'

*　　　*　　　*

This volume contains all the archives that exist of the Friday Club.

This Club was formed in June 1803; and got its name from the day of the week on which it used originally to meet. It was intended merely as a social institution, and has never been anything else. Learning, and talent, and public reputation, have always been prized in it; but the chief qualifications that have been looked to in its members are, a taste for literature, agreeable manners, and above all, perfect safety. There are two vices which have always been avoided entirely—conversational exhibition and religious narrow-mindedness; and a third—party spirit—which has been avoided as much as possible. The two first are held in established and uncompromising abhorrence, in all their forms and degrees. The opposite opinions of the members on public subjects, and the harmony that has uniformly subsisted among them, is best proof that the Club has always been open to the worthy of all political parties. But, owing to the prevalence of liberal opinions among most of the eminent men of Edinburgh in our day, the fact is that Whiggism has been its general creed.

We have never had any laws, or elections. The Institution keeps itself, and its numbers, right, by a prevailing feeling of propriety; and its members are kept up by a kind of growing together. Nobody has ever been rejected, for nobody has ever been formally proposed. Before a person can be supposed to be so worthy, so as to make it occur to any one to wish him among us, he must have been well known in the ordinary society of several of the members; and if, after being quietly discussed by a few leading associates, he is thought quite safe, and quite agreeable to all the rest, perfectly quiet, and free from offensive prejudices, of unimpeachable reputation, and adequate public consideration, he is gradually drawn in by some sort of natural attraction—an operation, however, which sometimes occupies years. Our tendency has always been to get stricter. Under this system the Club has gone on without a single jar, or dispute, or even motion, for twenty four years and a half.

It met at first every Friday about nine in the evening, but this was soon given up for a supper once a fortnight. Then the suppers and a dinner became alternate. But at last all-conquering dinner prevailed; and for above twenty years there have only been monthly meetings at half-past five or six in the evening during about eight months every year. There has scarcely ever been a meeting between the 12th of July and the 12th of November. After the regular dinner system was established, the day was changed to Sunday, and it has continued so ever since.

It was during one of the suppers that the memorable attack was made on Galen's Head. An apothecary called Gardner had a shop (which his son still continues) in the house immediately to the east of the Assembly Rooms in George Street. Over the door was a head of the Greek Doctor (was he a Greek?), which certain of our more intellectual members had long felt an itch to possess. But it stood high, and was evidently well secured. However one night Playfair, Thomas Thomson, and Sydney Smith, could resist no longer; and they mounted on the iron railing, and one of them got, or was getting, on the back of another, and had almost reached the prize, when Brougham, who had eagerly encouraged them to the exploit, but had retired, was detected in the dim distance of the old oil lamps, stealing up with the watch—for which he had wickedly gone. The assailants had just time to escape, and the gilded philosopher smiles a gracious defiance at this day.

We first assembled at Bayle's Tavern in Shakespeare Square. Bayle's was on the spot which is now occupied by the Westmost house on the North side of Waterloo Place. We then went to Fortune's, in the Eastmost division of Princes Street; where we remained for sixteen or eighteen years. This was the very best tavern that has ever been in Edinburgh; and was particularly remarkable for having, to an extent that few establishments of the kind have anywhere, the quietness of a private house. A graven image, like a New Zealand God, about a foot and a half high, stood on the chimney piece, and was long an object of much theological speculation. It was in the form of a sitting quadruped, though of what exact species our zoologists could never determine. Its essence was of brown clay; and it had large open eyes and ears, with a gaping mouth and wide nostrils. It was hollow; and when its body was filled with burning paper, the flames issuing from all its orifices made the Demon, in spite of a general graciousness of expression, very awful. Playfair and Jeffrey (such is the habit of devout habits) were apt to worship it, and it was long bowed to as a tutelary saint. Fortune died, and his widow did not long attempt to carry on the business. Since then we wandered about seeking dry ground for the soles of our feet, in vain, and by some carelessness we lost our deity. For some time past, however, we have resorted to Barry's, which is the Westmost house on the *South* side of Princes Street, and we have been so well—that is, so luxuriously

N

and quietly—accommodated that it is not improbable we may settle here.

We have no fines—no contributions—no presidents—no forms —no accounts. Some of these appear in our earlier proceedings; but they were scarcely ever attended to, and very soon disappeared entirely. The only officers of the Institution are a Secretary, and his Squire a chairman. John Richardson, now Solicitor in London, was the secretary from the commencement of the establishment to December 1805, when he left Edinburgh. On this the office was conferred upon, or assumed by, me, and I have discharged its duties excellently ever since. Our chairman has always been William—but, for his services in this and the Chrichton Club— raised to the dignity of *Sir* William Ross. His duty consists in collecting the names of those who mean to attend each meeting, and in levying at the same time the bill of the last one. All this, and the order to have the next feast ready to the tavern keeper, is done like clockwork, and costs no trouble to any body—Sir William, notwithstanding a little occasional unsteadiness of step, and a nasal blue of readily increasing intensity, being a correct careful man, well acquainted with our ways, and familiar without disrespect or obstrusiveness. My first official act was to print a card containing the names of the members and the days of meeting throughout the ensuing year. A regular series of these cards, which are the only documents I have had occasion to make out, is in this volume. I have hitherto been in the habit of leaving out the names of deceased members, but I mean henceforth to restore them. It is proud and gratifying to see though but the names of those whose society we once enjoyed.

When we only supped, Punch was our staple liquid. It used to be made by Brougham; who compounded a very pleasant but somewhat dangerous beverage, of Rum, Sugar, Lemons, Marmalade, Calves foot jelly, and hot water—a sort of warm shrub. This gradually gave place to iced punch, from which the Marmalade and the Jelly were omitted. When the suppers were exchanged for dinners, Claret became the standard. It was interspersed with other, and more delicate, productions of the grape; but at first this was done timidly. Indeed in those days there was a paltry prejudice against rarer French and German wines; which besides were very dear, so that their cost and their novelty made foolish people stare when they were rashly produced. The Friday had always a contempt of this, and an innate propensity towards good taste; which from the very first was evinced by a generous extravagance. But I don't think it was till the Peace of 1814, that, the continent being opened, we soared above prejudice, and ate and drank everything that was rare and dear—a principle which is still held sacred in all our convocations.

It is needless to add that our bills have always been high, or that their tendency has always been to get higher. Upon an average each dinner cost to those who partake of it from £1.18s. to £2.5s. In twenty-four years three of our members, and only three, have complained of this, which has generally made us more extravagant when they were present. For costliness is a good thing in such an association. It makes it more comfortable, and more select. And after all, the price at the end of the year is not more than what a prudent gentleman, aware of the value he receives in return, will always be willing to pay. The Club may date its decline from the day on which it has an election, or makes a law, or gets cheap.

The mere names of most of the members is enough to fix their identity and to recall their memories. But there are others as to whom it may not be altogether unnecessary to specify something more to those who did not know them personally.

The original members were as follows.

1803

1. Sir James Hall; author of the work on Gothic Architecture, and of several geological discoveries and publications.
2. Professor Dugald Stewart.
3. Professor John Playfair. Died in 1819.
4. Revd Archibald Alison; essays on taste, sermons, etc.
5. Revd Sydney Smith, an Englishman, and an English Clergyman; author of Sermons, the letters of Peter Plymley, various articles in the Edinburgh review.
6. Revd Peter Elmsley—An Englishman, and English Clergyman. Editor of several Greek classics. Dead.
7. Alex. Irving, Advocate, now Lord Newton.
8. William Erskine, Advocate, afterwards Lord Kinedder. He was the great friend of Scott, and wrote the review of Scott's novels in the Quarterly review, and the supplementary lines to Collins' Ode on the Superstitions of the Highlands. He died in 1822.
9. George Cranstoun—Advocate—now Lord Corehouse.

N*

10. Sir Walter Scott.
11. Francis Jeffrey.
12. William Clerk—Advocate—now first clerk of the Jury Court.
13. Thomas Thomson—Advocate—Deputy Clerk Register and Clerk of Session. It is he who has superintended the recent publication of the proceedings of the Scottish Parliaments, and by whom everything that has been done for unfolding and arranging our Public Muniments, under the name of the Record Commission, has been accomplished.
14. Dr John Thomson—Physician; author of Lectures on Inflammation and other medical works. He was Professor in the University.
15. John Archibald Murray—Advocate—Member for Leith.
16. Henry Brougham.
17. Henry Mackenzie—Senior—author of the Man of Feeling, etc.
18. Henry Mackenzie—Junior—his son—Advocate—now a Judge—Lord Mackenzie.
19. Malcolm Laing—Author of the History of Scotland. He died in [1818].
20. Henry Cockburn.
21. John Richardson, Solicitor in London.
22. John Allen, formerly Lecturer on Physiology in Edinburgh—now Head of Dulwich College. He is the author of the articles on the more difficult and learned matters on English constitutional antiquities or history that have appeared in the Edinburgh review.
23. Francis Horner. Died in 1817.
24. Thomas Campbell—Author of the Pleasures of Hope.

Those admitted after the original constitution of the Club are as follows:—

1804

25. Alexander Hamilton. He was secretary to Lord Cornwallis; and afterwards Oriental Professor at Haileybury. Dead.
26. Dr Coventry; Professor of Agriculture in the University of Edinburgh.
27. Professor John Robison; whose life Playfair has written. Dead.
28. George Strickland—son of Sir George, in Yorkshire.
29. Andrew Dalzell, Professor of Greek in our University. He died in 1806.

30. Lord Webb Seymour: brother of the Duke of Somerset. He died in 1819.
31. The Earl of Selkirk. He was the person who formed the colonies for emigrants from Scotland in the back settlements of America, where he went and resided himself. He died in [1820].
32. Lord Glenbervie. His original name was Douglas. He was the author of the English law reports, which are known by his name—and of other legal publications; and of translation of an Italian poem. He died in [1823].

1807

33. The Revd John Thomson; minister of Duddingston, and the finest landscape painter in Scotland.

1810

34. John Jeffrey, the brother of Francis.

1811

35. Thomas F. Kennedy—of Dunure, M.P.
36. John Fullerton—Advocate.

1812

37. George Wilson. A Scotchman by birth—but long, and very highly, established at the English bar. He was the great friend of Romilly, and would probably have been at the head of the courts, if he had not been struck with palsy about 1812; on which he retired to Edinburgh. He died in [   ].

1814

38. Dr John Gordon; physician, and lecturer on Anatomy and Physiology in Edinburgh. He died in 1818. His life has been written by Daniel Ellis.

1816

39. Andrew Rutherfurd—Advocate.

1817

40. James Keay—Advocate.

1825

41. Leonard Horner—brother of Francis; formerly a merchant here, now Warden of the London University.

42. James Pillans; formerly Rector of the High School; now Professor of Humanity, here.

1826

43. Count de Flahault. A native of France—friend and aide-de-camp of Napoleon; and now married to the daughter of the late Lord Keith.

1827

44. The Earl of Minto.
45. William Murray; Esq. of Henderland—a member of the English Bar.

Nobody can know Edinburgh without being aware that these are the most select and distinguished names connected with its history in our day. Besides these, the society of the Club has been varied by visits from strangers, though in general the feeling has been against this intrusion. I remember seeing Southey there—who was very bad company. But this was soon after he was beginning to feel the Edinburgh review, and Jeffrey was sitting opposite him. The stranger we saw oftenest, and with the greatest of pleasure, was old James Watt; who regularly told us, when we rose, that if we went on drinking as we had been doing, 'You'll all have stones in your bladders'.

Brougham and Sydney Smith predominated as long as they remained in Edinburgh; which, however, was not long after the club began. If there has been any ascendancy since, it has been acquired, over willing associates, by worth, steadiness of attendance, excellence of conversation, and agreeableness of manner. By these virtues we owed much of our pleasure formerly to Dugald Stewart and old Harry Mackenzie—who have been prevented by age and infirmity from attending for some years past. Scott too always was, and when he comes, always is, delightful: but though he has by no means given us up, his appearances among us are not so frequent as we all wish. But John Playfair was the person who, from our very first meeting till the summer in which he died, was unquestionably at our head. For sixteen years the Friday Club, for the pleasure which he conferred and which he enjoyed, was the favourite scene of that inimitable person. Not *next* to him—for this would seem to imply competition, of which we have never had a feeling—but *along with* him we have been indebted to Francis

Jeffrey and Thomas Thomson—in whose hands, more than in those of any other individuals, the institution now is.

Nothing more honourable could be written of any club than its Obituary of this one. But where these things are not done at the moment, they are never done. Many interesting men, and curious scenes, have been seen there, and many things have been said, which, if they had been judiciously recorded at the time, would not only have been gratifying to surviving recollections, but might have imparted a permanent value to the details of the biographer or local historian. Our thirteen deceased members were all worthy —but a more particular remembrance is due to Malcolm Laing, Francis Horner, George Wilson, and John Gordon; each of whom was not only eminent in public life, but seemed to prize his eminence chiefly as a source of gratification to his private friends. The interest of Wilson was greatly increased by his being a stranger—who had been obliged to leave his adopted country, the best London society, and great professional consideration, from illness; yet sat among us regularly, with his glass of water, excellent conversation, and gentle manner, as cheerful and resigned as if he had only returned to his natural sphere. It always struck me as the triumph of magnanimity over broken health and altered prospects. But what could be expected of the man, who, after being struck with his terrible disorder, wrote and consoled his friend Dr Gregory by saying, among other things, 'We bachelors have a great advantage over you married men—in *dying*'.

When Richardson went to London he left all his Club papers with me. I laid them aside and forgot their existence till this Autumn, when I fell upon them accidentally. On looking over them, I was much struck with the interest that comes at last to attach to any memorial, however slight, which recalls, or suggests, the private hours of conspicuous men, especially when they also happen to be mutual friends, in times gone by. I therefore arranged every thing I had, chronologically, and got it bound into this volume. It is a very inadequate record of our existence and proceedings. But I could not have resisted the pleasure of preserving it, had it even been more imperfect that it is. Nothing can be frivolous which awakens such associations.

H. COCKBURN
10 December 1827

15 January 1829. The Club has flourished all last year. There has not been an intermission of a single Club day; and our parties have generally consisted of from eight to ten, of whom Corehouse has almost invariably been one. I mention him particularly, because he used to be less steady than some of the rest. But he is one of the very few persons who have not been made stupid by being made a judge. Our only loss in 1828 was Dugald Stewart—whose memory will ever be cherished by those who knew him as a member of this association. It is an honour to us to have it in our power to say that we lost such a man. We are still at Barry's; and still very quiet, and very luxurious. An attempt was made to lower our bills; but the very next one was the very highest we ever had to pay.

7 January 1830. Still flourishing. But we have this year lost Alloway, who joined us late in his life, and in our progress, but adhered to us, during the two years when we were permitted to enjoy him, with the happy gaiety and kindness which always seemed to gush over him whenever he escaped from legal drudgery into rural or social ease.

Whiskey, too, has proved fatal at last to Sir William Ross; who demised last Spring; a respectful and attached Officer. John Stewart has ever since been on trials as his successor, and I suppose I may now consider him as more than a noviciate.

6 January 1831. Going on beautifully. We have this year gained the Honble Mountstuart Elphinstone, late Governor of Bombay, and the author of the book on Caboul, and the person described by Bishop Heber as the ablest man he ever met with. He is gentle, calm, natural, and so full of modesty that it is only by directly consulting him that his very great knowledge and talent are discoverable. He has the air and appearance otherwise of a poor worthy tutor, long oppressed in some great Highland family. But alas! we have been deprived of the excellent Coventry, the Professor of Agriculture. A most excellent person; learned, especially in science, more simple than any child, warm hearted, ludicrously absent, combining the plainness of a farmer with the knowledge of a philosopher. His whole time was spent going about as a Land Doctor arranging agricultural affairs. He told me that in nine months last year he only slept four times in the same bed. But all beds, and tables, and companies were the same to Coventry; for he was constantly happy, and so absent that he never knew one from another.

16 January 1832. Last summer old Harry Mackenzie died. But he had not been at the Club for some years. We have got no new member in 1831. But the attendance has been steady and the meetings regular, and Barry, at the British Hotel, is worthy of Fortune in his best days. Jeffrey has been almost entirely in London. So much for being Lord Advocate.

3 January 1833. Last year we have lost Sir James Hall, Lord Newton, and Scott. None of them had attended for some years, but their names were an honour. We have seen a good deal of James Abercromby. But he has a maxim against clubs, and won't become a member. It is surmised that Sir Andrew Agnew M.P., who is at the head of various Societies and Committees for checking the profanation of the Lord's day, has smelt us out, and means to be at us for the sin of eating our radish and our egg, and drinking our cup of cold water upon Sunday. Does he wish us to have a dinner extra at our own houses that day? The agitation of the Reform Bill, with the intense interest of its first popular fruits in Scotland, has made no odds on the calm, intellectual course of the Friday, which holds on its way, superior to these low terrestrial objects.

18 January 1835. We still flourish. Only two events have distinguished our Anchorite history during the last two years. 1. Abercromby has become one of us. He has a contemptible stomach; but he duly regrets this, and has probably spoiled it by past indulgence—so we endure him. 2. In November 1834 the King rewarded my twenty-eight years services to this Club by making me a Senator of the College of Justice. This prevented me from mingling any more among the crowd in the Outer House, and there arranging our social parties; and, besides, it was beneath the dignity of a supreme judge to be adjusting tavern bills. I therefore abdicated, and of my own authority named *Andrew Rutherfurd* my successor.

Fortunate youth! Thy character—thy fiery eye—thy morocco books—thy eloquence—thy bits of vertu—thy law—thy deep voice —thy virtues—even thy glorious debauchery, thy generous profligacy—will all be forgotten; like the taste of the feasts thou hast consumed! But this honour!—thy election by me—to be Recording Angel of the immortal Friday, this shall endure! Consuls have marked years—flavours vintages—discoveries epochs—cooks sauces—philosophers countries—druggists doses; but henceforth thy eternal name blazes on the Friday! Dean of Faculty Rutherfurd, Lord Advocate Rutherfurd, President Rutherfurd—even Andrew Rutherfurd; what are they? But Friday Rutherfurd!! Equal this,

Fame! At this very moment (one p.m. of the 18th of January 1835) you are on the Hustings at the Cross of Edinburgh proposing Sir John Campbell, late Attorney General, to be Member for this city. Honourable task, no doubt. But yesterday thou satest for the first time, overpowered with thy new glory, surrounded by me, Jeffrey, Thomson, Pillans, Abercromby, John A. Murray, William Murray, members, and Lord Abercromby and Campbell, strangers—and what a station was thine! I have given thee immortality—discredit not thy benefactor!

18 January 1836. No change last year. No death, and no admission. Abercromby has done better as Speaker than he ever did before; and if he were in Edinburgh oftener would probably become a fixture. I have been twice absent; from which it is suspected that the stupor of the bench is coming upon me. Our new Secretary has done well—considering the perfection of the predecessor, with which he has the misfortune to be contrasted.

12 January 1837. As we were. Except that last autumn Thomas Thomson, at the age of *at least* seventy-two, and after a long course of social virtue, took unto himself a wife. Friday groaned. A petticoat in yon library! Our small luxurious suppers! His never extinguished lamp—gleaming through the whole night—the Pharos of quiet friendly hospitality—ensuring a harbour to the castaway worthy, who were safe in risking, at any hour, a berth on his hearthstone, or round his board. His large paper copies! His antiquarian and literary manuscripts! Old worthy Miss Lockhart, the most exquisite of caterers, and seen only in her works! It is all gone. Oh! Thomas, Thomas! What had a petticoat to do there?

26 January 1838. Last year is marked by the death of James Keay. Honourable, amiable, judicious; social, hospitable, and safe—he could not be but a good member of any club. For though his talents were not high, and he had no learning, and no peculiar power of conversation, yet he was one of the men of whom a large infusion is necessary in every society, in order to form the public among whom the brighter spirits are to shine. He was so respectable in his character and conduct, both personal and professional; had such an unexceptionable plain manner, and was always so cheerful, safe and sensible, that he imparted an air of security, comfort, and propriety, into all his social scenes. He has been blamed by a few of late for inconsistency in politics since the introduction of the Reform Bill. I have always thought this imputation most unjust. He never mixed much in politics anyway;

but his friends being mostly Whigs, some of them chose to fancy, when his conservatism, which was always his faith, was called a little into action by the times, that he had deserted them; though I defy them to show one Whiggish act he had ever done, or one Edinburgh measure of this party in which he had ever even been consulted by his own Whig associates. He was an admirable counsel; not learned, or eloquent; but learned enough for practical business; candid even in litigation—and absolutely matchless for luminous verbal statement or argument.

Our worthy secretary forgot to print and distribute a Club card for 1837. To be sure he has his great practice to attend to, besides the Law Commission, and the general public charge of Scotland— but what are all these to the Friday!

Lockhart has (very foolishly) mentioned in his Life of Scott (vol. 2, p. 286) the only painful occurrence that ever disturbed us. It was when Scott allowed his temper so far to get the better of himself as to behave rudely to Lord Holland. It was the first time he had met Lord Holland after a discussion in the House of Lords, in which his lordship has given his opinion against a clear job of an office for Scott's brother, but in very handsome terms towards Scott himself. Sir Walter says in his letter to his brother that he and Holland 'met accidentally at a *public* party'. He must mean by this that it was at a club and a tavern, not in a private house; for it was at the Friday, the least public of all meetings, with only about ten or twelve persons present. He had not expected to meet Holland, though he must have known that he was in Edinburgh and that strangers were admitted; and evidently lost the command of himself from the first moment he entered the room. How sulky he looked! He hardly spoke a word except to his two neighbours, and I was always expecting to see him use his knife as his borderers would of yore—*not* upon the mutton. When Holland, the mildest of gentlemen, asked him if he would do him the honour to take wine with him, the answer was '*No*', uttered in a strong disdainful growl. After two hours, or so, of this childishness he suddenly pushed back his chair, and stumped out of the room. Richardson, who had been sitting between him and me, whispered to me that he was glad he was gone, for that his (Richardson's) knee was almost crushed by the action upon it of Sir Walter's, which had been shaking with rage ever since we had sat down. Instantly after he had retired, Lord Holland said, in his sweet blooded way: 'The Bard seems very angry at me, but I really don't know what it's for.

It can't be about his brother's business—at least if it be, he's misinformed; for what I said was, that if the arrangement was about an office, it was a job; but if it was meant as an indirect reward of Walter Scott, my only objection to it was that it was too little.'

I don't believe that Scott ever did any thing so unlike himself; except perhaps weeping over the Form of Process. The scene was painful certainly; but yet there was some entertainment in seeing the gruff feudal spirit fairly taking its own way. We smiled occasionally while it was going on, and laughed outright after the unkempt man had shut the door.

10 January 1843!!! A fearful, and shameful, pause of five years!— which memory cannot fill.

All 1838—1839—and 1840—we went on as usual. Our professionally and officially busy Secretary, Lord Advocate Rutherfurd, was too long absent, and too much preoccupied while at home, to enable him to whip us in properly—but still he by no means did his worst, and our meetings were pretty regular, and always quiet, cheerful, and luxurious.

But in June 1841 Jeffrey was taken ill, and went to England, where he remained till May 1842; and he has never since been so strong as to enable him to be regardless; and though his social propensities can be safely yielded to, in all their sprightly amiableness, in the domestic scene, we have thought it better not to put him within the temptation even of our philosophic Tavern. The partial quenching of this, our brightest, star, was enough to have abated our zeal. For the Club which Jeffrey used to irradiate, to abstain from meeting while his health prevented him from irradiating it still, was an homage due by it to him. But Alas! Another calamity of a different, and perhaps even severer, nature overtook us in the pecuniary misfortunes of Thomas Thomson, our next shining light. These misfortunes have, for a season, compelled him to live in privacy.

The consequence of these afflictions has been that it is now nearly two years since we have had a meeting. I think the last was in May 1841. But we are only in abeyance. If the institution be destined to die with the generation that created it, its duration cannot now be long. I trust, however, though I do not foresee how, that its existence may be prolonged into another age; and at any rate, even among those who be, there are many evenings which it may brighten.

10 June 1850. We have not met for some years. Our secretary, Lord Advocate and M.P. Rutherfurd, has allowed the contemptible cares of a senator and public accuser to interfere with his honourable duties as Secretary of the Friday; Thomas Thomson, besides marrying, got, for some years, into pecuniary confusion; and Jeffrey's health made his attendance impossible. So we have hung on—recollecting the past, and indulging in vague dreams of revival; till at last, *Jeffrey's death*, last February, seems to me to terminate the Club. Its continuance by the surviving members is scarcely possible; and with our recollections and habits, I do not see what new shoots could be engrafted on the old stock.

Let it go. It is a type of life—of which the brightest scenes close; and which, though they may be renewed in other generations, it is in vain to cling to after their Autumn has plainly arrived.

H.C.

Index